Ilon

Dolphins, Love and Destiny

Yoga for the Soul

Living From Vision

Published 2008 by
Living From Vision
Stanwood WA 98292
USA

Living From Vision®
is a Registered Trade Mark of Allied Forces, Inc.

Cover art by Amoraea Dreamseed
www.harmonicconvergence2012.com
Cover design: Don Paris Ph.D.

Selke, Ilona
Dolphins, Love and Destiny
Yoga for the Soul

1. Spirituality
2.Relationships
3. Dolphins
I. Title   II. Selke, Ilona

ISBN 978-1-884246-14-2
ISBN 1-884246-14-1

Dedication

To my beloved husband Don Paris Ph.D.

&

to the

Soul Star

in each of us

*In total union of our souls,
grace touches our hearts.*

*Love and the Union of our Souls,
brings us naturally into
the mystical experience
of the Sublime.*

*Together as One
we touch the face of God.*

Chapters

A Word by the Author

In the last few decades a plethora of spiritual books have appeared on the market, professing to be based on fact and lighting up the lives of many readers, but leaving a sour note when the stories were revealed as works of fiction. This has led some readers to feel deep disappointment. How can we know which books are true and which aren't?

Fiction is not nearly as compelling as a magical real life story. Because, if the miracles really happened to the author, they can happen to the reader as well. We reason that if one of us can do it, anyone can. This boosts a reader's morale and ignites the soul.

If the Bible were said to be a simple book of fiction, most people would lose their belief. If the writing is portrayed as a real life story, truthfulness is the author's moral obligation to the reader. Conversely, it took me a long time to decide to reveal many of my own personal stories from my life. But writing from personal experience makes the magical stories much more significant and effective for the reader.

I thought many times that I would rather dress up my real life experiences in the cloak of a novel, since it would allow me to hide behind the mask of fiction. Many of my experiences go beyond the taboos of our society.

Yet on the other hand, the stories that I tell have greater power just because they are real.

How effective would a story of shifting the Time-Space-Matrix be if it was only fiction? How effective would the lessons be on the trials of jealousy, attractions and love, if they were simply stories of fiction?

I decided to stay true to my life's experience and hope that by revealing my own trials, the truth will help to inspire you, the reader, to greater heights in your own life. My hope is to inspire you to greater powers of your soul and to enable you to shift your life into living in Heaven on Earth.

That said, I would like to add that some names in the book have been changed to protect the privacy of the individuals. All events happened as I have written them, but not all of the events happened in exactly the time progression as they appear, except for the ones which I marked with exact dates.

For the purpose of maintaining the flow of the story I have mixed and matched a few of the events, such as the healing of the dolphin in Florida which happened a few years later in real time. But all events happened to me as I described them. With that, I hope that you can feel confident that if I can do it, so can you.

Yours,
Ilona Selke

Prologue

The mystery of our souls is calling to the core of our heart like a mysterious flute from the heavens. As we grow in our ability to act as illumined selves, the age old questions about fate, destiny and freewill enters our thoughts.

On our path to becoming a greater illumined human being, we encounter questions like:

- Is there such a thing as a solidly formed reality
- Can we change reality? If yes, to what degree?
- Is the future predetermined and are we pre-destined to walk a certain path in our life?
- What is the secret and the implication of premonition?
- What is prophesy?
- Do we have freewill?
- Can we bend time-space?
- What happens after death?
- How do we love at higher levels of consciousness?

These are becoming increasingly important questions to be solved if we want to live more meaningful and exciting lives.

The Western understanding of soul, God and the material universe has gone through many stages of evolution.

The Western worldview, which has been dominated by a scientific view of the universe since the Renaissance, is now still largely dominated by an understanding of a clockwork-like and mechanical universe, in which soul is separated from the material world.

This understanding, though still popular, is already outdated by modern scientific research. Quantum physics and other theories have already made allowances for a more unified understanding of the universe in which *consciousness has a co-creative place*. This mirrors the understanding of ancient civilizations.

Both paths, the latest scientific, as well as the ancient mystical paths, tell us that we are co-creative, awake dreamers in the body of time-space and that our everyday lives are an expression of the divine. The outer life is a reflection of our inner life.

Yet we seem to encounter forces that are greater than ourselves. We often call it fate.

Fate is the script of our lives that resides in a dimension that is higher than the current residence point of our soul. Therefore we usually don't have significant access to these realms *unless* we rise beyond our current limitations and master time-space navigation through the evolution of our soul.

As our DNA evolves and as we become multi-dimensional beings, we discover that our relationships are undergoing serious transformations as well. Old norms don't seem to apply any longer, as we learn to love each other at higher levels of our souls. We are yearning for greater collective consciousness and love at universal levels.

There are unseen forces that we can learn to tap. These forces allow us to write new scripts of our lives, because we access dimensions hitherto beyond our reach, that allows us to interact with realms that were once delegated to the gods. In the process we become co-creators of our destinies.

As we evolve, we are able to navigate time-space more effectively, availing our lives to far reaching and magnificent destinies.

Happiness is a barometer in the process. We instinctually know that life can be grand, ecstatic and meaningful. And we also know that if life isn't yet that grand, or only occasionally so, there is still more in store for us.

The very nature of reality unveils itself naturally as we take one step at a time, living in this self-tutoring universe. Yet it helps to find guidelines, maybe roadmaps, of how others, who have gone before us, have experienced some of the same hurdles and questions we now may face.

It helps to get a few pointers along the road, some encouragement, some visions of what is possible from those that have walked the path before us.

If a few, or even a number of humans, have managed to live in Heaven on Earth, so can all of us.

The purpose of this book is to speak of the possible, to write about how to rise up within the finer realms of the multi-dimensional universe, and to show steps to take, in order to manifest your own higher destiny.

The Dolphin's Sonar Message

It was a beautiful sunny morning in early Autumn of 1995. The sun shone crisply into our dome house as I sat at our wooden living room table, looking at the Cascade mountain range across the water from our Island. I was in the process of editing the last few chapters of my book *Journey to the Center of Creation,* filled with stories about the magic of dolphins, the power of our imagination, and the holographic nature of the universe.

It told about how we live in a very mysterious universe, one in which we can make miracles happen. The book, as it turned out, inspired readers worldwide to create amazing miracles in their own lives. All the stories I had told about in my book were absolutely true and let the reader peer into the private life of Don, my beloved husband, and myself.

I was touching up the last few pages of the book before sending it off to my editor, who would polish my German-tainted English.

Sitting in this geodesic dome house was like sitting in a large cathedral. This was a house we had built with our own hands, and in which we could not allow ourselves the luxury of negative thoughts. We had learned to keep our expectations pure, as the structure of a geodesic dome is like living inside a pyramid.

I was on chapter 44. The story was compelling. I had written about how my friend Lorraine had called me one day in total excitement after she had swam with dolphins in a bay off the Big Island of Hawaii. That morning the dolphins had sent her a lot of sonar signals. Sonar is the dolphin's way of using echolocation.

"Ilona," she told me excitedly on the phone, "As I swam back to shore, I was trying to understand what the dolphins might have wanted to say to us with their sonar. I felt as though the dolphins were trying to tell me something! While I was swimming back I suddenly noticed a school of Talapa fish, swimming close by in front of me. It seemed like they were reflecting odd geometric designs. You know, they would rapidly shifted their positions underwater and reflect geometric patterns.

"You can't imagine what it looked like," she continued still in awe, "it was almost as if the sound of the dolphins was using the school of fish like an 'Etch-a-Sketch.'"

She told me that the geometric figures seemed to correspond to the sonar. The most amazing symbol looked like a donut.

"I couldn't make sense out of that shape, but got this intuitive hit today that you might know what it means." She finished.

"Amazing!" I said. "Because I have been writing about the meaning of the donut shape in my new book. It is also known as a toroid. It's the basic shape of the manifested universe, as far as I understand. But what's an 'Etch-a-sketch?'" I added.

She explained it to me quickly, "An Etch-a-Sketch is a plastic toy that functions as a sketching pad, where you can erase everything whenever you want to."

It dawned on me. In Germany we had used something similar but built much more simply. It had wax-paper that could be peeled back to wipe out the old images.

I kept explaining to her about the donut.

"I'm writing about the multi-dimensional aspect of the donut, the toroid in my book, trying to show how we live in a sea of black and white holes, called quantum foam, which allows us to enter any number of parallel universes at will. Physicists think of the toroid as a symbolic representation for the universe, much like the infinity loop, but more dimensional. It functions like a black hole that sucks everything in existence into itself and then spews it back out on the other end, which functions like a white hole. This recycling of energy creates the image of a fountain that caves in on itself. It really is like a never-ending recycling-station. Its shape can serve as a doorway for making quantum jumps, and it's the basis for the imagery transformation techniques which I teach in the book and seminars.

"If I understand you," I said, "you're saying the dolphins' sound had been turned into geometric designs, just like what happens when you put sand on a drum-skin and send a sound through the drum.

"Since each frequency has a different vibrational pattern, each sound can produce a different image. The dolphins were sending you the image of a toroid, a donut shape."

Dolphin communication. In view of all the extraordinary events that surrounded dolphins, I had no doubt that the school of Tilapia fish had acted as a sounding board for the dolphin's echolocation.

But here was the big question:

"Just what was the message the dolphins were trying to convey with this image?"

As I gazed at the Cascade mountains from our island home, I put my pencil aside. I was done correcting my chapter and I needed to leave for Seattle to see my dentist.

While driving I kept pondering the meaning of Lorraine's question to me: 'What was the meaning of the donut image that the dolphins had sent her?'

It was a sunny day and I adored nature. Life is so full of beauty! My spirit was soaring. Soon I just floated in the brilliant light as I flew down the highway.

The dentist visit had been easy and I was just on my way back home as life gave me one of its perplexing hints that not all is what it seems.

I had just pulled onto Interstate I-5 when I saw a gigantic 'Etch-a-Sketch' being erected to the left side of the road. It was serving as a billboard for an advertisement.

As I gazed upon the gigantic toy image, I stared at the message on the billboard:

"EVERYTHING IS SONIC "

I caught my breath! Here was the answer to my questions:
'What is an Etch-A-Sketch' and 'What were the dolphins trying to tell my friend, Lorraine?'

The message was loud and clear: '*Everything is sonic!*' Everything is vibration!

What a universe we live in! To this day my mind is boggled at the coincidental manifestation of that billboard. Life is truly much more magical when we start looking behind the curtains and it is not as solid as it may seem. Instead, life is an interactive, living, dream-fabric that answers to our calls, be they conscious or unconscious. It is a sounding board for thoughts, feelings and images we carry within. This multi-dimensional fabric weaves into visible form that which we may not be able to see with our normal eyes. The answer from the dolphins had manifested on an I-5 billboard.

I had never seen such a structure before. Nor have I ever seen it again. There was a manifestation to a question I just had.

Coincidence?

"*Everything is sonic.*"

Hmm… It reminded me of the movie *Delirious.*

Writing our own Movie Script

The movie industry must have secretly tried to teach the 101 of manifestation skills in the movie *Delirious*. In this movie John Candy acts the role of a soap-opera screen writer who suddenly wakes up one morning in a hospital bed and finds himself living the lead role of one of his characters. It takes him some time to understand what had happened.

"How did I get into the hospital?' he wondered totally bewildered at first. He couldn't recall. Strangely enough, he took note that the doctors

15

and nurses were acting identically to the doctors and nurses in his latest TV script. They even had the same names!

Slowly but surely it dawns on him that he's living the very life he created for his lead character in his soap opera stories. He had actually become the character and was now living the very stories that he had been creating in his mind. Much to his chagrin, he finds that he also has to live through all the pains of his characters as well. But soon, by sheer chance, he discovers that he can continue writing the script and most of all, that he can intentionally change the script into a much happier outcome.

I loved that movie. How true it was! How often do we daydream about how a particular event will turn out in our life! But do we take the opportunity and write the script with a pleasurable ending? Or do we write a "sob story" with us in the central role of a suffering drama queen?

I have caught myself so many times dreaming up a worst case scenario in advance. Again and again I have to remind myself to dream a positive future. In our daily lives we are faced so many times with that same choice:

Do we create a happy ending in our minds, or do we imagine ourselves as the saddest victims possible?

Here is a true story about Don and two mechanics, who used the power of imagination in two different ways to get a job done.

A few years back, Don and I had bought our first washing machine. It was a foreign model from Sweden, which only uses ten gallons of water per wash, compared to the normal forty gallons of ordinary washing machines used in the US. We felt good about our choice, although it cost us twice the amount of money. But buying a water-saving washing machine was our way to contribute to the conscientious use of the planet's resources.

The glorious installation day had arrived, which meant the end of using Laundromats. The installers managed to carry the heavy machine into the basement where they went to work hooking everything up.

"Shoot, I don't have the right tools."

"Damn, I don't have the right hose."

The installer's negative talk was hard to listen to.

It didn't surprise me to see that things were not working out for them.

Magic only happens when we expect a miracle, when we align ourselves with the higher principles of life. For example, when we know that everything is interconnected and that our thoughts and feelings have an effect, we are more likely to create positive outcomes. When we are out of phase with life, when we see ourselves as separate, alienated and alone, nothing seems to work out easily.

As we watched the installers fight their way through the installation, Don and I tried our best to cheer them up. We knew we could help by expecting the best out of people. But our encouraging talk didn't work miracles on them that day. Finally the installers decided to have lunch, to buy themselves more time. But to prepare us for the worst, they told us they probably would have to leave after lunch and come back in a day or two, to finish the installation.

I was really disappointed. That was not how I had wanted to celebrate our first day of owning a washing machine! I had waited long enough and really wanted it to be done that day!

One of our secretaries had been watching the whole scenario. Finally, she walked over to us and said, "Time for our genius to get to work."

She was hinting that Don should perform some practical miracles.

With both parts and tools missing, my hope for a working washing machine still that day sunk. But instead of giving up and taking on the usual tendency of seeing the worst before it happens, Don and I looked at each other and winked. And we went to work inwardly.

In my inner sight I rose up above the clouds to another layer of reality. I held the feeling and vision of walking into a different universe.

This universe, one of the many parallel options of universes to choose from, had everything we needed: Hoses, tools and the hook-up of the washing machine completed.

In my subtle perceptions I could sense Don moving into a heightened state of consciousness as well. It is OK to have everything work out, provided that the higher source of life doesn't have better plans for us. I asked for the highest good to manifest as I held the feeling of having a fully installed washing machine "now." I 'worked' inwardly until I could feel this feeling through my whole body.

Suddenly Don pulled a hose out of nowhere and found the right tools in his own tool box. Before the installers came back, Don had everything hooked up! We looked at each other with a glimmer in our eyes, knowing that we had just traded a parallel reality that didn't offer success in exchange for a better one.

What exactly had gone on? Was it just "chance" or was there really a quantum foam of which this universe is made, which allows us to change channels? How does one really manifest miracles?

Don had followed specific methods. He was working with a different belief system than the old science, which is still being taught in schools. When we understand that we literally have many parallel options of realities at hand, we can choose the one that suits us best.

If I am willing to have a positive outcome, I can hold that *feeling of a fulfilled future* until it manifests.

At times however, we either can't get high enough, can't convince our own emotions enough, or we don't know how to hold a field. We might also prefer to be sad, angry, fearful or a victim.

To rise up takes extra energy and practice of the imagination, and a belief that everything is changeable.

Having used the methods of Holographic Imaging and the Living From Vision course, we had gotten the hang of changing reality for the better. Since this had been a shift in a material world, it had been a little easier.

But how much can we alter reality when fate knocks at our door? Soon our lives were to be challenged to the core.

Dreams, Prophecies and Readings

It was now a few years later, in November of 1998. Winter was coming to the Pacific Northwest soon. As I woke up, the sun was peaking over the Cascade mountain range, turning the snow-covered mountains into radiantly shining golden cones. Fog was laying low over the water that separated us from the mainland and made it seem as if we lived on an island above the clouds.

My book had been published successfully and I was touring the USA, appearing on television shows and giving radio interviews, talks and teaching seminars. The German translation of the book on dolphins was scheduled to be published the coming fall of 1999 in Germany.

It was a cold morning and I needed to start a fire to heat our geodesic dome-house before we could start doing Yoga. Lighting a fire was a beautiful daily ritual. It reminded me of my childhood, when my grandmother had to light the coal oven every morning. Luckily the loft, which is where our bedroom was, got warm first.

In our geodesic dome we had a soft carpet to stretch out on and do Yoga, to slowly move from sleep to activity. I had a deeply moving dream that night that left me quite puzzled. It was a sort of prophetic dream, that heralded unsettling change in my life.

Throughout my life I have had many prophetic dreams.

One that was particularly interesting had happened years ago, when I was still married to my ex-husband Rick while I was studying philosophy on the East Coast of America.

Rick and I we were friends with Don and his former wife. I had dreamed one night, that all four of us were walking on the edge of a beach of an island. The odd part was that in the dream I was married to Don!

As we meandered down the beach, Don and I hand in hand together, I pointed to a house up on the high bluff and said: "Look, Don, that is our house up there."

At that time in my life, I was writing down all my dreams.

When I wrote this dream down, I thought "What a nice wishful dream! There's no chance Don and I would ever get married, live on an island and build a house together." But dutifully I noted all parts of my dream.

Seven years later, Don and I took a walk on the very same beach, not too long after Don and I had actually finished building our house on an island overlooking the water of the Pacific Northwest. As we were walking hand in hand along the beach, I turned to look up to point out our house on the high bluff to Don. That is when I suddenly recalled my dream from seven years ago.

As I rushed home to find my dream diary, I could hardly fathom the implications of that dream. Could it be that I had dreamed in great detail ahead of time the kind of life we now lived?

The dream was just as I had remembered it. Don and I were living that dream!

Many questions arose: Do we have destinies? Can we dream prophetically of our future even that far in advance? After all, how many twist and turns had my life taken to arrive at this reality with Don now.

Do we even have freewill?

As Don and I finished our Yoga and the fire was starting to heat the house, I pondered if my dream from last night was another one of those prophetic dreams? I really hoped not.

I had dreamed that I was walking downhill on a forest path. Sunlight streamed through the leaves and created a very vibrant play of lights. Suddenly a voice from above, deeply godlike, said: "You are done with Don, your lessons are complete. You need to leave him."

Don and I had been together for nearly fourteen years by now and had known each other for almost sixteen years. Was a fourteen year cycle coming to an end?

Was there an unconscious clock in the universe of relationships that ends in seven year cycles?

I was utterly shocked as I realized within my dream what I was being told. As I pondered what I had just heard, all the while still dreaming, I wanted to know my options.

Don and I loved each other deeply. We were the best spiritual partners, and we had a very grand life together. All the workshops we were teaching had grown out of our collective energy. We were in love and happy. The dream made no sense emotionally.

In desperation I asked the voice in my dream: "What can I do so we can stay together?"

The answer came in form of words and pictures. As I descended an earthy trail down a mountain slope in my dream, walking from a wooded forest into a village, I was told: "If you want to stay together, you will need to let other people into your relationship."

The next thing I knew, I was holding an older man in my arms in my dream. He had shoulder length grayish hair, and was thinly built. As I held him in my arms, he died. Was the an image of Don in his old age at the end of his life, and was I given a preview of our life together, if I followed this alternative suggestion? Or was this a different man altogether. It could not tell. The man certainly had the same body style as Don.

The message in my dream was clear: We needed to allow others into our relationship, our marriage. Needless to say, I was very perplexed when I woke up. I was deeply concerned about the depth of the dream, because the type of dream had those prophetic qualities that comes once in a great while.

Don and I talked about the dream after Yoga and didn't know what to make of it.

Soon, life took on its normal course of events and we let it all go. Neither Don or I wanted to change. So we didn't.

But that was all destined to change.

For the coming Spring of 1999 I had been invited to give talks at a number of conferences. One such talk to be given was in Florida at the Global Science Congress.

After finishing my talk and book signing at the Global Science Conference in Florida, a woman who was also on the speaker's panel approached me. She was a medical intuitive with a lot of authority, massive experience and an amazing success record. Her name was Patty Conklin: http://www.patticonklin.com. Patty offered to meet me for dinner and even do a reading for me.

To receive a reading from such a renowned psychic sounded wonderful. I'd had a health problem for nearly a year after taking antibiotics. Candida had nearly incapacitated me and it had taken most of the last year to get well again.

I was almost totally back to normal health, thanks to the help of Dr. Bob Beck's "Blood Cleanser," an electric pulser, which miraculously seems to help the body fight illness, as people told us. But I was curious what she had to say about my progress, and the cause of my health problem.

As we sat down to eat we chatted about her work. Doctors often called upon her help when they couldn't find anything on an x-ray but knew that the patient had a real problem. And she would find it. She was one of the best medical intuitives in the country. I was in good hands.

After eating together and chitchatting about her life, she began the reading for me, right there at the dinner table. Don had retired early, and I was eager to discover more about myself.

"Well," she said after a few minutes of silence, "what I have to tell you may shock you. Your health is fine, just 3% left of the Candida, but what started it all, and what your system is telling me is that you are not to be in a monogamous relationship."

This news set off an emotional ripple effect of grand proportions in me. Just three months ago I'd had my dream that had given me a similar message. And now she repeated the message again.

"If you want, I can talk to Don," she said. "I can imagine this isn't the easiest news to digest."

She was very certain of herself and she knew how unorthodox her reading was.

What was I going to do? My dream. Her reading. It all added up to one giant message I wanted to ignore.

The next day I told Don about her reading. We just took it all in, and made no plans to change our lives.

We were scheduled to teach at the Prophet's Conference to be held at the Spring Equinox in Mexico near the Chichen Itza Pyramid. We had no time to change our lives.

Accepting the Past and Changing the Future

Patty's message had deeply shaken my foundation. My dream had already felt ominous enough. Her reading confirmed the message of the dream: Let others into your heart.

But I was reluctant to make any changes in our life, despite the information I received from my dreams and the medical intuitive.

I was looking forward to our time in Mexico. I had worked "ahead" to prepare for the Prophet's Conference where I was to speak. Besides doing all the left brain work, such as writing outlines for the various talks and experiential seminars I was to give, I had spent time 'working' inwardly ahead of time. By entering the holographic dimension I sought out those images in the future that represented a luminous and awakening experience for us all at this conference.

The day had come to fly to Cancun Mexico. Don and I settled into our seats and soon found ourselves flying high at 33,000 feet above the Earth.

I took advantage of this higher altitude, in the heavens so to speak, to get in touch with higher states of consciousness. Imaginary or real, high above the world I often entered deeply meaningful reverie states. Slowly I rose high above Mexico in my mind's eye. I tried to sense if there was anybody that I needed to meet. Sending out an echolocation beam of sorts to the area of the conference I located a being that I felt I had a connection with and whom I had known for a long, long time. I sent a light beacon out to him or her along with a message that if we needed to meet he/she could find me in the conference halls of the Prophet's Conference in Cancun, Mexico. We met in a higher space and already were in contact now.

I love living in this kind of dream world. It seems to me that whenever I prepare reality from a higher vantage point, whenever I rise to a higher "seat of perception" and pre-create reality from here, things work out better in my 'real' life.

After sending out this call I opened my eyes and took in the sights of the clouds floating beneath us. Don and I started talking about our past lives and recollections we had of the land we were going to experience anew.

The hotel where the Prophet's Conference was being held was very tastefully decorated. The entire conference was a collage of presentations by lecturers and authors, experiential seminars, field trips to pyramids, music performances and sacred ceremonies.

The organizers had collected a great body of teachers and a wonderful crowd of very educated attendees. We were all looking forward to a very varied pilgrimage of our souls.

Mingling with the attendees as well as presenters proved to be equally as exciting. At lunches and dinners we exchanged amazing stories of supernatural experiences, new research and stories of the heart and made friends for years to come.

Only one dark cloud was hanging over this otherwise very eclectic meeting of shamanic teachers from North America, elders from Mexico, and Indian representatives.

The organizer had fallen ill from what he felt might have been a psychic attack. It seemed that there had been an upsetment about their unorthodox bringing together of shamans from all walks of life. Some were modern, some worked along the ancient methods.

There were misgivings from people who felt that life should stand still, and be forever the way it was. There should be no mixing of shamanic teachings, no modernization, no progress nor change. This was the way many of the old tribes used to function, very conservatively.

I could relate in some way: I wanted 'my Tibet' back the way it had been as well. I was still Tibetan somewhere inside of me, and I resented the invasion of the Chinese. But the Dalai Lama was wiser. His emphasis is on living *with* the change. His view is that this historic drama has allowed Buddhism to flourish all over the world as a result of the Chinese take-over. He preaches compassion and happiness and the middle way approach not to a separate Tibet, but an autonomous Tibet.

True I reasoned, we do need to evolve with the times. In the end we all change bodies through many lifetimes, and our soul doesn't belong to a country, but is a spark of God, that lives outside the identification with borders, planetary systems or even galaxies.

The day before the Equinox had arrived in Mexico. Knowing that famous pyramid of Chichen Itza was going to be swamped with tourists, we decided to visit one day ahead of time. We were going to hold a special ceremony on the site as well as witness an amazing display: A shadow-serpent climbing up the side of the pyramid.

This dance of the serpent only happens on the Equinox in Spring and Fall. On that day the sunlight hits the pyramid at just the right angle to create the mirage of a shadow-serpent walking the slopes of the steep pyramid, with the head of the serpent at the bottom. This pyramid truly was a masterpiece of celestial time keeping.

The Mexican Shaman who was a member of the lecturers, had accompanied our group to the pyramid. Near a special Cenote, a sacred waterhole, he had invited us to sit on the ground to go into meditation. He talked to us about parallel time portals and worm holes and spoke of the ancient history of this special Cenote. Soon I fell into a deep trance. The extraordinary energy of the time-space matrix at this multi-dimensional waterhole was drawing me in. I felt irresistibly pulled into a different universe and was mesmerized. Unable to move, I entered into this vision and allowed myself to enter another parallel reality. Rich and complex imagery filled my mind. It was one of those journeys, where I wondered if I would come out in another universe at the other end of the tunnel. Was I entering another reality this way?

I had not heard anyone get up or leave and only slowly returned to somewhat normal consciousness. The energy had been so strong that at first I could not move my body. After some time, I felt Don standing behind me, pulling on my spirit and eventually I pulled my fascination away from the waterhole and got up. This waterhole truly was an amazing portal.

In reverent silence Don and I walked the trail back to the pyramid. All the experiences here at the conference were starting to feel like a pilgrimage of my soul. Pilgrimages, even in the costume of touristy attractions, help shift our inner ruts, allow more expansion, and more light into our soul and daily life. Aspect were changing within me, and yet I didn't notice it. I had no conscious understanding of where I was going.

At the right moment Don and I found the rest of the group standing at the pyramid of Chichen Itza. The magical display of the sacred serpent was about to start. Mesmerized we watched the shadow-snake walking up the steps, celebrating the Equinox. It was a stunning visual effect. The stepping stones cast a continuously moving shadow which looked like a serpent moving up to the top of the pyramid.

Now and then my eyes kept wandering over to another group of people, just a little distance away. I saw a younger man with long, blond hair standing next to a very tall man, with dark, longish hair. Nothing yet warned me of the impeding events to come.

This day had been rich. Satisfied we returned back to the hotel and spent the evening sharing stories with attendees and presenters.

Don and I had not forgotten the reading and my dream about the potential changes that were ahead of us. They were beckoning us to address them.

What changes were ahead of us at a time in our life when we had exactly what we wanted?

Myths and Metaphors Guide our Lives

Don and I had just taken our morning shower. The lighting on the walls, the flowers looked so beautiful. The stucco walls, so typical for Mexico, surrounded us in an exotic field of energy that spoke of another era.

We were looking forward to take time to dive deeper.

I got in touch with my feelings about my health struggles for the last year. I had led a nice 'straight' life. But somewhere, I had parts of me in conflict with this 'straight' life.

Dr. Vernon Woolf had shown us how to enter the time/space fabric, the holographic pattern of the co-creative universe. As I had described in my earlier book *Journey to the Center of Creation*, Don guided me in the exploration of the rich inner landscape of my unconscious.

Don asked me if there was a place in my body where I could feel the difficulty, the challenge. I told him I felt it in my entire front, belly, heart, and sexual area.

A mixture of images came up. Getting stoned to death, as well as an image of a big 'A' inscribed on my forehead. It stood for 'adulteress.' Images of Mary Magdalene who had almost gotten stoned, and images of her deep love of Jesus arose, followed by images of Queen Guinevere who had been branded for her illicit love with Lancelot. And finally I felt a heavy burden on my chest.

"Does this feeling have a color, a shape?" Don asked compassionately. In his inner mind and heart he too had entered with me another world. This was the metaphorical world. Somehow I could feel his presence here and I felt a greater sense of closeness.

I dove deeper into my imagery.

The color of this feeling was dark, like a large rock. I remembered how a gypsy had given me a reading when I was a teenager, saying that I would always have two men in my life.

The burden I felt was heavy. I felt my own judgment against myself as well as the imaginary judgment from others, not to mention the weight of past lives that added to the feeling of heaviness on my chest.

When I was completely in touch with the feeling and image of this issue, Don asked me to place the image/feeling in front of me so I could perceive it objectively. I did, and the feeling of the burden on my chest eased.

Next Don guided me to ask the image what it really wanted.

"If this feeling could have what it really wanted, what would it be?" Don asked me in a sweet voice.

The answer came floating in, surprisingly easily. If we just would ask ourselves that question more often: 'How would it feel like IF we had what we really wanted!' We would get further in our pursuit of happiness more easily.

I saw an image of an orange-blue silken bedspread floating in my mind's eye. I had seen the same quilt at the home of my friend Roger in Hawaii. Above his bed, covered with this luminous bedspread had hung the famous painting of Radha and Krishna. It is the image of the divine beloved couple sitting on a swing hanging from the branches of a large tree.

That's what I wanted: Divine Love.

In the relationship of Krishna and Radha, Radha is almost always depicted as the supreme Beloved of Krishna, his greatest divine consort. Quoted from a dictionary: This was a love that happens not while married, but is rather an expression of the spontaneous love of God, not of the mundane, sexual nature.

The painting showed that although Radha was not married to Krishna, internally and eternally she was his most loyal consort, his Beloved.

Somehow I knew that this new image heralded a new future. But I couldn't fathom the depth that this metaphor would take on in our lives.

Don asked me if the image needed something else. "Do you have any other needs?" Don asked. Yes, I did.

Judgment – from others and myself – needed to be addressed. Somehow I knew that the silk bedspread image and the image of Radha and Krishna I had received from my subconscious mind invited other loves into my life. Their purpose was to raise my consciousness to God.

Though I felt that Don and I were living in high consciousness, more was being asked of us. Maybe I wanted to find my Krishna, a master of sorts, that would ignite me yet into higher dimensions. Or maybe this was the kind of next step we are asked to take, once we have mastered the previous steps of love. Life doesn't seem to favor homeostasis, but rather seems to continually invite exploration and evolution.

However, I still recalled the persecution in other lives due to adultery, and I felt restrain in myself to open to love in a grander scope.

Yet if I were to allow myself that kind of expansion, and if I could have what I wanted, I wanted society's support for all the adventures of my heart and soul, which went beyond the norm of society.

"How would you feel if you had that wish already fulfilled?" Don asked me.

Instantly a new image popped into my mind. It didn't make any sense, but I knew that it was the image of completion for me.

In this image I saw cobblestones in downtown Bonn, which had been the former German capital. These cobblestones formed the market place. It was where the courthouse was situated.

I smiled at the image. The stones were no longer used as weapons now, such as for stoning an adulteress, and they were not the sight of public disgrace, or of judgment. Instead they now represented the foundation for support of all I was to experience that lay outside the norm.

This collage of cobblestones, now dotted with palm trees, and floating above it all the orange-blue silk blanket, represented my new holographic reality.

I could see that this entire image was allowing me to have the experience of divine love, and that this would now be socially accepted. This I knew deeply in my heart and body. The holographic images speak to us holistically.

I was flying high with energy from the images. Deep waves of joy rushed through me. I thanked the old images and the feeling of the heavy burden and shame for wanting such a joyous fulfilled life, and I felt waves of gratitude.

By asking the old images what they truly want, they are free to show us what the deeper underlying wish really is. As bizarre as it may seem, dark energies, in the end, always want to give us a new positive future.

Usually the old energies try to fulfill our wishes, often though in a painful way. And if we follow their suggestions we usually wind up not getting what we really want. But by asking the fundamental question of what the negative symbols within us really want, we are shown their deeper truths and it opens the doorway through the black hole into a new future. All we need to do, is to image and feel such a future fulfilled.

After I thanked the old images of the stones and the letter 'A' for having wanted such an amazing future for me, I asked them if they were willing to transform into the new image of the cobble stones, the palm tree and the floating orange-blue silken bedspread. The new image was more likely to fully express my wish fulfilled than continuing to carry the images of being stones. That was for sure.

The images were willing to transform and I let the transformation proceed in my dreamy mind.

As soon as it happened, my body was extraordinarily ecstatic. I was so joyous I could hardly keep still. There was a deep release and transformation I felt throughout all my cells.

Don guided me to take the new images to my inner place of peace, and to introduce them to my highest Self. There the images would work together holographically to create a better life for me from the inside out. These new images were now my holographic steering committee of my subconscious mind.

I asked the images to go through any past experiences connected with the old image and to let all cells in my body be healed by the energy of the new images. As I let this happen, I felt an effect like dominos falling in my cellular memory of the past. My body started to feel the new energy.

Next we asked the new image to go into the future and prepare my new life. Little did I know what was coming. Soon the entire process was complete and Don gave me time to start moving my body slowly. I opened my eyes and looked into Don's deeply open blue eyes.

Don and I felt a great love for each other. We had shared a deep tracking session and I was so very grateful to have the love of my life and also my best friend and councilor in Don. It had taken a lot of practice to be good friends and lovers at once, and many times we had wanted to give up. But we never did. Even when I felt like screaming, or Don felt like walking into his "cave," we kept on keeping on. And here was our reward! My heart opened even wider and my love for Don was overflowing.

We were ready to have breakfast now, so we got up and went outside to meet the real world. The breakfast buffet was still open and we were guided to a wonderful table at the edge of a terrace, with two Mexican wooden chairs at a little table. There, in the rays of the sun, with flowers around us, we were in heaven. Don and I beamed at each other. His eyes were brilliantly blue, and my heart flowed like a huge river. We were speechless from all the love we felt.

If I hadn't known what the central theme of my imagery session and the message from the medical intuitive was, namely: 'To integrate the message of my dream to allow others into our married life,' I would have thought I had just had a session to fall more in love with Don. Maybe I had.

The First Kiss

The next day, after Don and I had finished our imagery session and we had had our breakfast, I sat as a member of the lecturers on a panel discussion. These gave the audience a chance to interact with the presenters. Together we discussed the emerging shamanic wisdom in all cultures, modern and ancient. Next on the schedule was a lecture by a well known Native American.

Don had decided to take a walk outside for a while, and I sat alone in the audience. A gorgeous young man sat next to me. His jet-black, straight hair flowed over his shoulders and he looked Native American. I couldn't keep from glancing over at him from time to time, and as he noticed he leaned over to comment on the bad lecture we were privy to.

The lecturer was hitting my buttons. Although he was a well respected Native American, he was hard to listen to. He was accusing anyone, other than Native Americans, of being bad. I did realized that the personal and collective history of his people had hardened his heart. In his upbringing, he kept being told, that he was bad. And these were the words he now repeated to us.

Generations of oppression by white occupiers in America were guiding his tongue and heart. Every other sentence he offered us was, "You are bad!" Whether directed at us or not, knowing the power of hypnosis through the use of language, as taught in NLP, I knew how powerful his message was to our subconscious mind, and how damaging it could be, whether it was directly aimed at us or not.

Again I looked at my handsome neighbor, and we both nodded at each other in consent that this was a bad lecture. Just as I looked over at him again, blaring white light fell into the conference room, straight into my eyes. Someone was opening the door over and over again, stepping out and out of the hall. I became annoyed at the unconscientiously intruder. "Who is the inconsiderate person that keeps coming in and out of the room, opening and closing the door?" I wondered. I tried to watched who opened the door over and over again. Lo and behold it was the young man with the long blond hair that I had seen at Chichen Itza! How dare he let this much light fall into this dark lecture hall!

I would have laughed at myself, had I noticed the deeper meaning of this metaphor. Luckily, the lecture was soon over and we all got up and milled about.

The young, very good looking Native American that had been sitting next to me, tried to strike up a conversation with me, as we stood near the entrance. Since my early childhood I had loved Winnetoo, the Native American, played by Pierre Brice in the Karl May Stories featuring the friendship of the last Mohican Indian with a white man by the name of Leather Stocking. Whenever Don would spot a man with long, black hair he would tap on my shoulder and say with a smile, "Look, your ideal image of a man is standing over there."

Suddenly, the young guy with his blond, long, curly hair tied back in a ponytail and hippy shorts, who had opened the doors incessantly, came up to us, looked straight at me and said, "I'm supposed to find a woman at this conference who has something to teach me. Can you help me to find her? She supposedly knows about the Mayan Calendar."

He had come to the conference on someone's recommendation, because he wanted to find some woman he had met earlier.

Although he was the exact opposite of my ideal image of a man, something inside of me stirred as our eyes locked onto each other.

His name was Merlin and he was born in Germany. He had lived in Mexico for the last four years, working as a massage therapist.

As I talked with him, all my annoyance left me, and I was riveted. This man summoned my attention above and beyond the ideal image of a man, who was still standing next to me. Everything faded away as we stood and started to talk.

I walked over to the exhibit tables nearby where I had books for sale and I introduced Merlin to Don. I wanted to make sure I gave Merlin the right impression, being married and all.

I was delighted with Merlin and wanted to keep in contact, so I signed a copy of my book and gave it to him as a gift, hoping it would give him a reason to stay in touch with me.

Unfortunately he needed to leave soon, to keep looking for the woman he wanted to find. So I let go, and let fate take its course.

Later that evening a number of speakers and attendees had gathered just outside a restaurant. Buzzing with aliveness like a pod of dolphins, we all talked about going out for dinner. To top this excitement, Merlin suddenly showed up out of nowhere and wanted to join us. I was ecstatic to see him again. But since he had been camping, his dress code wasn't up to the standards of the restaurant and he was asked to find new clothing and return later. He left in a flash to his car find better clothing.

As we entered the restaurant, a film crew from New York came up to me and asked me to do an interview. I agreed somewhat reluctantly.

Gone would be my chance to meet Merlin again. In a hurry I grabbed a bite to eat and soon rushed out to find the room where the interview was to be held. The sun was setting and I had to cross the parking lot to find the right building for the interview.

I sighed and thought of Merlin, wishing he was still here. He really had caught my attention. Suddenly, out of thin air Merlin appeared in the parking lot in front of me.

He walked up to me as if he had been looking for me all along. We hugged gently and my body melted into his. Needless to say, I invited him to stay for the interview, and promised we'd spend some time alone afterwards. He accepted.

I felt stiff during the interview, not my usual self. Somehow, though I knew what I wanted to get across, I couldn't focus. Merlin was sitting to the side and I felt distracted. It was getting dark and I couldn't wait for the interview to be done. As we stepped outside the warm night's air greeted us. Stars were shining brightly above us, as we strolled outside, winding down pathways through the greenery of the hotel grounds.

Since I was a public speaker I felt I needed some privacy for this encounter. Everyone knew me as married with Don, and I was walking with a handsome young man alone.

We found a small river that flowed through the hotel gardens and stopped atop a small bridge far away from where all the others were.

After a few moments of chit chatting, we fell into a deep silence. Standing across from each other, we started to gaze deeply into each other's eyes. My mind fell into an ancient silence and gone was any need to talk. Our communion was more complete than many talking could ever produce.

As I looked into his eyes I started seeing a deeper light. My eyes gazed at his face and at once at the inner world. I imagined rising on a beam of light together with him, to "find" the true residence of his soul. He had the refined energy of a kingly being.

As I rose higher, opening myself to his deeper layers of his truth, I saw an image of a large palace. It was an open space with marbled floors and marbled columns. It looked like it could also been a temple in the mountains somewhere. I entered his palace and walked slowly towards him. Merlin showed himself as he truly was, he let his pure essence shine. In this inner experience I felt like we truly met.

I felt that he had been very lonely for quite some time, waiting for someone to come and find him, as if no one had come to visit his soul in his true dwelling place. I had risen quite high on the beam of light and understandably he hadn't had too many visitors that were able to find him in his true dwelling space. Most humans are satisfied to talk but not really meet. But the deeper parts of us, our soul, resides in a world much finer than our egos and we want to be seen, met and found.

It can be lonely down here on Earth when we don't find others with whom we can really connect with. It is all the more breathtaking when we do find someone we can commune with at a deeper soul level.

True, it was odd to be silent together and to start feeling the subtle nuances of meeting in soul. We don't usually do this with strangers, or even our best friends.

Think about how uncomfortable is it to be still and in silence together for more than one minute. It is usually awkward in social and even family settings. We hardly open ourselves that deeply even in our long term relationships. Getting that close in our souls means letting someone into us, really letting ourselves be seen, and to allow someone to penetrate us to the core.

I felt drawn to open my soul and Merlin cooperated. I could see the light of his eyes sparkle back at me as he felt me meeting him. It was a meeting somewhere in a world far above the ordinary human world.

With a few words here and there we shared what we were experiencing.

He told me that he had been attached emotionally to a woman from Germany, who was now living in Australia. And though they didn't have much contact anymore, others around Merlin felt that she was his fiancé. He had done this kind of eye gazing with her often.

What was I doing? I never ever let any man in my life get this close, so quickly. Yet feeling our souls touch, I felt like we had known each other for ever and had waited for this moment.

I recalled the energy of the being that I had sensed ahead on our flight to Mexico. Suddenly I felt myself let go.

Merlin had held me in his arms, as we swayed back and forth to the Spanish music that was floating in the air. A sultry female singer's voice drifted over to us as we stood on the bridge, letting our hearts follow the sound of the music.

Merlin took my head in his hands and pressed our foreheads together, keeping our eyes open. His nose touched mine and being this close his eyes looked like those of an eagle. He felt innocent in doing this, like a child in wonder and awe at the close up look of our eyes gazing at each other.

Yes, I liked this. We stared at each other for a long time, walking through gates of inner realms, breathing each other's breath.

Slowly his face came ever closer to mine and the side of his lips parted ever so lightly to touch my face. Soft, without tension, his lips touched my cheeks, slowly inching downward to seek my lips. He rested softly on the corner of my mouth, inviting me gently to respond.

His mouth opened wider, beckoning me to answer his call. And then I did what I never did with anyone but Don. We started to kiss. I don't even kiss good friends or family members on the mouth, and certainly not a stranger. Being married kissing others was out of question. This was a new 'me,' and the new images in my subconscious, my new holographic imagery, was busily at work. Five hours had passed since Don and I had completed the imagery session, where we knowingly opened our doors to other loves in our lives. And here was Merlin!

As he softly touched my face with his lips, he pressed his hips against mine, wrapped his arms around me and pulled me even closer toward him. My hips were already pushing against the railing behind me and I felt our arousal climb.

After some time Merlin pulled his face away from me to look at me in awe. He told me that he had made a prayer the night before. He wanted to find a woman who could show him how to love. His heart had been closed down, and he wanted to learn about love. What a great line that could be. But I trusted him. His eyes were true.

Just today had I done the imagery session myself with Don. And he too standing in front of me was maybe the answer to my prayer. Both of us seemed to have called each other in. Although it was socially uncouth, I felt good. It was not right to be this open to another man while married in ordinary human terms, but I knew that this was the right step in my life right now.

I had been in love with Don so deeply and this morning we had felt more love than ever. At the same time I was in an embrace with a man I barely knew, who had come to find a woman to teach him to love.

As Merlin shared his heart with me, I told him how beautiful he was. He replied, "That's what you say now, when you don't know me, but you may not say it later." I had no idea how much I would be tested!

Later on we said "Goodbye." In two days time we were going to try to meet up again. Both of us were going to join the ceremonial march to another pyramid. We hoped to be able to see each other again at that pyramid.

The Truth Shall Set You Free

As Merlin and I parted, I was leery of going back into a crowd that knew Don had been without me all evening during a music performance. Everyone had asked him: "Where is Ilona?" Luckily he had not been quite alone. He'd been holding hands with two beautiful women, one on either side of him during the performance. He could tell that something was up. No interview would take that long.

Although Don had guided me through the imagery transformation and we knew that some things in our lives were about to change, and although we had an agreement that allowed us to open to other people more intimately than before, I still needed to check with Don every step of the way. This was a way to honor each other's feelings. We were walking as partners through life, sharing our abilities, strengths, as well as our weaknesses.

Our commitment to each other had the highest priority. Asking Don for permission is all my steps of communing with others along the way, gave Don the chance to veto what I was doing, if he didn't feel right with it. By letting him know what was going on, I gave Don the power to say NO if he needed to. It gave him the chance to ask me to stop in my tracks. If at any moment Don would have said "Drop it!" I would have.

We are not superhuman, and our need for security is a strong byproduct of our human bonding behavior. Helen Fisher has done a lot of research on the chemical and hormonal mating and bonding pattern in animals and humans. The need for security and at the same time the drive for freedom form the two polarities we encounter when we enter a bond. We need to come to terms with these. Don and I were trying to unify these opposing drives in our hearts consciously. Most people do this in secret, or even try to suppress their opposing needs just to find themselves leaving the relationship inwardly or even outwardly sooner or later.

I took a deep breath as I stood with Don about to tell him of my recent encounter with Merlin. It had helped me to imagine what I would face if I didn't tell Don. Secrecy produces distance, which to me is far more painful.

Instead, I took the plunge and presented my facts to Don in a playful way. I admit, I didn't make my experience sound terribly disturbing. That was my way of squirming around the edges of truth, but I shared the general story of my experience with Merlin, and it gave Don a chance to tell me to stop.

He didn't and instead told me about his experiences. His freedom for the moment didn't feel undesirable to him either.

The connection between our inner holographic work and the outward manifestation of Merlin that afternoon had come very quickly. Barely five hours had passed and voila, my life was about to change.

The reason many, if not most, people are secretive about such extracurricular encounters as I had experienced, is, that they don't want to hurt their mate's feeling, and that they don't want to experience the predictable jealousy. And we don't want anyone to interfere with our newfound joy either. Ideally we want our partner to keep feeling secure, to stay with us, all the while we engage in a potentially threatening encounter of freedom with another person. We want to assure ourselves that we can have our cake and eat it too. But by lying we never create security, instead we create a huge distance between us and our partner, as we can never truly share our entire truth with them once we started lying.

A kiss in not even necessary to create havoc in the fragile fabric of love. Intimacy of souls can be much more disturbing to partners than a kiss or even sex. If we wish to open our lives to deeper and more meaningful soul contacts, we need to develop new ethics, new understanding and new maturities.

In our modern world we want to think that we are totally independent and free of one another. Our possibility to survive alone financially has brought with it a lessening of the need to bond. More and more people are single, and plagued by it, because they wish to reaffirm their personal identity, without compromise.

But once we start to co-create an energy cocoon together, as we enter into a union of sorts, we become interdependent. At first this union is not that noticeable, and our cocoon is not that large either. We only need each other's emotional presence a little bit. But as time goes on we start to depend more and more on each other. This is especially true when we move-in together, as we form a marriage, or start a family. We create a veritable ball of energy together. Although invisible to our mind and our physical eyes, we start to depend on each other for more and more of our needs: be they emotional or sexual, mental or related to our soul, or our very home.

Even in lesser committed relationships it is foolish to think that a partner is independent from us. Trust only grows in the environment of a mutually created field of energy. With time we live increasingly in this cocoon of energy with our Beloved if both partners feed it. As this cocoon grows in depth, its ability to nurture us, and in its ability to stimulate growth in both partners expands as well. Such expansion of our capacity results from the combination of our souls.

We are not an island unto ourselves. If we try to remain 'free' we should really not enter any deeper connections. Some people are truly only interested in momentarily diving into the most superficial, impersonal union, the impressions of which behave like water that pearls off the back of a duck. Such unions are for gigolos or flirts at best, or for a person who is phobic of commitment, but does not carry the ability to co-create a cocoon in which they can care for another being.

Quick unions are for people who don't want to lose their imaginary freedom. Those relationships never transform us. They don't require the depth of love that makes our soul grow and glow. Being independent, we never have to give to another being anything that goes beyond fulfilling our personal needs and wants. We never need to learn the art of surrender or give of ourselves to a higher cause in such quick merging of soul or body.

But when we want to create a bigger energy field together, either to raise ourselves to a higher platform as souls as can happen in union, or to have a safe haven in which children can be raised, both partners are in fact totally dependent on what they each do, and where they spend their energy.

When we create a cocoon together, an egg of energy, this union continues to nurture and stimulate us, whether we are physically close or apart.

As such, a partner should have the right to say "Yay, or Nay" when we choose to spend our energies elsewhere. This would apply to a question of whether we take on a second job, start night school, or all sorts of others ways to spend energy.

If he/she approves, fine. If our partner doesn't approve we need to negotiate. Either we can listen to his/her needs and find a mutually satisfying answer, working on fulfilling both party's needs, or, if that proves impossible, we can leave the relationship.

But we can't steal the energy away from our partner and expect them to remain present with us. Even if they did, unconsciously they will seek the energetic balance elsewhere sooner or later too.

If we don't say anything about the facts that we know all too well would hurt our partner, all we do is to try and protect ourselves from a possible loss of our mate. We should give him/her the fair chance to say 'yes' or 'no' to our extraneous energy exchanges, be they related to work, friends, loves, or spiritual encounters.

To keep silent, and to keep such energy exchanges secret, keeps the partner puzzled as to what is really going on. They sense that the energy is moving elsewhere usually unconsciously. But not knowing what is really happening, he/she will not be able to make adjustments in their life, if they are not told. With time they may feel more and more uneasy, unloved, and disconnected and it may leave them feeling paralyzed and unable to move their energy productively forward.

Lies have a way of hypnotizing us. Somehow we as humans are ill-equipped to handle contradictory information. Our gut level instinct may tell us one thing, but when we hear a lie, some part of us goes into a trance and doesn't know what to do. Lying is a very toxic behavior, that stops true development of our heart and soul. Lies build walls.

If I may paraphrase Erich Fromm from his book *The Art of Loving*:

"In the beginning of our love relationships, we let go of all walls, we drop all protection. We let ourselves be seen. This feels exhilarating and we feel loved. Maybe this is the only time, when we let the other see us so clearly. We glow, we shine, and we open in love.

"After that, if the little lies set in, the wall goes up, one brick at a time. Each lie is a brick in the wall between us and our lover. In having lies we cannot share our true self. We can only share half of our selves. A wall grows that is so thick that love and intimacy get lost."

I did paraphrase liberally. But that is about what he says.

So how do we keep love flowing?

By allowing our partner to see us as we are, to keep defenses down and truly listen to the needs of each other.

The bottom line of all arguments seems to be the question: "Do you still love me?" and "Can I get my needs met and still be loved by you?"

Lies seem to be a way to try and keep getting what we want and not to lose what we want to keep as well. To have our cake and eat it too.

We all have a primitive brain center that wants to protect the nest. The chemicals our brain pours out when we bond emotionally and sexually partly want to make sure we keep our mate. Some of us have these hormones flood through our bodies more strongly than others, and women seem to be have more bonding hormones than men. Men are designed to spread their seed, women are designed to keep the nest going until the young are raised.

This mix of hormones and the drive to be secure and free are in great contradiction to each other. But if we want to live in an integral, powerful, soul-realized relationship, we need to come to terms with truth, our biological nature, and our different needs.

In truth we are all transparent. Any higher developed being can see the truth about anyone, anytime. Even the subconscious knows, and reacts. The body knows and doesn't lie. But we twist ourselves many times, because we want to avoid the conflict of telling the truth and dealing with the consequences.

The maturity that it took for Don and I to give space to each other to allow other people into our close-knit marriage, without running away, was and is hard earned each step of the way.

Fears, insecurity, the emotional reaction of our primal brain, are all aspects that add into the equation of relationships, whether we like it or not.

Love, as an absolute strength of selflessness, is not a given ability in any new relationship, but rather a strength earned through trial and error in the voyage of love. Don and I wanted to stay in love and be willing to expand our limits.

After I was done telling Don about my meeting with Merlin I felt better. It seemed that Merlin had shown up by chance, but in a bigger perspective it merely mirrored the transformation we had finally allowed within ourselves. The higher design was trying to birth itself. Don and I saw the bigger picture and we were willing to keep walking in the direction we had started our new voyage.

I was relieved to see that my somewhat harmless meeting with Merlin didn't seem to threaten Don, as he had given me his permission beforehand. Don also reasoned that soon we would be leaving Mexico to return to Hawaii, our island-home away from home. So we thought ourselves to be safe.

The Voice of Fate

Two days after the Equinox celebration the entire conference group and its faculty members went on a ritualistic walk to another pyramid. I was really hoping to meet Merlin again.

In a large opening in the forest just a few hundred yards away from the pyramid we formed a circle and held hands with tribal elders.

The faculty members had been asked to perform a blessing ritual and share a special drink of Kava juice during the ceremony. My job was to perform a blessing and to pass out small portions of this sacred liquid. Merlin had arrived too, but alas, he had found "the woman" he thought he was looking for. He stood in the circle next to her like a ghost. Gone was his light and fire. I could see he was struggling. Maybe he didn't feel good being seen with her and knowing how we had spent the evening on that bridge.

I was perplexed, sad, and unsure what to do. It was clear that they were together and I had to let go. Was the past evening a onetime event?

After the ceremony, Don, I, Merlin and several others took the short walk to the nearby pyramid. A special chamber had been carved into the pyramid near the peak. One woman who wore a crystal on her shaven head, was sitting inside this cave, and hummed a silent mantra as we arrived. I joined her in the silence. Merlin had climbed yet higher to sit on top of the chamber, on the very top of the pyramid. A few other women had climbed with him to the peak. It was clear they all wanted to be near him.

In that case, I thought, I was definitely not going up on top to join the gopis! Consequently I stayed on the platform below, where a camera man took the opportunity to take pictures of me. Soon Merlin noticed that I had not followed him like all the others, and he leaned over the edge to ask me to come and join him. But I stayed where I was. The day was not as magical as I had hoped.

One by one we slowly left the pyramid and started on our way home. Don and I climbed into the bus that was waiting for our group and drove off. As I sat in silence I dreamed of seeing Merlin and wished he was with me.

Attracted by the colorful art ware at the side of the road, we asked the bus driver to stop at a shop on the side of the road to look at some of local pottery. Lo and behold, Merlin pulled up in his car right next to me as I entered the parking lot. I caught my breath as the sunlight reflected off his golden bronzed arms leaning on the open window of his car. Crouched next to his car door I laid my hand on his arm gently, looking at him in hopes of recognition. Astonished, he looked at me, and tried to introduce me to the woman he was traveling with. 'Was I too forthright?' I wondered.

Apparently he wanted to establish a hierarchy, and it was clear that I was at the bottom of this totem pole.

I made sure to tell him however which hotel we were moving to next for our dolphin excursion, which was to follow the conference.

I was scheduled to lead a wild dolphin excursion as part of the Prophet's Conference, and we were going to move to a hotel near a beach. Merlin took note of the hotel's name and drove off, while I was wishing I was in his car.

Our dolphin excursion was to last for a few days, and I hoped Merlin was going to join us. But he was nowhere to be seen. 'He is probably not going to show up again,' I reasoned. 'After all, why would he want to see me, when he found the woman he was looking for?'

On the second day, early in the morning, a group of fifteen participants plus Don and I met at the pier. We were going to take a boat ride out into the channel to look for dolphins. They had high hopes. Last year dolphins had been sighted in the deeper channel and the captain felt fairly certain that we might see more of them this year.

I had taken Dramamine, because the waves were high. Everyone was dressed in beach clothing and the sun was shining from an azure blue sky. The water sparkled in purple and turquoise colors that made me feel as if it was from another dimension.

After about 45 minutes of looking for dolphins I began to get a sinking feeling in my stomach. We gathered to meditate in a circle, but the waves were too high to allow us to hold hands. I saw people closing their eyes and trying to call out to dolphins in their minds. This was a scenario nobody wanted. We were looking and looking but the waves were too high, which made it hard to recognize any dolphin fins. Another hour went by and we all started to feel low. The waves made several of us queasy and our hopes sank even lower. The captain asked me what to do. I didn't want to tell him that months ago I had been told that it was going to be hard to find dolphins in these channels. How lucky we were to have found them in Key West, where they appeared every day. There, the water is shallow and I didn't have to deal with large waves at all.

After looking around the circle, we decided we had had enough of the rough sea and asked the captain to return to land. Disappointed, we tried to make the best of the situation by gathering on the beach and working on our ESP skills.

People had paid extra money to be with dolphins. But wild dolphins are not on a schedule. Finding dolphins and swimming with them is not a certain event.

Finally we had time off, and Don and I took the opportunity to rest from the strenuous experience on the boat. But I couldn't sleep. Images of Merlin ran like a fever through my mind and body. I deeply wanted to see him again.

Suddenly we heard a knock on the door. I got up, looked through the viewfinder and nearly fainted. It was Merlin. He had remembered the name of the hotel and made a trip on a whim to find me.

He entered the room as if we knew each other well, and stood at the end of our bed as if it was the most natural thing to do. While he chatted with Don, I jumped up to get dressed so he and I could go for a walk – alone. I had checked with Don quickly, and he had nodded in agreement.

Downstairs, Merlin introduced me to the woman he had taken to the ceremony.

"It must be serious," I thought, and took an inner step back from him.

As we walked away from her, I asked him straight out, "Are you with her?"

"No way," he replied, "we just camped together, nothing more."

Hmmm, so he could be close and not feel much. But somehow I felt delighted. There was still a chance.

We walked alone along the white sandy beach, away from any prying eyes, and found a dune of pure white sand with the sun setting behind us, silhouetting the palm trees. The ocean glowed in turquoise and purples and the moon was rising.

"A picture perfect moment," he said. It really was. My heart was singing, and as if to complete this perfect moment, he took me into his arms. As if I was in a movie, he embraced me and started sensuously moving his body against mine. Soon we were rolling around on the sand, but something was amiss.

It was all too fast for me and I felt nothing. No excitement, no love. Nothing.

I asked Merlin if we could just sit in front of each other and be silent. We tried to look deeply into each other's eyes, to find the same connection we'd had before. But I could not feel his heart.

Although it had all seemed so perfect, I had to let it go. I had never been one for a short fling. Having been married I was accustomed to connecting deeply; not playing on the surface. Instead, Merlin and I sat side by side and felt the evening's cool air touch our skin. Merlin had no jacket so we shared mine. In a way, this was more intimate than rolling in the sand. As it got darker we went back and joined Don and the others for dinner.

Merlin's companion was there also and we all took our seats at a large round table in the Mexican style restaurant. While everyone was scanning the menu, at one special moment I looked up at Merlin to my right. He had the most amazing light in his eyes as he returned my gaze.

He looked very princely at that moment, and a deep loud voice said in my head: "This is your future husband!"

That is the kind of moment you remember for a lifetime. As if a narrator from above gives hidden messages to an actor on the stage of life.

"Excuse me?" I nearly said out loud. "I am very happily married," I thought to the voice. But there were no more comments.

Everyone was talking a lot at the table, while I staggered inwardly. Was this the voice of fate, the voice of a director from a higher vantage point than mine?

My dream a few months ago, the session with the medical seer, and the session with Don just days ago to allow myself to change my holographic field, all seemed to work hand in hand.

Merlin had shown up at the right moment. But nothing had really happened, except that I heard a promise for the future in my mind, a prediction of sorts, that I didn't really want. I really wanted to stay with Don, as I had said in my dream. In a way, I rather wanted to allow others into our relationship, but at the same time stay with Don.

But was there such a thing as fate? Did I have other lessons to learn? Was there freewill?

Merlin seemed to be the person of the moment to me. He seemed to be having fun in the moment. I preferred to think long term. But I also knew of prophetic powers, of destiny.

Finally it was time to get up, and we hugged each other goodbye after dinner. Merlin and I took a while to say goodbye to each other. Before he left I memorized his email address just in case I wanted to stay in touch.

Don seemed happy to let it all happen and had walked over to the side a bit, so that I had some space alone with Merlin. Don surprised me deeply with the love and allowance he gave me. In my imagery, days ago, I had pre-created a holographic inner energy field in which the stones that would have been used to stone a woman to death in this kind of scenario were now the cobblestones of a market place.

The image of the cobblestones with the freedom of the palm trees and the orange silken cloth were all symbolic of receiving the support of society and my husband, in everything I was doing on this new adventure. So far the image was creating a harmonious field. It was as if I was being guided from a higher dimension.

The next day we left, having made amazing connections with all the participants. Although we had not encountered dolphins, we had spoken of ETs and dolphins and had been transformed by the magic of the whole week.

We flew home to our dome house on the island in the Pacific Northwest. In six weeks, we were to lead a week-long seminar in Hawaii. I had mentioned to Merlin that he was welcome to attend our seminar for free, before we parted ways, if he could make it to Hawaii in time.

Mother Mary Comes to Me

Don and I arrived home to a load of emails and office work. Don needed to do extra trainings for the SE-5, a radionics instrument, on the phone, and our office workers had missed all our extra help. It was still cold in the Northwest. But tulips as well as hyacinth were blooming and greeted us with deep, fragrant smells when we walked up the steps of our dome house.

I loved Spring in the Northwest, with its spray of colors. We stood admiring the trees, loaded with blossoms and the view that overlooked the water. White apple blossoms amidst the rhododendron in fuchsia and pinks let us know that Spring was in full celebration. Nature was a true witness to the life-force in action.

In six weeks time we would be in our warm Hawaiian paradise. It was just enough of a time gap to really enjoy the cool Spring here in the Northwest, since we knew that very soon we would be surrounded by balmy warmth, the oceans, dolphins and Summertime.

One late afternoon I sat down to meditate by the fire. The woodstove was still needed to keep us warm and cozy. The flames of the fire flickered next to me as I slowly I entered my inner worlds. This ancient form of heat nurtured me deeply.

First, I felt the field of the air and space around me as I started to relax. Air was touching me and if I really paid attention I could feel it, which led me to feel space as energy around me. Soon I became aware of a greater field of energy surrounding me like a vast cocoon. Feeling more and more layers of refined vibrations around myself, I started to take on the feeling of becoming an increasingly larger field of space. It was at once around me, as well as filling me with more light. A feeling of well-being entered me as I gave way to this softer sense of being "me."

My breath started to flow deeper, and something inside of me let go. I accepted the moment as it was, letting life simply surround me. As I continued to focus outwardly, I started to feel as if I went upward within the cocoon. I was becoming a column of light, reaching higher into the cosmos. There was no real movement as such, yet a shift of perception happened. I felt as if I was "moving" through layers of clouds, rising to find finer vibrations of whatever it was that surrounded me.

I rose upward and outward in size and scope. Layers of space fell behind me or beneath me, as new ones came up. I ascended into continuously finer layers of the universe, or rather of consciousness.

I knew I was calibrating my frequency upward, which appeared to me as moving through layers of light upward. In our language we refer to space and time, and we describe any change of perception as a movement through space and time. In this case I felt like I was going up. Another person might say she was going inward, deeper, down, inside. I could also say that I expanded and became ever larger.

Our minds are accustomed to recognizing only the obvious, that which exists in time-space. For many of us the perception of subtleties in emotions is already a difficult task. How difficult would it then be to perceive something that is beyond the ordinary measurements of time-space? How can we adequately describe *becoming* the knowledge that is harbored *in space*? How do we describe the feeling of simultaneousness?

Through likening inner experiences to our three-dimensionally trained mind of perception, it will always sound as if the inner frontier is linear, like the outer universe appears to be. But when we practice subtler perception, we learn to distinguish realities, and we get accustomed to the finer nuances of Is-ness. Soul is the origin within all of us. But just how in touch are we with this core of us, that is a question of practice.

How fully alive and lit is this unit of consciousness, our soul, that steers our human ship? Our level of awareness depends on us. The more we bring this unit of awareness, our soul, into full alignment with the source, God, or whatever you want to name it, the more we feel large, fulfilled, and expanded.

Being expanded gives us the feeling of floating, since we no longer harbor our identity within our body-suit. Floating is a feeling that we get when we go beyond our known limits, when we expand. It is a feeling when we reach beyond the confines of who we have known ourselves to be.

We like to be in the flow, connected to a larger state of being. Being expanded gives us a feeling of ecstasy. This then is the universes' way to reward us.

That day, as I was deep in this inner state of awe, it seemed like outer space came to surround me. Suddenly, Mother Mary appeared in my vision, holding a baby. Deep blue veils that covered her head were gently draped around her face. She held her arms out, as if to give the baby to me.

In my mind I asked her who's baby it was. Don had had a vasectomy so it couldn't have been from him. Besides, Don really didn't want to have a baby.

Her answer was very clear: "It will be from Merlin!"

"WHAT?" I was floored.

The voice in Mexico had said he would be my future husband, and now Mother Mary was giving me his baby. Maybe my subconscious was having a heyday, concocting a new future. But during both experiences I felt as if a higher force was at work.

In realistic terms though, I had no plans to visit Merlin. He was living in Mexico, and we'd had only scant contact via email.

"You will see," was the almost audible answer I got from Mother Mary.

This was a real vision for me. I don't know where my archetype of Mother Mary came from. I was not raised Catholic. But here it was. I knew it was a real message.

The vision left me feeling perplexed, moved and in awe. But it seemed too unrealistic for me to give it even a second thought. So with that, I filed the vision away as "very interesting!"

Weeks later, just before we were to leave for Hawaii, Merlin called. He wanted me to know that he had made plans to sell everything in Mexico, including his car, and fly to Australia, via Hawaii. He wanted to attend our workshop that I had invited him to.

"You are still planning on it?" he asked.

This was too much. There had been no indication of a realistic future with him. I had not been very warm to him on our last evening on the beach in Mexico, and I doubted that it was either me or my subconscious that was pulling him to come to Hawaii.

"Yes, of course," I told him on the phone. "We are about to hold a *Living From Vision*® class and of course you can come!" I told him he had to fly to Hilo, the biggest town on the Big Island of Hawaii and that he could stay at our house during the seminar along with two other women friends who were planning to attend and would also stay with us.

I had wanted to have a pod of dolphins in human form at our house, and it was now looking like it was about to manifest. The seminar participants were all staying at the "Kalani Honua" retreat center, on the other side of the forest next to our house, about one mile down the road.

What a surprise his call was! I could hardly believe it. It was almost as if events were being organized by a higher force. Were they?

The days flew by. There were lots of details, paperwork and emails to attend to. The seminars and the one-on-one sessions were where my heart and soul soared. But the nitty-gritty details of organizing and emailing were also part of my work. At times I felt like I only wanted to do the fun things, like meditate and teach guided imagery. But that was to come soon enough.

Off we flew to Hawaii.

Shape-shifting the Time-Space Matrix

When we walked up to the customer service counter at the Los Angeles Airport, crowds of people were squeezing in on us from all sides. El Niño's rain had delayed many flights, and this "Act of God" was merciless. We had just flown in from Seattle and were about to change flight to take off to Hawaii. Don and I needed to teach our seminar in Hawaii in three days and we had missed our connecting flight.

Hoards of people had also missed their connections and were frantic. Everyone tried their best to be on top of the pile, to get a re-routed flight. I made my way to the customer service desk of our airline. The lady in front of me got to the counter as I was taken by the next agent to her right and I overheard her plight. Unfortunately, due to the weather, there was nothing that could be done. She was screaming, threatening, bargaining and lastly using guilt on the customer service representative, who finally had enough. I was getting a bit concerned when my customer service rep with her red hair told me that all the flights to Hawaii were booked to the brim for the next three days.

"Impossible," I thought. "We need to be in Hawaii to teach the seminar. Too many people are coming from afar. We have to get there!"

I took a deep breath and did something that shamans and shape shifters do: I moved my feeling of being, my center of presence, into another world. Right "here" in all this turmoil existed many, simultaneous realities. Nothing was utterly solid in the quantum world of potential.

Slowly, I moved in my awareness to a higher, faster vibrational point. I felt myself become my greater illumined light-body. Next, I contacted the higher essence of the customer service woman in front of me. She too could be seen at many levels, and what I chose to focus on had an effect. In each moment we can either live in a lesser intensity of presence or a greater one. It will have an effect on what we manifest.

The tirade of negative words next to me continued. "Sorry Madam, we are not responsible for an 'Act of God.' All I can say is, sleep at the airport and go on stand-by on every flight until you get out!" Her words hung in the air like a verdict. The harsh reality of sleeping at the airport with hundreds of other people, or staying at one of the rather costly hotels nearby was not a pretty future.

In my mind and heart I held a higher vision. I knew that the laws of physics do not hold up at all times. Rather like in a dream, the outcome depends on what kind of feelings we hold in our minds and in our hearts. In dreams as in "real" life, our energy determines our reality. The law of resonance applies to our thoughts and feelings just like it applies to music. I had to hold a harmonious field in my mind and heart and work with the loopholes that exist everywhere in the matrix of our time-space universe. I just needed to feel that there was a possible wormhole in time and space through which Don and I could slip.

I could see my customer service agent glow inside as I looked at her with my heightened awareness. From this higher vantage point I also showed her my true inner essence. Luminously shining and vaster than the physical body appears, I met her in this subtler dimension. In the heart of my heart I truly felt the need to be in Hawaii, on time for the seminar.

"Sorry, all the flights are booked, and many people are wait-listed already," she shook her head. Remaining with my attention in this hyper-dimensions I said, "Ah, maybe you can do some magic," knowing that my continuous support of her and the suggestion to her subconscious would only help. I was kind to her and heartfelt, since I knew I was in the hands of the larger universe, a very flexible one in which things will always work out, one way or the other. I continued to hold the field, "the field of dreams," the field of great potential in my mind.

"Wait," she said suddenly, "what about getting you to Maui? The flight won't leave until tomorrow morning, but from Maui you could take an Inter-Island flight to Hilo on the Big Island. You would have to pay for that portion of the flight but at least you would get there." She felt hopeful.

I didn't object and remained kind and loving and appreciative of her efforts.

She could sense that spending the night at the airport and paying for the inter-island flight wasn't my idea of fun. I kept searching the inner dimensions for heightened interconnecting filaments, which would indicate visually to me on the inside that an outer coordination of the miraculous was possible.

I stayed with this altered state of awareness while I was smiling and occasionally chit-chatting with the customer representative in a cheery way.

Then she made some calls. I overheard some words as she mumbled, "She is really nice. Yeah! Coupon. OK!

"Well, I got a supervisor to OK a free flight-coupon for you and your husband, to make the inter-island connection from Maui to Hilo. And we will also give you a free night's stay at the Sheraton Hotel with coupons for your dinner and breakfast. We're sorry that you have been inconvenienced, and as you know, we don't really have to do this. But you have been very kind and we hope to see you again!"

I nearly jumped up and down for joy. I let this lady know how much I appreciated her incredible kindness in the midst of this zoo.

Then I noticed a diamond covered pin on her jacket. The pin looked like an airplane and its wings reminded me of an angel. When I pointed to my pin-on angel made of Rhinestones on my jacket, she smiled at me and said, "We recognize each other, no matter where we are, right?"

In the end we found out that we both had taken a stray cat under our wings on the same day two month earlier. Indeed, it takes one to know one, as the saying goes.

Maybe we are being watched over. Maybe we are able to rise to the level of angels in disguise. In my mind I had searched with my subtler mind through the multiple parallel dimensions for a reality that would allow us to get to Hawaii on time. We had a real "need" and it was met.

Many of the people at the airport rushed into the obvious massive vibration of chaos, anger, and feeling victimized. What we can do in situations like that is to remember, as best as we can, that everything works out for the higher good, that we co-create reality, that the laws of nature are flexible, and that we can walk between the cracks of the cosmic egg. Co-creating heaven on Earth is what I like to do, something all of us can choose at any moment.

I am aware that some people are more interested in taking responsibility for their lives than others. "Waking up" takes excitement and willingness to be responsible for what we experience, and a strong belief that greater things are possible.

What I had done at the airport was to shift my "reality within," so that I would allow a change in the physically manifested world "outside." The techniques we had learned from our Time Traveler, which I wrote about in the book "Journey to the Center of Creation" created veritable miracles in the three dimensional world. I had practiced these imagery methods until I got satisfying results. Eventually it became so satisfying to shift my inner imagery that I did it as often as I could when faced with obstacles.

We need to realize that we are much vaster beings than our physical bodies. Our energy body, mind, and finally our soul-essence, each exist at increasingly subtler vibrational levels of existence. Through our imagination we can tap these higher worlds and manifest physical outcomes that are more fulfilling.

We can either choose to contract our energy field, or to expand it. If we contract, we feel pain. When we expand, we feel pleasure, often love. The more we practice expanding, acceptance, and love, the more we will express our core, our soul essence here on Earth.

Heaven and Hell are side by side. The lady next to me at the customer service center desk, who had been screaming at the agent, was literally kicked out into the rain. She had chosen to be in a world with no satisfying outcome, one where she was going to suffer and live to tell about it. Her energy had contracted.

Instead, I had chosen the belief that there are many possible outcomes. I have learned from experience that we live in a living dream. Our solid reality is very mutable. We set up the conditions we will experience with our expectations, with our belief in the possibilities.

It takes knowing "how" to access the world of choice. Just repeating to ourselves: "I am happy, rich, and wise," will not get us there. That is not enough. To produce real miracles it takes using real roads – learning to access the deeper subconscious, as well as learning to navigate the invisible higher dimensions. Our lives will begin to reflect to us the kind of vibration we actually hold onto. It is something we can experiment with, and in time we build our faith by getting results.

Each of us determines the channel of reality we choose. Living in Heaven on Earth is a lot of fun.

Soul awareness has much to offer us. Greater happiness; better lives; dreams that come true; deep love and deep relationships; miracles that happen daily; the deep satisfaction of union with God.

That's what our trip to Hawaii was all about.

The Vibrating Universe

The thought of spending a night at a first class hotel near the Los Angeles airport was invigorating. A very polite waiter greeted us as we sat at our dinner table and I felt like I had been transported into heaven.

The napkins in our laps, an exquisite dinner menu, and sparkling crystal glasses filled with fresh water, all reflected to us the rich reward for dreaming awake in the form of a gift from an angel at the airport!

I could see the airport lights from our room, and I pondered how incredibly generous the universe is to those that recognize that we have a choice.

We can choose how to react. We can choose what to create, and to live in heaven on Earth. We can choose to live in greater harmony, that this 3-D reality is truly much like a dream.

We can write the script to our lives every moment anew and live on cloud nine if we want to. When we live in higher vibrations, in alignment with the universal laws, there will come a time when normal ordinary laws give way to higher laws. But how exactly can we get in touch with those higher laws?

A few weeks earlier, when we had returned from the Prophet's Conference in Mexico, Bojilina, our neighborhood in her seventies, called me. She wanted to take a walk along the high bluff on our island in the Pacific Northwest.

Her white hair and blue eyes made her look radiant. If I ever knew a person who was getting prettier with age, it was her. Vibrant, active, and very spiritual, she was dedicated to making the best use of her life on Earth.

She had been to Peru to help teach about her master's teachings, teachings that focused on working as a laser-light for the good of mankind. We had stories to swap and decided to do it under the open sky among the trees.

The cool spring air was laden with mist and earthy smells. How I loved to be outdoors! And how amazed I was to hear the story of Bojilina's return.

She had felt a clear guidance to fly home just prior to Easter week-end. When she landed in Dallas Texas, she was surprised to find that due to intense rains so many planes had been canceled that there seemed no chance of catching a flight, especially with a stand-by ticket like hers. But she too had learned to realize that we are connected with invisible rays of light to a much grander scheme in the universe. So she simply closed her eyes and traveled inwardly to the worlds of luminosity and grandeur.

In her heart she felt supremely guided and just "knew" that everything has a purpose, and that the delay and a possible over-night stay at the airport did not fit into her sense of rightness.

As she sensed the inner worlds fitting beautifully together, she felt her connection to all that is right and to her angelic guides, and finally opened her eyes.

At just that very moment a customer service lady walked up to her, looked straight into her eyes and said, "I happen to know that an airplane is about to board going to Seattle, and they have 45 seats available. Go quickly, right now to exit 23 and you'll get on."

Without questioning, Bojilina turned and walked right to the exit and got a seat. The impossible had happened! She had simply held the vision and the knowing that the universe works from a much grander perspective and that we are not peons in a senseless game.

We are divine sparks of God-essence and we can wake up to the fact that life operates differently depending on what we believe in. The energy with which we vibrate in our lives and especially in the very moment we want to shift reality, determines our outcomes. We can live fully alive in our multi-dimensional selves and become who we truly are: Co-creators for living in heaven on Earth. Or we can believe in the trappings of a 3-D world, and believe ourselves to be slaves of the limitations we perceive. Bojilina's story reinforced my understanding once again of an awake universe.

The next morning, after a great night's sleep at the Sheraton Hotel, so graciously extended to us, we flew off to Maui. Hawaii, with its balmy breezes, was about to receive us again.. The coupons from the customer service woman worked for our onward flight from Maui and we were transported quickly to the Big Island.

In three days we were going to hold our *Living From Vision®* seminar and now we were able to have just a few days to relax beforehand.

Our house, where we stayed during the seminar, was just one mile from the Kalani Honua Retreat Center, where we were teaching the course.

The house itself was truly a dream we manifested with the very tools which we were about to teach to the seminar participants. With the imaging processes of *Living From Vision®* we had astounded ourselves and all our neighbors.

The flight to Hawaii felt as if it was guided by higher forces. I realized how much we carry the responsibility to lift our souls up high in any given circumstance.

On one hand we have a body with a brain and on the other hand we have a psyche. Both are run by our imprints and habits. As we learn to rise further up the spectrum of vibration, we start to interact increasingly with the laws of creation and as we rise higher beyond duality, we become aware of a point of singularity, which is the residence of our soul.

If we take a step away, we see that what "we" really are, is a continuum of frequencies living in a sea of frequencies. We don't live in a solid universe but rather in a constantly changing one, in which we co-direct the outcome by the images we hold.

Our journey to Hawaii was about to ask us to put more of that into practice.

Arriving in Hawaii

As we stepped off the airplane in Kona, we were greeted by palm trees, warm, soothing winds and the smell of flowers in the air. Instantly, Don and I felt the change within us. Smiles embraced our hearts.

Hawaii has a magic that is deeply transforming. Maybe it's the moisture in the air or the smell of the ocean, but within moments another "me" surfaces when I get off the airplane and I start to slow down.

The hectic pace of the normal world dropped away and we felt ourselves enveloped in the arms of paradise. We were greeted by our house sitter, who had kept our house safe, the weeds picked and the flowers watered.

Pink bougainvilleas lined the side of the road as we left the airport. Lava fields and hot sun are a perfect environment for those radiantly colorful bushes.

During the several hours drive over the volcano to the Hilo side where we lived, we saw many different landscapes. Moon-like surfaces, changing to bare lava fields, to windswept grasses, greeted us as we drove over the volcano on winding roads, taking us high above the clouds.

We were at 19.5 degrees latitude on our planet. Richard Hoagland, the well known scientist/researcher has done the math. If you place a tetrahedron inside a sphere, such as a planet, the place where the tips of the triangle touch the sphere will always be at 19.5 degrees latitude.

This will always be a power spot on any planet. And indeed, the pyramid of Giza was located at 19.5 degrees. So is Hawaii. The eye of Jupiter is located at the same position. Here on Hawaii it was the space where the earth spewed forth its hot lava. Don and I live within a few miles of this active spot.

On the way down to the coastline we drove by many waterfalls and valleys filled with trees crowned with orange flowers. The ocean crashed at times in great blue frothy waves onto the lava and at other times lapped at the rocks that lined the shore. The water took on hues of turquoise, and white foam frothed over the rocks like crowns of wispy wings.

By the time we got to our house it was dark and the stars were shining, covering the sky like a brilliant canopy. Huge cities were far, far away and it was so very peaceful here. The frogs had started their evening ritual of sounds, and these new strange sounds, the warm air and the silence that surrounded us, lulled our hearts instantly into a new rhythm.

Don and I hardly had any time to be alone, because the next day our friend Aimee was to arrive already, followed by Irmi and then Merlin. What a wonderful pod of friends we were to have at our house to help us with the seminar.

Aimee arrived like a goddess. Draped in a sarong and silky top and her long flowing hair, she smiled a huge heartfelt smile as she got out of her car. After long hugs, and deep feelings of gratitude to see her again, she quickly passed all ordinary forms of greetings. "Sit down," she told us, "I have to show you something." She pulled out a double Indian flute from her bag and shook her long, flowing golden hair in the wind. Don and I sat down on my favorite meditation bench on our balcony, overlooking the forest as we closed our eyes. Longing sounds flowed from the flute that echoed memories from ancient times. The melodies floated in and around our hearts as Aimee played the sounds directly at our bodies. Don and I sat transfixed on our couch on the balcony while she played songs to our souls. It was a great welcome. This was what I had been hoping for – dolphin pod living.

Gone were the conventions of "hello" and "how are you?" We just opened our hearts, and after she stopped playing we took turns looking deeply into each other's eyes. My heart was full of joy for this magical moment. I closed my eyes and imagined that higher up, in the vast sea of the cosmos, all three of us were seeds of stars.

Aimee was unconventional. She came from Maui and had the "Maui feeling" about her. She was a free spirit, living in the moment, dancing with life, young at heart, and ready to play. Her heart was deep, and she was here at the workshop to look more deeply into her soul and to play flute for our group every day. And she wanted to find answers: How could she love? How could she bond? How could she find a fulfilling relationship?

Irmi arrived a few hours later. She was also staying at our house for the workshop, came from Switzerland to facilitate the Watzu, treatments. Watzu is a water therapy where one floats in the water in the arms of a trained therapist. It's an amazing way to let go into the arms of the universe, which everyone in our group was going to experience in the natural volcanic pool.

On the Big Island we had the goddess of the ocean and the goddess of the fire creating harmony together. They were usually rivals, as water puts out fire, but here on this island we had the blessing of water being heated by the volcano to create a naturally heated pool. The warm ponds! Irmi was assisting with the LFV course and the water treatments with excellence.

Later in the afternoon we made a great orange pumpkin soup together, grown in the belly of our permaculture garden. The next day Merlin was to arrive.

Feeling like a Pod of Dolphins

Aimee, Irmi, Don and I all got up at the same time as if our inner clock was already adjusted to living in a pod. The bird's loud songs had woken us early. Nature's energy is still strong in this more rural part of Hawaii and dictates the flow of life. As I stood on the balcony I could watch the sun breaking through the clouds. Millions of sparkling diamonds on the leaves reflected the sun's light in the fresh dewdrops. I played some flute on the balcony, to invite Aimee and Irmi to come upstairs and we started to make breakfast together.

This was pod-like living. No one seemed to have to say anything, all our actions flowed harmoniously together. We had opened our hearts and now telepathy took over. Timing was a matter of following the feeling of what was right to do at each moment.

When I felt myself running to fast. I took time to breathe and to slow down long enough to listen inwardly as to what was needed in this moment. It was so different than my otherwise German hostess behavior. But this was Hawaii to me, living in the flow. Planning events and being on schedule was nearly impossible here. I had to learn that just when I thought I had figured it out, things went differently, but always in perfect timing, if I could get my ego out of the way.

Today I had to go to Hilo, to pick Merlin up from the airport. He was flying in from Mexico to be with us, and to come for the seminar. The music I listened to spoke of ancient times. The singer sang of not running from the shadows and when we dealt with our shadow we would realize that we always had been the light.

I was excited to meet Merlin again. My most daring dreams started happening. Merlin had given up his life of four years in Mexico to come to see me foremost; so I hoped. We had kissed before, and I hoped more would come. Long forgotten was the vision of Mother Mary.

At the Hilo airport, the doors finally opened and Merlin came down the escalator. He smiled like an angel, his long blond hair flowing like the mane of a lion. Unlike others who jumped and screamed for joy, he took me quietly into his arms and we stood in a silent embrace. Again we touched our foreheads together and gazed into each other's eyes like we had done just a short while before, in Mexico.

His eyes looked like those of an eagle as we looked at each other so closely. Our breath flowed into each other. That was how ancient Hawaiians exchanged their 'Hellos.' Aloha stands for the sharing of breath. Here on this volcanic island, we were drawn to this ancient form of greeting.

In the subtle feeling of my awareness I started scanning for our meeting point high above. Being simultaneously aware of our bodies, as well as sending a sonar beam of consciousness higher up, we found the spot where we met in union at yet a higher octave of ourselves. It was as if both our resonant light beams came into synchronization and touched. As they touched they allowed a certain docking into each other, and the space between him and I, as separate beings, vanished.

It was a deep experience, right the first moment we met. The fact that we had just greeted each other in exactly the same way we had left each other didn't surprise me. With a heart that could have jumped for joy I gave him a lei, a wreath of flowers, and slowly laid it around his neck.

"Welcome to Hawaii," I said with a soft voice and a sparkle in my heart and soul. This could be a grand time, I thought.

We held hands as we drove home. Briefly, I told him who was awaiting him at our house. On the way we stopped at the dolphin beach just a few minutes from our house, and Merlin opened his heart to the large vista of the ocean.

White crests made a crescendo as the waves struck the lava, frothing and churning about ten yards below us. The sunlight shone upon the water and reflected itself in hues of brilliant turquoise.

Silently in my heart I formed a prayer: "May all experiences we would share together be guided by the higher forces, above and beyond my personal wants or desires." This was important to me, because I could feel my emotions reeling. In silence we returned to the car. Little did I know what awaited me.

At home we were greeted by the lively three. Aimee was very open and charming to Merlin right away and I felt him enjoying the extra attention. Irmi was smitten by him too, and I felt a twinge of jealousy. But at least Don felt safe. With that much competition over one new guy, Don didn't need to worry about me getting to wrapped up.

Evening was soon upon us and dinner had to be made, so we all pitched in. The kitchen was very small and we all flowed smoothly around each other, We enjoyed the excuse of such a small space when we had to squeeze by each other to get to the sink or the stove. The mystery of Merlin turned everyone up a notch and it made us feel like one pod of dolphins. Touch seems so natural when our hearts are open. No one was sexual toward one other, but we felt a buzz that energized us all.

I remembered seeing dolphins in the wild behaving like this. They touched each other a lot. In groups of two, three or five, they often swim together, whooshing their tails across each other's chests, touching each other's fins, fanning water across each other's bodies as a way of expressing closeness. Altogether the dolphins are a very close-knit group, using varied modes of water touch as a way to stay connected. They depend on each other for survival and touch may be a way to help create a field of harmony amongst themselves.

That evening we were all joyful, flowing, and we laughed a lot over dinner.

The next day the seminar was to start, and we were going to share one week together, with a group of like-minded beings. I was very excited about this week.

The Magic of Manifesting

"Welcome to the *Living From Vision* Course here at 'Kalani Honua.'"
I said to the group of seminar participants while the soft evening light of
the setting sun was flooding into our room.

"'Kalani Honua' means 'Heaven on Earth' in Hawaiian. That is one
of the most rewarding experiences we can create in our daily life with
our manifestation skills." I added.

The group was dressed in summery, colorful clothing, a welcome
reprieve from the drabber colors of city life. A circle of flowers created
our center, with a candle shining gently in the middle. We had gathered
in a circle, seated on cushions on the floor. Don and I gave each
participant a colorful flower lei as a greeting. A lei is the traditional
wreath, usually made of flowers or greenery, that newcomers are
welcomed with upon their arrival to the Hawaiian Islands. Music from
Ulalena, with its beautiful Hawaiian drums, conch shell and haunting
voices played in the background as Don and I went around the circle to
gift each participant with this splash of flowers.

As we finished our little ceremony, Aimee started playing her Native
American flute, and we closed our eyes, letting our minds fly into the
land of our souls. The octagonal meeting room where we were gathered,
had screened-in windows instead of windows made of glass, allowing
the balmy evening air, the smell of the tropical flowers and the sound of
the ocean to enter our meeting space. Nature was still very much around
us, even being indoors. As the song of the flute ended, Aimee sat down
with us in the circle and I started to speak from my heart.

"We are about to enter a new world together." I looked at each one as
I spoke. "You neither have to believe anything I say, nor change your
spiritual outlook, or believes. You can simply try the techniques which
we are going to practice in the next week, and keep those that you like. If
you see results, you know for yourself that you are on the right track," I

said, knowing that each of us have different beliefs, which need to be honored.

I was more like a mystic in that I liked to experience spirituality instead of just taking other people's words for it. So my introduction was an invitation for each of us to test the new ideas, and if they proved to be useful, to keep them.

"The methods I am about to share with you have been tried and tested by us for many years. We have been teaching these techniques since 1989 in Europe, America, Asia, Australia, India, and the course has been translated into four languages so far. I say that just to let you know, that this method has been around the block, so to speak, and proved to help thousands of people create miracles in their lives. We will practice steps, some of which you naturally use in your daily live already, others that you will want to remember over and over again in your life. We easily tend to forget to pre-created our reality from the inside out. But with the CDs you get to take home, you can continue to do these very effective exercises daily at home if you wish. They can make the difference from living a life that is a reaction to everything around you, to starting to live extraordinary miracles in your daily life. Believe me, I still always need to remember, and rehears all these techniques. But when I do, my life, our life, is a miracle!"

I hoped by sharing these words that the participants would realize that we need to remember over and over again to rise to the center of our power of creation, and that neither I nor anyone possessed an automatic membership to permanent miracles. We earn them ever day over again.

It was an honor to be with a group of people who were dedicated to increasing their light within, and dedicated to discover the greater power of their minds and souls. Merlin sat next to Aimee across from me and looked steadily at me. Irmi sat to Don's left.

"Life is much like a dream," I said. "We each get to write our life script. The more lucid we become, the more conscious we become of our ability to co-create, the more we can allow our lives to become expressions of our greater beauty.

"During this week here on Hawaii we will be studying the techniques from the *Living from Vision* course, making dreams come true. We will be studying the art of co-creation. Soulful living is about mastering many layers of our reality and frequencies. Most of all, we have to learn how to make use of our minds.

"Co-creation is not only about making things happen, acquiring material or emotional goods, or forcing our will on reality! Rather, co-creation is the art of becoming a greater soul, expanding in our soul-awareness, and learning to navigate within the laws of the universe. As a result, we create a more magical life where we fulfill our dreams. As we practice the art of living as conscious co-creators, we understand the design of lives better. In turn, we live more in harmony with our souls and realize how much life is like a dream. Eventually we use the same methods of creation to become enlightened beings.

"We live in a vast ocean of possibilities. We can either live in a solid world, as a physical body, abide by all those laws that apply to solid objects, or we can expand our awareness of reality and become a vaster being of energy and light.

"Once we rise up to a higher or larger 'space,' we begin to experience a life where different laws start to apply. Suddenly we can co-create, we can heal, we can find hidden information and we can make miracles happen. It is possible because we occupy a different 'space.'

"We live in a multi-layered universe of a magnitude of all possible manifestations. Each one of us has the chance to shift ever so slightly into a greater and grander version of life, until we live in a grand celebration of the divine.

"We each have already realized that the matrix of creation is co-creative and interactive. That is why we are here. Once we realize that life can be much like a dream, we also realize that life is not simply a sequence of haphazard events. We recognize that the external events are closely related to our inner states of consciousness. Our feelings, our subconsciously held images, our innermost fears and beliefs all shape what we experience outside in our 'real' world.

"The universe can be seen as a giant hologram and what we do as a small portion of this hologram can and does affect the larger picture. The holographic plate can be shattered into a million pieces and yet each little piece still holds the image of the entire picture in it. Let's just say we live in a holographic picture show that is alive and has two-way communication, the way that life actually is.

"Now imagine that you make a change in the small piece of the shattered holographic photo. Can you guess what will show up in the big image if you were to put all the pieces back together?"

I saw some people nodding their heads and I said, "That's right. When you change the pattern of the small piece, the large picture will reflect the same change. In other words, you can change the image of your boss in your mind and you'll wind up having a different boss. Either the same person starts changing or a new person will fill those shoes. You may even work in a new place. Either way you will live out the end result of what you inwardly energize. You can make a change in your own mind and you will see the change in the world around you. It all depends on your degree of focus and most importantly your definition of your Self.

To illustrate the power of co-creation I shared the story of how we had found the "Kalani Honua" retreat center and how we came to live in Hawaii.

"One sunny day, a few years back in the mid nineties, Don and I had decided to drive to Eastern Washington to look for a place to build a retreat center. Everything looked favorable. People seemed to walk into our life at the right time. Very auspiciously a Permaculture community designer joined us for the ride over to Coleville in Eastern Washington. The word 'permaculture' was coined by Australians Bill Mollison and

David Holmgren during the 1970s. It's a contraction of **perma**nent agri**culture**, or **perma**nent **culture**.

"Community living seemed like the next step in our evolution and 'Intentional Communities' were sprouting up everywhere. I feel it is in response to an unconscious knowing of coming global changes, that drives so many to seek a life in self-supporting communities. On our drive over to Eastern Washington we learned a lot about living in harmony with nature and designing human habitat so it would cooperate with nature. We spoke of our visions for a community to the auspiciously arranged community designer on our long ride to Coleville. We had a sense of coming changes on our Earth and in nature. Our guide, who was helping us find the right land was teaching us about Permaculture principles. He gave us one most important message:

'Never move away from something, always move toward something you want,' he said. 'You will always take the energy you carry in you with you, and recreate the same. It is most important that you move toward what you want,' he repeated with emphasis."

"That day in Coleville, Washington, in the USA, Don and I made a choice. Though it seemed reasonable to buy the inexpensive land there, I realized that the world would be very dismal for me if I were to live so far away from the ocean. Should life ever be different and things not as easy, I would much rather live by a dolphin beach.

"For years we had been swimming with dolphins and at that time I was writing my first book *Journey to the Center of Creation* about the amazing world of the dolphins. Though the property prices in Hawaii were outlandish, I said to Don in one magic moment, 'If this was by a dolphin beach I would say YES immediately.' It meant that we had to say NO to the Coleville experience, because, although it all looked good, my heart was not truly singing about that land.

"Inside our hearts we know what our truth is. When our cells sing YES, we know. There is no guess work involved. All I had to do was be sensitive enough to my inner nudges and follow what I could sense as truth in my body. Don and I are so similarly tuned that he found it easy to relate to my YES feeling. We heeded our guide's advice not to move away from something, but rather toward something."

I paused. My story was really showing the Living from Vision principles in action.

"So it happened that one rainy day in 1995 we found ourselves visiting Roberta Goodman on the Big Island of Hawaii. She was a dolphin researcher who had worked with Dr. John Lilly. We had met each other on a sailboat, shortly after I had read about her in Lana Miller's book *Call of the Dolphins*. That afternoon I asked her lots of questions about dolphins for my book I was writing then, and I memorized every word she said. Suddenly, out of the corner of my eye I saw a real-estate magazine on her coffee table.

'Affordable houses by a dolphin beach!'

"I jumped up. I got very excited about my long lost vision. It had been about two years since we had looked into buying land in Eastern Washington. We called a real-estate agent and before we knew it we drove off into the hinterlands, the boonies, a place where no electricity and running water existed. It was still the old world of Hawaii, an area away from the modern world, where people wanted to live simply and voluntarily rely on natural resources. But the house we looked at was not to my taste; it was too square and I didn't like the layout.

However, the owner, a white haired older gentleman, was a spiritual artist, a man who had designed the gardens of many country's kings in his long life, and the paintings on his walls were of spiritual masters I recognized. Although the house was not the right one, I felt we were on the right track.

"As we walked outside onto the deck of his house, I saw the purple trim on the octagonal house next-door. 'Don, I want a house like that!' I said with enthusiasm. 'Well, I don't think we have another house like that in this area,' said the real-estate lady. 'Of course not!' I thought, 'but maybe we could build one?!'

"Let's look at some land instead of houses," I suggested, and opened the big real-estate book on the hood of her car. The book, as big as a city's Yellow Page phonebook, flipped open accidentally to a section with pictures of houses. My eyes caught the photo of another octagonal house.

'My goodness,' the woman said, 'that house is just three streets up from here!'

"Miracle upon miracle, there was yet another octagonal house for sale right in this alternative neighborhood. The house was situated next to Hawaii State land, which gave us privacy, and a dolphin beach was only a few minutes away. Don and I decided to buy this unfinished house, especially since we could do our dolphin research right from our own back yard.

"Originally, we had wanted to purchase land and build a retreat center in Eastern Washington. It seemed prudent. Yet this little house seemed to call to us instantly, and at first we didn't know that the universe had conspired to arrange for all of our wishes and needs to be met.

"To our surprise we discovered that an Eco-Resort-Retreat Center, called "Heaven on Earth' in the Hawaiian language, was located just on the other side of the forest preserve, about one mile away from our house!

"Life is indeed grander than we can imagine. Once we let go of a limiting view of what we think is possible and start living in a larger universe, one that is alive and intelligent, we experience a different world.

"We really wanted to be near dolphins and not trapped in snow and cold winters. We had wanted a community nearby and a retreat-center to teach seminars! All of this had manifested by simply going forward with our vision, instead of what we thought would be reasonable or proper.

"Although we hadn't known how this would happen, we held the wish as a vision. Instead of being resigned to a less than satisfying choice, just because it seemed logical, we had opened our hearts to something much greater, and something we thought could never come true, did come true.

"Instead of building a retreat center ourselves, we found one nearby. Living near such a center was much easier. We didn't really want to run a hotel anyway, but rather be with people in high vibrations.

"This entire manifestation had been a co-creative process with the universe.

Individually, with our limited human consciousness, we do not always see the entire picture. We had provided the general design of a wish and turned it over to the universe. We don't usually know all the possibilities there are, nor do we always know clearly what is best for us. But something much greater and vaster is always at work if we co-create. By co-operating with this greater wisdom, the new design emerges and we get our needs fulfilled as we develop our spiritual nature. We become not only programmers of a great dream, but rather, in conjunction with the higher forces, we discover a bigger possibility. We are truly co-creators with the wisdom of the universe.

"There are parts of our super-consciousness at work that we often do not have full access to. There is information at work that is so subtle that we don't usually hear its nudges. It may be that we think of it as God, as our guides, as our Soul, or as destiny. Those layers that are all beyond the grasp of our consciousness are indeed helping us to shape our lives.

"Now, here we live on Hawaii, within minutes of a dolphin beach, and our house is only minutes from the 'Kalani Honua' retreat center.

"Who could have thought of all this?" I asked.

Everyone was still paying attention and now seemed eager to learn how to perform such miracles in their own lives. I had wanted to paint a picture of the vastness of how our choices are really a co-creative process with the larger universe, and how we grow in our capacity as we cooperate with the higher laws of nature.

At school we were taught that we live in a material universe which operates under specific laws. But Einstein had to change a lot of the previously held perceptions of reality in order to discover a mathematics that could apply to this vaster understanding of the universe.

Einstein found that the laws of Euclidean Geometry were not sufficient when looking at the larger universe. Suddenly, the straight lines that made up a triangle would not suffice to explain the curvature of space. Straight lines only apply when we look at a small sample of space, on the street so to speak. Space appears to be fashioned by straight lines, unless of course we look at space from a vast enough vantage point. Now we can fly to the moon and look back at Earth and see even with the naked eye that space is curved. But not too long ago that was impossible. Some adventuresome geniuses took a look at life outside the box, and discovered new dimensions which allowed us space travel.

The same understanding of curved space applies once we get into outer space. Here we have curved lines, because light travels in curves, time bends and gravity changes.

The same is true when we become a 'galactic' traveler. We can no longer apply the laws of the 3-D world. We can no longer rely on the five senses of our physical body; we need to put on the garment of an inner space-traveler to explore inner galactic space. Luckily, outer galactic space and inner space share components, which scientists are still trying to figure out. For this exploration we don't need a space suit, but we need a different suit to explore our inner time-space dimensions.

Scientific research has proven that thought is an energy which influences matter, time and space. The 1984 Maryland experiment that I had written about in my first book was a good example. It was first postulated by Einstein, Podolsky and Rosen and is known as the EPR experiment, to prove that Quantum Mechanics was incomplete as a theory.

But Einstein was proven wrong, and non-local effects were proven to exist. Something far away, A, that had no connection to another physical object, B, could indeed influence the outcome of B at a distance. Non-local behavior is the term for this phenomenon.

I wanted to share a story with the seminar participants that I had heard first hand from one of the top remote viewers in America, Joseph McMoneagle. He proved something very similar, by using the human mind to effect change at a distance.

"Back in 1995 I stayed for a week at the Monroe Institute in Virginia, to take a week out of my busy life and focus on Out of Body Experiences," I told the group.

I had gone on that trip by myself and encountered an amazing person on the airplane. It was an extraordinary event. A friend of mine that could not join me on the trip, but had really wanted to, spoke to me via the person that sat next to me on the airplane. I had written about this deeply moving event in my last book as well, and everyone remembered the story.

"As part of the week-long training at the Monroe Institute, Joe McMoneagle was invited to give us a lecture one evening. He was one of the top six remote-viewers in the US and had worked in the government. He could 'see' at a distance, thousands of miles away, with incredible accuracy. He could be given the coordinates of a location and could report what he saw. While he had worked for the government, he participated in an experiment that proved we can affect the past. Can we change time and space with the use of our imagination? Can we change the past with our imagination? That was the topic Joe McMoneagle was going to talk about."

We took a small stretch break and gathered together again. Everyone leaned over to listen, and I felt as if we were sharing ghost stories by a campfire.

Remote Viewing and Changing the Past

Joe McMoneagle was a man in his fifties. With his gray hair and weathered face he was at once approachable as he was very knowledgeable. Vibrantly, Joe told us the story of how he had been part of a project where he was asked to change the past by using his imagination.

Here is what he told us:

"Several psychics had been invited, including me, to see if we could alter a pre-determined computer-driven outcome." Joe had a fabulous history of psychic research with an all-star performance. His words rung like crystals in the room.

"A random photon generator was driven by a computer, to beam single photons onto a photographic plate. The program was designed so the photons would shoot out at random, but in the end they would always make a diamond shape. In other words, the computer chose random numbers that allowed only photons that would create a diamond shape to be sent onto the photographic plate."

He was a fabulous story teller, and continued to draw a picture for us in living colors. He continued: The psychics were asked to influence the computer. Despite the predetermined or predestined formula, the psychics were asked to concentrate on the random generator, to coax the computer into sending some of the photons outside the boundaries of the diamond.

This was a controlled study, to prove that without the influence of the psychics, the computer would only generate the diamond shape onto the photographic plate, as predetermined by the random number generator.

When they checked the photographic plate which the psychics had influenced, they found photons which had *escaped* the rigid predetermined path of the computer-driven formula.

Voila! Thought can bypass machines and change the minds of computers. Predetermination is not the end all of everything.

But the plot thickened!

A scientist reasoned that if the psychics could defy natural laws, they could possibly also defy time. Two photographic plates were bombarded in the usual manner to produce a diamond shape on the plates. Before the plates were viewed by anyone, the plates were then sealed and kept in a time-capsule safe.

"Six months later I was invited to take part in the experiment," Joe continued as we held our breath. "I was asked to go back in time and alter the computer generated image; to create photons that would shoot outside the diamond shape, but now in the past!"

I was rephrasing the story to our group in Hawaii. "In other words, Joe McMoneagle was asked to change something that happened six months before, but only for one of the photographic plates.

"Joe used his imagination to enter the timeless dimensions and imagined that the photon generator was sending photons outside of the predetermined path. The computer formula was the same as before, the one that allowed only a diamond shape to be created by the photons. But when the time-capsule was opened, photons had shot outside the predestined diamond path, and left their imprints on the plate for everyone to see.

"The other 'control' plate showed the image as it was supposed to be a neat diamond shape. Joe McMoneagle had managed to go back in time, with his mind, and change the computer program, or somehow create photons to shoot outside the predestined path.

"What did this experiment prove?" I asked everyone in our circle in Hawaii.

I was hoping the hour was not too late, as most of our participants had come from many states on the mainland, and we'd all had to deal with some jet lag.

We all agreed that thought and consciousness can affect both the physical world and time when applied with enough focus. When we navigate the holographic universe through the power of our imagination, we can touch events in the past and future, which in turn can bring about changes in the present! All it takes is a heightened ability to focus our attention. By focusing our attention, using the imagination is much like an astronaut using a robot's arm on a spaceship. We can navigate through the many dimensional layers of reality. The past is mutable, and so is the future.

To navigate with more accuracy we also need a broader understanding of how the universe operates. We need to have a reference point, a map of how the universe works, one that we can deeply believe in order for us to make miracles happen.

"The old mindset of Newtonian beliefs that mapped the laws of nature and the universe, didn't have a place for human interaction with the mechanics of the three dimensional universe. This belief left us much like cogs in a wheel: predictable and dispensable.

"But our subjective and objective understanding of the universe is interwoven with the quantum universe, and the holographic nature of the universe gives us permission to navigate the inner realms of dreams and the imagination. This understanding allows us to expect change to happen in 'objective' reality by changing our subjective reality.

"Mystics have always known this. Eastern healers, yogis and seers of ancient civilizations knew this. Tribal people live with this knowledge. Our western culture has been a little slow in understanding this," I added. I had seen enough proof in our seminars, where we had participants re-create their past to give them a different "now."

Time and space are so amazing. Reality is really a training ground for us all to realize that veiled in the cloth of time and space is a great luminous essence, whose origin is divine. Each one of us is this essence and we each can, if we choose, awaken to the greater dream.

We can awaken to be a co-creative dreamer, and to the degree that we are aware, we can become an agent of the higher order. Wherever we go, the matrix will change.

On our journey through life we learn that the higher our coherency of our consciousness, in other words, the more focused we are as radiant laser beams in our inner energy worlds, the more effective we are on all levels of reality.

"As you sit here in this room at Kalani Honua, your presence calls all other particles of the surrounding time-space matrix into coherence. So choose goals that make your heart sing.

"The more highly focused you are, which is determined by your consciousness, and the stronger your coherence-factor is, the more you shift the surrounding matrix to match your holographic blueprint.

"You can see this displayed by sand that has been spread on the surface of a drum. At first you might expect a random design or no design at all. But if you vibrate the drum's surface with a specific sound, which is a frequency, you can expect to see a pattern emerge. Each time the same note is played, the same pattern emerges. A softer sound will have a lesser effect than a stronger sound, to call all the sand particles into coherence and create the same pattern.

"A stronger sound can be likened to our stronger focus of our energy. In my mind I experience this as being able to move upward on an imaginary beam of light and as I do, I go through different layers of dimensions," I explained as I turned my attention inward.

As I was sitting in the circle I was also focusing on my higher essence all the while I was speaking. Ordinarily we only move into true Alpha brainwave states, when we have our eyes closed, but with training one can also move into altered states with eyes wide open. Moving into a heightened space, I became softer, becoming aware of existing beyond my body and extending higher than the room's ceiling.

Whenever we do this consciously we help set up a higher resonance for the world around us. This field becomes a subtly higher vibrational world, a replica of the one we were in a moment ago, but now slightly higher. It is like we begin playing in a higher frequency spectrum of the same Earth, now a slightly higher one. Parallel Earths, that is what could explain miracles.

I paused and just let the words become feelings and images. It takes time to grock these concepts. We were sitting silently together. There was something bigger amidst us now, and everyone looked so beautiful. One by one we slowly started gazing around the room and started to see that there were beautiful beings sitting across from us. Merlin glowed at everyone. I wanted to see if he was looking at me too, but for now we were in a group and I could not focus on personal needs.

"Would you like to practice seeing each other at a higher state?" I asked.

Everyone was ready. In reality we always yearn to be seen for who we really are, and to see into each other more deeply. Soon we would each become a great psychic. Utilizing our multi-dimensional mind brings out our psychic abilities.

"Let's do that tomorrow." I suggested.

For tonight we had heard enough, and we ended the evening hugging each other good night. It was time for sleep, and for inner silence.

"Tomorrow we will practice being in touch with each other's Higher Self," I told everyone. "Sleep well!"

Journey to the Higher Self

The next day all of us met for breakfast on the open lanai by eight o'clock. An exquisite breakfast bar was inviting our hungry stomachs. Papaya, pineapple, guava and star fruit called to us. Pancakes, granola, eggs or tofu and a huge choice of herbal teas pampered us early in the day. A short rainfall had refreshed the morning air, and sprinkled light on the tropical plants as the rain drops glistened like light jewels in the morning sun.

We gathered again in our octagonal seminar room, with its screened windows open to the lush tropical air. Today we were exploring the dimensions of our inner selves. I turned on some music so that we could all start to travel the inner seas. I looked over at Don who was smiling at me as he was ready to start on his journey to his Full Potential.

In my mind I felt myself rise upward. The music made it easy to relax and float into a reverie. Slowly, I asked everyone to go to their place of peace, a beautiful place that they could make up in their minds. My place of peace was in the Himalayan Mountains, in the world of snow and silence, but in my vision were highly refined temples and masters, and I floated in mid-air as a being of light.

"Now imagine a brilliant being walking toward you, radiant and flowing," I whispered. It seems to be easier for us to imagine someone else being radiant, and then to step into that image in order to get in touch with our own higher potential. By first imagining it outside of ourselves, we don't get our egos involved. But everyone is different, and some of the participants instantly started to glow just by being reminded of their higher selves. After we had sufficiently entered this inner state, I allowed a time of silence so we could experience this inner state more fully.

On my journey upward or inward, I have different ways of seeing my Inner Self. It depends on how high I rise. We literally exist in different levels or versions of "Beingness" at different stratospheres simultaneously. But how we affect the world around us depends on the vibration of our souls at any given moment.

At any moment we can just be aware of the body, be emotionally or mentally more present, or be a combination of them all. We can also go further, or deep into our essence and become ever subtler, and eventually become just a brilliant ball of consciousness. From this state of being we are able to move back and forth in time, as well as move through space-time barriers. Higher still, we can unite with others in the same field of light, and eventually experience God and a total sense of unity.

I originally experienced this when studying an eastern yogic path based on the Light and Sound. As you ascend into heightened states of reality, you traverse various levels of Self. First, you find your physical body, a three dimensional version of Self. Next, you can experience yourself as an astral body, the one with which you have Out-of-body experiences, and the one you fly with at night in your lucid dreams. At this level, the laws of time and space are slightly different. You can manifest yourself somewhere else almost instantaneously.

Then there is the mental body. This is the perspective that remote viewers use. The advantage is that you are not tied to a specific viewpoint or location. For example, by looking a table when you use your astral body, you would only see the table from the specific position you are in. But when you use your mental body as a way to perceive, time and space are a lot more fluid. You can zoom back and forth. When you view the same table with your mental body, you can see all the information regarding the table; the people who originally made it and stories of people who have had significant experiences around the table.

In remote viewing one is using the mind and looking at the information only, rather than feeling all the stories and being involved in the feelings. You can also go above the time-line and make changes in the time-line of your own life, either in the past or in the now.

As one keeps going up in one's refinement of perception, it is almost like traveling into the higher stratospheres. Our manifested essence is more like a beam of light which has many different stations. We can stop at any station and become the focal point at that particular frequency by taking on the form of a Self of that frequency, or that dimension. Eventually there comes a point where it may feel like we make a jump into another way of being. It is almost like breaking through the gravitational band around the planet and suddenly "poof," we are a star.

It may feel like we are above it all, as if we are something, and yet we are not anything specific. Usually it is a feeling of beingness above the crown chakra, where we feel a sense of lightness permeate our entire being, accompanied by a feeling of letting go of all attachments of who we are.

Here we taste the first stages of simply being a free being of awareness. From here on out we can "travel" with freewill. We don't really move, we just become more refined awareness, a more refined thin focus of beingness, which seems to rise ever deeper into the zero-point in consciousness. Here we can travel to the Center of Creation, and feel that we arrive at yet another point at which we burst through. Here we can merge with another soul, and we can become ONE in this free space of no-identification. Together we can enter the most wondrous union of Soul, and feel like we touch the face of God.

Whenever I enter into the frequency of my Full-Potential Self, I rise as high as I can at that moment on that beam of light. At times I become a master being, or a swirling being of star-dust, looking much like a galaxy, in rose-colored hues. Or I become a magnificent angel. At other times I rise above my head into a focal point of light. I don't pull my energy body there but I place my whole awareness in this spot of beingness. It may be a few feet above my head at first, and then at times I place it high above the clouds, or even into a space all its own in the cosmos.

I looked at Don while I was guiding our group through the imagery journey of meeting our Full Potential Selves, and saw him as the radiant pillar of light that he is. Here we can see another much more fully.

Usually daily Don and I both move high up, out into a star point, where the two of us meet or merge to become one; one star. This is where I fall in love with Don over and over again.

Don must have felt me focusing on him, since he ever so gently opened his eyes and beamed at me with gloriously jeweled blue eyes.

Everyone else had their eyes closed. For a moment, Don and I hovered in that space of super-luminosity surrounding our physical world, or shall I say inside this luminosity, and we were undulating in our heightened essence. As if we were playing a game of catch, both of us zoomed up even higher on a beam of imaginary light, seeing each other even more and more as light, until we started to feel our essences swirl around each other. In this swirling and being still at the same time I feel the most alive, the most true to my core.

This dance looked in my inner vision much like the spiraling of the DNA. Our essences seemed to be wrapping around each other right then. Don and I rose higher yet, and then suddenly our light points got ever so close and as we touched our stars, we burst into one luminous Oneness. I experienced an overwhelming feeling of love permeating my entire being. My heart overflowed and Don and I felt closer than ever. Although we weren't even touching, we had entered a point where we could no longer tell if we were ourselves or just a big Isness. Don looked at me in sparkling light. He was in the same state of union with me, as I was with him. Although we had a group of people around us, we were at once in total union.

This point of total surrender is one of the most glorious doorways to God. Here Love finds its resolution. The yearning of two to come so close as to no longer be separate, finds its answer in this precious union of two souls into one. This is the moment we feel ourselves no longer separate from God.

We need only traverse into very heightened states of being aware of our essence and almost automatically we unify duality into oneness. This happens to anyone who places his attention on the inner journey upward. But it requires that we stay awake and notice.

It has taken some practice for me to be able to be in such spaces at the same time as being consciously awake. Being able to tell when another is keeping up with me, is way ahead, or joining fully with me has also taken some practice. But with time and getting used to the refined light in such non-dual states, one can develop the sensitivity to know or see. The truth is, we already exist at such levels now. All we need to do is become focused enough to become aware at such a level of existence.

As I had been guiding the group to see their own and each other's Full Potential, I also looked at each one of them in such a purified way with my inner vision. How much light we each radiate, often without even knowing.

We spent time seeing each other in our inner vision, and slowly, I guided us back to our daytime consciousness. First we wrote, to give our left-brains time to adjust to being active again. Next, I wanted us to practice with another person.

I asked everyone to pick a partner, to practice seeing each other's Higher Self. We used a similar guided imagery journey but now we were not only to feel our own higher energies, but to also pay attention to our partner's.

Afterward, everyone shared with their partner what they had experienced. One could literally feel a holiness in the air.

With a sense of reverence, everyone shared their vision of their place of peace, the qualities of their own essence, and what feelings and visions they may have had of their partner's Full Potential. Amazingly, people are able to see deeply into one another. It is as if they have turned on a switch for being psychic.

We often do this exercise in a group, and the collage-like image that a group weaves of what they see in a person's Full Potential touches each participant deeply. People feel seen, and can finally share what they carry in their most sacred dreams.

Let me remind you here that we are looking at the Full Potential Self. Many times in the course of normal living we look at each other with the most critical eyes. We see the flaws, the mistakes, the lack, or the impending doom. But if we focus on flaws, we only magnify the very potential we attempt to avoid. Not to say that we should gloss over the obvious. But let us remember that we make a ladder for one another. What we see in each other will help to stimulate this very outcome. It is a fine balance between being too negative and too positive. It is very useful to have a sense for what is real and what is the deeper potential. When we remember that "how" we see the world around us determines how we feel in our lives, we will take more care to be the very vibration that we really want! Each vibration is possible now.

We all know our mistakes, and yet we all hope to aspire to greater heights.

By setting up a resonant field within us that invites the angelic to come alive around us, we set trends for the subtle manifestation of a higher world to exist around us. Let us be trend-setters and believe in those around us.

What we do inside with our attention and energies determines the outcomes we experience.

When Don and I need to get closer, we invite our souls to join by tuning into that part of ourselves at that higher level. We actually beam light to each other from a state of soul union. A little further "up," where we enter the ultimate state of bliss, is when we join into complete oneness.

In the old teachings, this state is known as becoming one with God. It really is that. Built into the nature of life is a natural carrot to draw us closer to our source. Built into love and relationship is the desire to become One, one unit. It is part of our biology. It is part of the most basic program of life. We can make use of it at the subtlest of levels of reality. Our souls want to become one, because at a higher level we co-create another reality. Oneness is God's way of calling us back home. Enlightenment comes through many paths. Love and union is one of easiest ways.

Next I asked everyone to pick a new partner from the group. Merlin picked me to practice with. I had not shared much time with him. The short drive to the retreat center was usually such that he had shared the back seat of the car with the other two women, and I sat next to Don in the front. They all frolicked and laughed and it was obvious they were having a great time with the male-female energy. I had felt very left out, and silently I was crying.

Mexico had been so much fun but the kiss seemed all but forgotten. This week was getting really hard on me when I thought about Merlin. He hadn't given me any signals that he had had any special feelings for me.

A New Understanding of Plato's Cave Allegory

Merlin had settled on a cushion in front of me. He had been very attentive to everyone else since his arrival, except for me. It seemed that he had wanted to play and flirt as much as he could with everyone and I was now more a hindrance than a joy. I couldn't blame him. After all, Don and I were married and what was I to do with another male? Maybe the psychic had been wrong about my new lifestyle, and my visions were just desires of my own biology.

As we sat across from each other, we went into silence together, looking into each other's eyes. I had asked the group to practice seeing another person's Higher Self, and the energy between Merlin and I was starting to take on a different tone.

Suddenly I felt a grander energy engulf Merlin and I. Transfixed, we looked at each other and it felt as if the lid of the universe above our heads had opened up. Immense spaces expanded before my inner sight and we entered into a vast sea of light. There, I saw Merlin as a very large being of light. I had not expected that. Apparently Merlin wanted to show me his innermost, truest self, and it felt like I was sitting in front of an enlightened yogi. Tears came to my eyes and all boundaries dissolved. Brilliant light engulfed us. This was a different Merlin than I had seen before. We were in an enlightened space of consciousness together.

For a long while we sat silently, engulfed in this heightened state. I was sure that Merlin was experiencing the same breathtaking reality. For a moment I felt as if I was going to be lost forever in this luminous envelope. But then I saw Merlin blink, as small tears had gathered in his eyes as well. He smiled ever so gently, and slowly took my hands into his. His warm heart was very present in his touch, and his light shook my heart to the core.

"Who is this man?" I wondered in awe. If the kiss had gotten my attention, this experience surpassed it. I could see how attractive we are when we shine our light toward another being; it brings with it a responsibility in our human encounters. His light had lit my heart and soul and had pierced my protective boundaries. I wanted to be his, to surrender to him like a moth to a flame. This, I now saw, is the most challenging aspect of becoming so luminous with another human. We are just not accustomed to that much light in our relationships.

If a being outside of our marriage ignited our soul that much, we could easily interpret it as a sign of greater love, and want to follow that flame. Luckily, Don had a luminosity that surpassed all. However, Merlin had the magnetism of Krishna to my soul and I was willing to be one of his admirers.

Gopis were said to adore Krishna, wishing for the slightest gesture or attention from him, each wishing they could be the Radha, the most beloved of Krishna. The intensity of Merlin's light captured not only the attention of my soul, but my heart started to catch fire too. We were both speechless.

As we started sharing verbally we compared notes about our experiences. I realized I was seeing more specific images than Merlin, since I was a visual person and he was mostly kinesthetic. That means he primarily gets his information by feeling, and I get it through inner seeing.

For the kinesthetic types of people, inner journeys are harder to decipher. They feel a lot but they don't see as much, which makes it harder to get an overview. Visual types usually perceive more details. It makes the kinesthetic type often feel unsure of their abilities, but their experiences are just as valid.

Merlin was deeply moved by the depth of energy we had shared. Not too many people dare go this deep, precisely because it is so intimate and opens us up so much. From deep within our hearts we both felt we had a connection that was ancient and timeless. We felt moved to bow to each other at the end of our exercise. A meeting of our inner essence had happened, that was for sure.

I called the group back into the circle and we shared our varied experiences. It brought me great joy to see how deeply satisfied people felt by meeting each other in a heightened state. We love to be seen for who we are, and to share a sacred space with another. Not everyone had clearly seen or felt the Higher Self and I thought it to be a good time to share my interpretation of Plato's Cave Allegory.

In the Cave Allegory, Plato describes people living in a cave . They believe that the shadows on the wall, cast by fire, are the only true reality. They don't realize that all they see are shadows and not the true objects, since that is all they have ever been exposed to.

Eventually, a daring person ventures out of the cave, into the "light." At first he cannot see anything because he is blinded by the intense amount of light cast by the sun. In due time his eyes adjust and he can make out forms and shapes within this massively luminous amount of light. Later yet, his sight adjusts even more and he can make out reflections upon the waters of lakes as well.

The world of shadows that dominated his reality in the cave has been transformed into the experience of a colorful, luminous world of real objects. Naturally, he returns to the cave and wants to tell as many of his co-dwellers of a much grander world, beyond the opening of the tunnel. But few could follow him. Only the most adventuresome ones were willing to expose themselves to the blinding light and endure the time of learning.

By looking at the 3-D world, humans too are used to recognizing only the world of shadows as reality. But the adventuresome souls seek a higher world. Although the inner light can be blinding at first, or hardly noticeable, with time and training our sight will adjust until we can make out more and more details of the inner dimensions. Fuzzy at first, our perception gets refined over time and our world of shadows is superseded by the reality of the inner light.

Our normal physical sight has been adjusted to seeing the "shadows" and not the actual energy. Some people may need to take time to get used to the way things look inwardly. Subtleties and nuances eventually become commonplace, and even navigating through time becomes easy.

Plato, according to my interpretation, was hinting at this very inner development. Usually, Plato is said to hint at seeing the world of Ideas, and not as I might interpret it, as seeking the experience of inner dimensions. But the world of Ideas is the mental realm, which is part of the many dimensions. And who is to say whether scholars can grasp the truth of dimensions beyond the physical? Their interpretation of Plato might be just what a cave dweller can manage to understand.

One of the easiest ways to learn to distinguish subtleties in the inner realms is by setting up an inner "Place of Peace."

Each person had gone to their place of peace during our seminar's guided imagery. This is a place we can make up in our minds, a place we can go to again and again. Near-death survivors have often described a very peaceful place where they are met by family and friends upon leaving their bodies. There, the newly departed one can regroup and gather light and strength. Later on, they meet a very dear guide where they review their life's lessons and understand the deeper meaning of their life experiences.

We don't have to wait until after death to meet our guides! Instead, if we willingly cooperate with our inner guidance while we are still alive, we can alter much in this life for the better. Imagine the delight of our guides at seeing us so much sooner! They can help us now, and our conscious co-evolution then happens every moment we engage in heightened awareness.

In the process of creating such a place of peace, we actually enter into another dimension. We use our inner senses, such as the imagination, to navigate there, and that activates a higher part of ourselves.

By shifting into a heightened level of awareness by simply going to a place of peace in our minds, we create peace as a frequency around ourselves. Just like the sand on a drum starts reflecting the pattern of the sound-frequency, so does the three-dimensional world start to conform to the frequency we generate within ourselves.

By having a place of peace, which we can create in our inner minds, we will measurably generate the frequencies of peace in our body chemistry, in our aura and finally it will reflect itself in the holographic world around us.

It is a perfect launching pad for all sorts of inner activity. Later on, we can choose any place of inner peace, in any dimension we choose to go to.

Placing our awareness at the place of peace may be imaginary at first. As we progress in our awareness training, this place become more and more real and eventually we can actually use this image to enter a different dimension.

We are often led to believe that we live in one world, namely a physical universe. Our five senses are very strong and receive an incredible amount of input, translating this input to our brain all the time via electromagnetic impulses. As in Plato's Cave Allegory, our brains translate all the physical data first. Subtle things are not so real to us at first but as we train our perceptions to higher forms of reality, subtler than the physical impulses, we will find that there are many more dimensions that we can perceive and act within. Since the advent of digital photography, cameras are starting to capture such subtler worlds, often now known as Orbs.

Our imagination is the bridge and doorway to subtler perception. Our brains translate the impulses from the subtler dimensions as electrical impulses, which are then translated into feelings and images to our cognitive minds.

To many people these impressions may come in the form of floating images, like misty clouds in a mystical forest. To others, who are more kinesthetic types, these inner perceptions come in the form of feelings. To still others, these perceptions come as auditory messages.

Whichever way you perceive the subtle impulses, you can start mapping your inner dimensional experiences. It takes repeated experimentation but with time you will realize there are repeatable stations that you can navigate to at will.

What happens in our mind is that we "translate" these subtle impulses into a representation that we habitually use in our normal lives. If we are very visual, that is how we will perceive the inner worlds. Images, knowing, hearing and feeling are representations of perception, whether of the outer or the inner realms. Perception is a navigation tool.

A fly, for example, receives the image of our world through its infrared eyes. What the fly sees is vastly different from what humans see. If we were to put the two images on a screen next to each other we would see very different representations of the world. But they are only a different visual interpretations of the same 3-D world. Humans and flies utilize different frequency spectrums to perceive the same reality. However, both allow the fly and the human respectively to navigate accurately through the same 3-D world. Infrared seeing is a consistent representational mode and the fly can navigate well in its version of the world, just as well as we can.

What we don't see so easily, and yet what still affects us, lies beyond our five senses. These worlds from beyond are indeed influencing our daily lives.

Plato's Cave Allegory gives us a description of the difficulty of perceiving anything when our sight is not accustomed to light filled spaces. We have to get used to subtleties. This requires training our inner sight.

As the seminar progressed, we started feeling the tropical surroundings with increasingly heightened perceptions. Of course the balmy air was a welcome treat for everyone. We were really entering a feeling of being in a "Place of Peace" from the inside out, which made the entire seminar feel even more magical. Pretending, like children do, is one of the easiest ways to improve the use of the imagination. Somehow, when we play in these inner worlds instead of trying hard, it becomes much easier.

The distant sound of the conch shell gently called us to dinner. After a great afternoon we were looking forward to a tasty meal. We had asked Roberta Goodman to give us a talk on dolphins after dinner, since the next morning we were going to try to swim with dolphins.

It was a treat to be with a woman who had worked for years with Dr. John Lilly, the famous dolphin researcher. Roberta had a lot of stories to tell, and Don had already filmed many of her stories about telepathy with dolphins. During her years of being with dolphins, she had realized that they listen to us with their minds. They seem particularly able to see our inner images, and those images and feelings are real to them. Her experience had spanned thousands of hours with dolphins. In the evening, we were to learn about dolphin etiquette in the water from Roberta.

As she gave her talk we learned foremost that we need to be gentle in the water, by not making big waves with our fins, since dolphins see bubbles as solid objects with their sonar. And to give dolphins a general respect, we were also instructed not to touch them in the wild. If they wanted to, they could touch us. With every move they make, they know exactly where they are and where we are. Their body awareness is so amazing that we didn't have to worry about getting hurt, even when they came very close to us, as long as we didn't overstep boundaries or provoke them.

I had been surrounded by wild dolphins swimming within inches of my body, and never got touched or accidentally splashed by them. We were to give them the same courtesy. We would not likely go up to a stranger at the a food market and say "Hi, you look cute, why don't I just touch you?" while running our hands over this stranger's breast, or legs, or face!

In the same way, we weren't to do that to wild dolphins either.

Also, Roberta explained, we would do well if we just relaxed and did not chase after them. They can out swim us with one kick of the tail. It takes very little effort; one kick and they can be gone, faster than we can think. They can dive and easily get out of reach, leaving us floating like corks on the surface of the water if they want to. She told us that if we chase them they tend to just swim a little faster and farther away from us. It was much better, she said, to go into ecstasy and let the dolphins feel our light. They seemed very attracted to that energy, more than anything else.

"Let them come to you, while you make invitational movements. Swim to their sides and then away, but keep contact in your heart," she said. "They will come to you if they want to. Leave the contact up to them but invite them with your energy and grace. When they come straight toward you, swim around to their side. Get into the same direction as they are swimming. Open your heart to them. Make your Higher Self big and bright."

Roberta took a deep breath and finished by saying: "What I am doing is really teaching you the dolphin secrets:

"The first three are: Relax, Be Present in Eye to Eye Contact, and Go in Grace." She paused to allow us to etch these words into our minds.

"If you can remember this in the water you will be in the best condition to attract and enjoy your contact with dolphins!" she said.

She had given us beautiful insights into how to swim with dolphins, and we all applauded. Roberta had had amazing experiences with dolphin telepathy. She promised us she would come back another night and tell us about them. We began to prepare for our beach experience the next morning.

Swimming with Hawaiian Dolphins

Each morning I spent some time alone in meditation before everyone else got up. Nearly every morning since Merlin's arrival I had cried over the distance and disinterest I felt from him. Although we had shared a great meditation together, as soon as we were done he seemed to forget that special connection, and gave his energies to everyone else but me. He walled himself off as soon as we had shared a moment of closeness, so I worked on letting go of the feeling I had from the day before.

"Your future husband." Those words that hung over my head in Mexico were now pale memories of a personal fantasy. The part that felt so frustrating was that letting go seemed very hard. I had to do it over and over again every morning. My heart ached anew every day, as if at night I had forgotten everything. It was as if the feelings in my heart and soul had a desire of their own; but no one seemed to notice and luckily we had a great seminar group.

Before the sun rose, the birds were singing their morning songs. Little by little I pulled myself out of my attachments and eventually I was able to meditate. I loved the morning doves cooing to each other, and today they soothed my heart.

As the sun rose above the tree line and the sunlight lit up the water droplets on the leaves, which I could see from the balcony high above the tree line, I was determined to have a great day. I had started my menstruation in the middle of the night and my weepiness was over.

Soon we all were up. One by one we took a shower in our lava rock enclosed outdoor shower. The Ohia trees with bright red flowers stood tall against the blue sky next to the shower, and the orange blossoms climbing over the shower wall added a brilliant splash of color to the glorious morning. The rainwater that we collected was heated by the sun and now splashed over me, washing away all my sadness. I thanked the ingenious inventors of solar hot water.

"Maybe the dolphins are in!" Don said with so much enthusiasm that we all got excited to go to the beach. He had such a sweet smile as he looked at me that it melted my heart.

"Thank God for Don's love!" I thought. Why was I worried about Merlin? Don seemed above it all. My apparent attachment to Merlin and my tears made no dent in his love for me.

Off we drove after breakfast to pick up the seminar participants who wanted to join us. Some of the other participants drove with Irmi to the Hot Ponds to receive their Watzu, Water-Shiatzu treatments. The rest of the seminar participants came in our cars to the small beach in the bay near our house, where dolphins and whales visited regularly.

It was a hot day at the beginning of May, and palms graced the black sand beach. High lava cliffs protect this secluded beach from the rest of the world. Slowly we climbed down the steps that had been worn into the black lava wall. Steps by step we descended to an overlook. The vast sweeping view of the ocean took my breath away. The sun's myriad of brilliant little sparkles beamed off the ocean with blinding light.

We checked for dolphins but couldn't tell if there were fins breaking the surface of the water or if it was just our imaginations. Within minutes we walked down the rest of the steps and found a shady spot.

As we laid our blankets in the shade of the palms I couldn't help but feel that I was in another world. Heaven is truly within us. Often, just before I see dolphins, there's a change in the feeling of the air. It feels as if a more magical world starts to envelop me.

I felt the glow of light in the air increase and I searched the ocean, looking for the fins to surface, or for the little baby dolphins to jump up high and spin. That's why they are called "Spinner" dolphins. They swim in large groups of twenty, fifty, or even up to one hundred. They come to the bay to rest, play, and mate.

At night they go out to sea as a pod, to catch fish. When they rest, they swim in large S-curves or figure eights, coming up for air in synchronicity. Then they dive down in a steady motion and stay down for a long time, up to eight minutes.

To sleep, they close one eye at a time, and research has discovered that they rest one brain-half at a time. While the group rests, one or more dolphins will swim along, acting as watchful guardians. Whenever they swim like that they are in a meditative mood and we try not to disturb them. Don and I just swim above the dolphins that are swimming maybe seven to twenty feet below us, and we join them in this very meditative state in our minds.

Today we kept our eyes on the vast ocean, and Don spotted the dolphins first. Before I knew it, he had his flippers in hand and his mask and snorkel ready. Not everyone was ready to get into the water. Having just arrived at the beach, they preferred to wait a little while and just watch. Since I had just started to menstruate I chose to stay on the beach as well.

Don got ready to go in by himself. White foam playfully lapped at his feet to greet him. Small waves washed onto the sand and Don glided elegantly into the water. Today was a good day, as waves were flat and I wished I could go with him. Instead I sent Don off with my love and my best wishes.

I had seen at other times that when one person stays on shore and wishes well for another who's swimming, both benefit. Even when we were in Florida, where we went out with a catamaran to swim in shallow, warm water with the dolphins, I noticed that those that wished others well, unselfishly, got rewarded by a visit from dolphins. Today I simply stayed on the beach.

In my mind I tried to communicate with the dolphins.

"Don is my Beloved. Please go swim with him." I imagined and felt that my message was reaching them. I saw Don get closer to the dolphins that were swimming back and forth in an S-curve. They were coming up for air and then diving again, staying down a long time, which is typical of their resting behavior.

As we don't have sonar, it is harder to locate dolphins when swimming in the vast ocean. When dolphins rest, staying under longer without breaking the surface, it is harder to find them. Since I wanted to use my telepathy to help Don make contact, I closed my eyes. Don had gotten pretty close from what I had seen.

Dolphins are wild beings just like any other untamed animals, but they seem to have a greater awareness that somehow lifts our human spirit when we come in contact with them. Dolphins' telepathy, their amazing timing and their ability to voluntarily make contact with humans has proven to be very different from the behavior of any other animals in the wild. To me they are more like angels of the sea. They are free to choose if they want to be with us. This is why I only support contact with dolphins in the wild.

If a dolphin swims up to us and looks us in the eye, he or she does it because they want to, because they are free to choose. This is why we were willing to take the burden upon ourselves to swim with dolphins on their terms, in their home territory.

As I sat on the beach with my eyes closed, I tried to imagine swimming under water, being a dolphin. By sending that kind of image I tried to entice a dolphin, who by nature is very telepathic, to copy what I was imaging. I had seen this method of communication work many times and now that I was sitting on land, I wondered if I could send the same message to help direct the dolphins toward Don. The more I fully felt what I was imagining, the better were the results. Just like in real life with real wishes, we need to feel the future fulfilled.

As I imagined swimming as a dolphin in the ocean, I felt myself coming closer to Don. Suddenly I "saw" Don underwater. "I" swam up to him in a spiral and saw Don's eyes in his mask as they gazed back at me. I realized that "I" was a dolphin. We were both transfixed, and "I" as the dolphin felt an incredible amount of love and honor for this human, Don, who was looking equally intently back at "me." I felt, as a dolphin, that it was a great gift to be this intimate and connected with a human.

I felt a love surge in my human heart that I was not accustomed to. It was almost as if the love I felt was now greater than what I was used to as Ilona, the human. I felt the feelings of the dolphin meeting Don, the human, and I was feeling an amazing love as I gazed into his eyes and soul. Time stood still. Eons may have passed while I just felt love. This Love was between two beings in the water, yet I, as Ilona, was feeling it was just as real in my heart at the beach.

I opened my eyes after a while, still stunned by the beauty and depth of what I had just experienced. I felt high, just like I would have had I really swam with dolphins. How much was my imagination, and how much was real? I really didn't know. But if it was real, we don't need to go into the waters to feel the contact with dolphins!

As I opened my eyes I could see Don swimming on the surface of the waves along with the dolphins. It seemed like an endless time. He moved fast, as if in tow with the long sweeping moves of the dolphins.

Finally Don came out of the water. He was so excited. "Ilona, guess what happened!" Don exclaimed. "One dolphin came up to me and spiraled around me and gazed at me with such intense eye contact. I felt this immense love come from his eyes. We were so very close." Don was visibly moved. He had felt such a personal contact and an extraordinary love, as never before.

My heart was glowing as I listened to him. This was exciting! His story was exactly parallel to my experience, and I was now sure that I had been in the dolphin's mind as he swam with Don. This showed me again that our minds can cross the boundaries of space and allow us to unite at a distance.

I had piggybacked onto the mind of a dolphin and I had experienced very likely what he or she had felt when Don and the dolphin actually made contact. The love was so strongly felt between them.

Don had just experienced a melding of hearts, a union with a being from another species. If a mate had experienced this kind of intensity of love with another human, it could have been cause for emotional upset between marriage partners. But we don't perceive any threat while sharing love with a member of a different species. Don was not going to leave me for a dolphin!

How strange we are as humans. We are afraid to share love and the depth of soul with anyone but one person, our mate, in life.

As I could tell with my feelings for Merlin, I understood why we could get anxious. For reasons beyond my mind, I had very strong feelings for Merlin, but somehow Don didn't feel threatened by him, just as I wasn't threatened by the dolphin's love for Don. Instead of feeling alienated I was able to partake in the love they shared because for a moment I had gotten into the skin, mind and heart of another being and taken on that being's identity. All I felt was the love they shared. And Don came back to me with an open heart. How much we still have to learn!

Humans have different brains. The old brainstem, the limbic brain, and the old mammalian brain, which is also called the emotional brain, are very territorial. When we mate and have sex, certain chemicals are triggered in our brains, which makes us bond in order to ensure that we are attached to our mate and will raise our young.

Bonding ensures we are less selfish. When we bond, we want to give of ourselves to something greater. We are willing to create a family and do everything possible for our offspring. The same applies to us serving a greater cause, such as a nation. When we feel love, we will do whatever it takes to preserve it. Human survival requires the support of adults to raise the young for a period of time, which requires that we be attached. But feeling attached has its downside because we feel pain if we lose that source to which we are attached. So we are willing to defend it. Such behavior ensures that we have the safety of a family or whatever kind arrangement of a unit that works for current economical needs, just long enough to raise the young.

Jealousy really has a purpose. It ensures there is safety and a continuous supply of the love that we have opened ourselves to and have become dependent upon.

But raising the young has become almost secondary in our society. Many people have come to me over the years and expressed a desire to have more soulful connections in their marriage and with others. They ask questions like; can we commune at higher levels of our soul, share love and feel safe? How can we walk like angels in human form? How can we be full of light and open our soul to others without having to mate with them or without feeling that if our mate shared his or her inner light with others, that we have to protect our territory?

After Don returned to the water to swim with the dolphins again, everyone noticed that the waves were not too high, so they jumped into the water too. It didn't take them long to find Don and the dolphins, and it was a great morning for us all.

When they finally returned, everyone was buzzing. They told stories of how close the dolphins had come, how they played together and other special moments. I loved to listen to them all. It was as if by being with dolphins, everyone had shared a group-mind. The feeling of love and belonging was strong. The sunlight passing through the palms created a subtle interplay of shade and light on our faces, and the beauty of the mist from the waves rising in the sunlight dazzled me. The shadows of the trees played on the sand. After the stories we got dressed, so that we would be back in time for lunch.

At home we met Merlin, who had been at the Warm Ponds with Irmi. Two carloads of happy beings had returned from a blissful experience of floating in the warm waters, being held in the arms of the great mother.

In the afternoon we were going to work on the purpose of our lives in the Living From Vision course. I was looking forward to the understanding that I would gain for my own life.

The Light Beyond the Higher Self

After swimming in the ocean in the morning we were very hungry. A great lunch buffet awaited us on the lanai, the open-air restaurant with a view of flowering trees and hibiscus bushes that had lusciously large clusters of pink flowers.

The tropical air, the large green lawn and the sound of the ocean made us feel very much like we were in paradise as we ate our healthy vegetarian food including fresh salads, nuts and fruit in the sunshine.

After lunch we had a little time to rest on the lawn, by the water fountain, or under the shade of the trees. I looked to see if Merlin was nearby, when I spotted him doing some yoga stretches in the sun, just outside our *hale*, the Hawaiian name for house or home.

Soon one of our student teachers that was going to lead the afternoon's session called us. We went upstairs into our octagonal *hale* and took our seats in the circle of mats on the floor. Gently, our spirits were lifted by the Indian drone flute that Aimee was playing as we settled in. She slowly walked around us while we closed our eyes and let the sound of the flute carry us into a deep space of peace and relaxation.

Having a teacher in training lead the afternoon's group allowed me to sit back and participate as a group member. I looked forward to letting my spirit soar when the student teacher would be guiding us with imagery exercises.

Gaining access to the inner dimensions is a real work of art. It takes time, perseverance and dedication to come into one's own higher potential. By tending the garden of our inner worlds we develop greater awareness of our souls. This comes in many stages and changes over the years in depth and clarity.

We were developing our intuition during the week and started to understand the mechanism by which we manifest our goals and wishes. It seemed to me that quite a number of the participants were really getting the bigger picture. It is very exciting to start seeing the three-dimensional "real" world begin to shift, and to experience signs of real, miraculous changes.

As I sat in the large octagonal seminar room with its open windows that allowed the sounds of nature to surround us, I became aware of the bigger field of energy around me that gently touched my body. As I slowly breathed in and out, I let go of all that I had unconsciously held onto. I expanded my attention and felt myself becoming more open to the field of energy that was surrounding me, and I became more aware of subtleties.

Letting go of much unneeded tension I felt a cocoon of energy envelop me and everything around me started to feel more alive. My breath became even slower and I felt my body become a vessel for life energy. I noticed that this energy that was flowing through me was making up "'me," and that it could be contracted or expanded.

Slowly, I was able to feel energy around me at various distances. There was no distinct "me" but rather an awareness or various spheres or sizes of "me." I also started noticing all the sounds around me. I noticed how everything was chirping, buzzing, singing and rustling. Paying that much attention to details made the world much more alive. There were birds, the wind, the ocean, and the sound of the waves crashing into the lava rocks far away. I took that moment to expand my sense of aliveness even more, and my sense of self became larger and larger.

I like to remind myself to do that kind of attention-opening exercise as often as I can. In a beautiful book on Tibetan Tantric exercises, which was a book that had nothing to do with sex but all to do with aliveness, the French author suggested doing this mini-exercise for maybe fifteen seconds at first, whenever we think of it. It quickly brings us into blissful feelings, and the sweetness of the experience will draw us into wanting to repeat this short vacation for our souls many times a day. After a bit of practice, this state can last for minutes, and later can fill our days with long moments of rapture and aliveness if we do this kind of exercise as a path to awakening.

That moment, on Hawaii, was a good moment to get started on the path. At home during our regular work schedules, it took some extra attention to remember to expand. But when we make this bathing in expansion a regular practice, we can enlighten our subtle energy bodies quickly.

Still in my reverie, I heard the voice of our teacher starting our class with some guided imagery. As part of the beginning exercise we took time to practice self-appreciation. As I sat in silence my heart started to expand and I thought of all the things I liked about myself. I felt love filling my heart and this love expanded into the space and the room around me.

It was a very magnetic energy. We like being around people whose hearts are open. And to appreciate one's self, or appreciate anything at all, is a great exercise to open the heart chakra. Love is the best magnet and gift there is. We love to open to people when they exude love. We can become such a magnet when we exude love, something we do if we practice seeing the good in others and ourselves.

We started our day with: "What has gone well, and what hasn't?" After writing down our observations we were asked to envision and feel what we had really wanted to experience instead of the things that hadn't gone as we desired.

We were reviewing our experiences from the day before. We learn a lot by reviewing. How seldom we take time to stop and see how life is going! But it is good to pause and review. We start noticing our successes more easily and we can step back and learn from our mistakes or difficult experiences.

I took a deep breath. It is really good to be honest with oneself, to look at what works, what doesn't work and most importantly to focus on what we really want. I realized that with each day in Hawaii we started to have more things that worked, and fewer things that didn't. When we focus on what we really want and learn how to train our imaginations to set up the holographic template from within, we start to experience more and more small miracles daily.

Next we began reading about the nature of the self image. It is good to emphasize that we are neither our negative nor our very positive self-images. This message became very clear to me during the next imagery exercise that explained this concept from the inside out.

After a number of preparatory writing exercises we went inward again to begin listening to our inner worlds. With music in the background that lifted our spirits, we were asked to make up a new self-image. I closed my eyes and imagined myself to be a masterful, galactic being, angelic in nature, wise, loving and with a great ability to serve others in reaching higher states of God awareness. I radiated white, golden and pink colors. But what came next was a most illuminating experience.

We were asked to take a moment to look beneath our new self-concept, since we were not really either the old or the new image of our selves. Our unconsciously held imagery greatly affects reality. Through that imagery we can change our appearance, our health, make miracles happen, amplify our abilities and live more happily. Yet truly, we are not the images, the successes or the forms we dream ourselves into.

With closed eyes, we allowed ourselves to look behind the images. Suddenly I saw a supernova of light expanding. It was just that. Or should I say: "I was just that: a big light." It was so brilliant and devoid of form in the common sense, that it took my breath away. I understood from the inside out that I am the light behind all forms. It was as if the sun had been covered by clouds, and as nice as the clouds looked, what really shone forth was a brilliant, luminous light. And that was my true nature.

It was an extraordinary moment. I was not Cleopatra; I was not the man in the moon but rather the light that animates all of me. In that moment I became the witness to my true inner self. For some reason my perception rapidly raced around our circle and I saw a few of the others in the group in exactly the same light. I was overwhelmed at the beauty of our presence. Merlin was a radiant light himself and opened his eyes for a brief moment and looked at me the instant I had looked at him. Had he felt my presence in this supra-dimensional space as well? What was our connection about?

It had been a holy moment for me. I was grateful I was able to sit in the circle as a participant and do my own inner exploration. The teacher was new but she did a wonderful job guiding us to our innermost truths. Even though I had done these or similar exercises many times, this time it took me deeper than ever before; as deep as I was able to go.

The rest of the exercise that our student teacher guided us through allowed us to pre-create successes in advance and see the most capable version of ourselves. We made up new and wonderful self-images. From my own experience I knew how important it was to live with a capable self-image.

Our self-image changes continually. When we encounter difficulties and experience setbacks, it is easy to slide into some kind of stupor, a reactive feeling of unworthiness or feeling unloved. But it is important, especially in these moments, to stop, look at any downward spiral we find ourselves in, and just recreate ourselves anew, in splendor, with the feeling of "I can!"

What we feel we can do, we actually start to become. Whenever I remember that I am a masterful being, I actually start occupying a larger field of time-space. I feel myself walking taller, and suddenly other subtle realities come to my attention. As if I am walking with my head in the clouds with my feet on the ground, I can actually feel a shift around me. It is only after I actually feel such a shift within me – not just telling my mind that, but actually when I feel this shift of energy in the back of my spine – that I also start to notice how the laws of nature start changing, and miracles begin to manifest.

The beliefs that we often hold unconsciously about ourselves, our abilities, our identity and our worth, all shape the manifestation of our reality. We design that which we allow to manifest by the blueprint of our inner, but often unconscious, visions of the possible.

Again and again I need to enter a heightened field of what I feel to be "me." Once I rise above the stupor of the daily human humdrum and let my wings become larger, I see a new version of reality take shape around myself. Once I start living in a larger energy field and I can truly feel it all around me, it is as if the coincidences start piling up and I can live in as many choices of realities as I can imagine. The one where I live in Heaven on Earth is my favorite dream.

We shared our inner experiences with the group, to the extent that we felt comfortable. The more courageous participants talked first. Once we got a taste of how wonderful it was to listen to someone else's innermost light, we all wanted to join in. We felt closer when we shared our feelings, our innermost dreams and beauty of our experiences with each other.

A glow surrounded me when we went outside onto the lanai to eat dinner. The evening's tropical scents filled us. Slowly I walked across the lawn to dinner and savored the feeling of space and light within me. I had invited Roberta Goodman to speak to us again. Tonight she would tell us about her telepathic experiences with dolphins. We were all looking forward to her stories after dinner.

Experiences with Telepathy and Dolphins in Captivity

Dinner was very healthy and rich. Salads, vegetarian food, fruits and great deserts filled our thankful stomachs. Merlin had taken a seat next to me, which was a special treat and my heart was fluttering. Don, who was seated a little further away kept eye contact with me, and we winked at each other as if to say "I am with you."

While eating the dessert, Merlin got excited and wanted me to taste some exotic Hawaiian fruit he had found. He placed the food on his fork in a masterful way. Then, ever so slowly, with the movement of a connoisseur, he inched the fork toward my mouth. I felt embarrassed to be watched by everyone around me. One of our group members got his camera out just to capture the moment. We were a spectacle for everyone, and yet simultaneously we were meeting each other in a most luscious way.

What is more primal than feeding another person? My lips gently opened and as we looked at each other I was aware that this small action carried so many other little nuances, so many little meanings. I fully received the piece of fruit he was feeding me, and it gently slid into my mouth. As if he was in no hurry, he gently pulled the fork out of my mouth, with just enough extra energy for me to notice.

The fruit exploded with a thousand stars in my mouth. It was sour-sop, a sweet and sour fruit I had never tasted before in my life! A shiver went through me and I felt clearly that Merlin was a very sensuous person. I opened my eyes and looked at him. His golden hair had been freed from the hair tie that had tamed his mane into a tail. Now it was flowing freely, surrounding his face with angelic locks. He smiled when he saw my response and for a moment our eyes locked onto each other, and all was still. It was as if in that moment we were more than just our bodies sitting there.

Luckily, everyone else just saw the funny feeding part, the picture was taken, everyone laughed and we finished our desserts.

My head and body started spinning. So much in me responded to this man! He looked like a flirt, but somehow I responded as if there was so much more.

We gathered upstairs in the octagonal meeting room, and Roberta Goodman introduced herself. She was here to tell us about her dolphin experiences. She had worked with Dr. John Lilly, the famous dolphin researcher, who was trying to break the communication barrier between dolphins and humans. As Lilly's project director, Roberta initiated the release to the open ocean of the research dolphins, Joe and Rosie.

She told us many stories about being extremely intimate with the dolphins. All her experiences had taken place in captivity. Although the conditions of captive dolphins appalled her, Roberta gained what knowledge she could from her close relationships with dolphins in tanks. Now she chooses to do her research with wild dolphins. But she told us of her earlier amazing experiments with the dolphins at Marine World. Don set up a camera and filmed her, so we could carry her stories. They have since become available on video and DVD.

One day she was on duty to clean and scrub the pool from algae, which would grow on the walls. She had a pool brush in hand, and had to work her way around the pool with a snuba setup, her regulator receiving air through a 100' hose attached to an air tank that sat outside on the edge of the pool. All the while two dolphins were racing around her.

One of the dolphins was a male, Joe, who had taken great interest in her. He would rub up against her, keeping her from working, insisting that she play with him. Needless to say, she didn't have much choice. He was a bigger being than her, with bigger muscles, about 25 % more brain mass, and more convolution of gray matter, which was thought to be a sign of high intelligence. Only humans and elephants, as well as some chimps share that feature. So she let go of her brush, which dropped to the bottom of the pool, and let Joe take her for a ride. She held onto his dorsal fin and he took her round and round in the pool.

After ten minutes she had played enough and felt the urge to resume scrubbing the pool. She wanted to get back to work, but the water had become so murky green from all the algae scrubbing that she could barely see her outstretched hand, and the brush was nowhere to be seen. In her mind she told Joe "You have to help find my brush!" Joe continued swimming around the tank, pulling her along the bottom, until he stopped. She put her hands out in front of her and found the brush right there!

After another ten minutes his patience for her work-driven behavior was exhausted and he wanted her to play with him again. What could he do, such an intelligent being, captured in a concrete tank? Any human would go stir crazy in such an environment. Since Joe's only entertainment was Roberta, he kept nudging her until she dropped the brush again and raced around the pool with him.

He was wild and happy. Eventually she had to go back to work. Again the brush was missing, and again she asked Joe for help in her mind. Again he swam with her along the bottom and tilted his dorsal fin to drop her off exactly where the brush lay.

This exchange happened a number of times in a row, until there was no doubt in Roberta's mind that he was able to hear her thoughts and respond to her needs by very politely doing what she asked for. How was a dolphin able to do that? They can indeed read our minds; some of them better at it than others.

Frank Robson had written a book on his experiences as a dolphin trainer, *Pictures in a Dolphins Mind*. He had trained dolphins by simply using his imagination, by using telepathy. If he wanted the dolphin to jump high to touch a ball, he would just imagine it and the dolphin did it. He never fed them fish as a reward, as so many trainers do. He just gave them love and total respect. He also noted that if a trainer expected the dolphin to be a dumb animal, the dolphin would behave like that too.

Roberta had experienced firsthand that the communication block, the wall of silence, was being broken. Not that she was able to read Joe's mind, but at least he was able to read hers.

Another day she was to dive down 20', to pick up small steel nuts that a worker had dropped into the tank. It was the end of the day and Roberta had put her 24 pound weight belt, mask, and fins in her locker. Wearing a wetsuit, which gave her buoyancy, she would have a hard time getting enough momentum to dive down and stay down long enough to find and collect the nuts without a mask to enhance her vision.

This time it was Rosie who came to her rescue. Rosie pulled Roberta to the bottom of the pool and placed her *nose* beside the little nuts. Roberta had just enough time to scoop them up before her buoyancy brought her back to the surface.

This was getting spooky. What enabled the dolphins to know exactly what she needed? How smart did they have to be to take the right action and do something as abstract as help her collect foreign objects from the bottom when she didn't have all her gear?

Roberta also noticed that when she was in the water with dolphins they expected her to behave according to rules they had taught her. Not fear, but rather absolute trust in them, was required of her.

When strangers came to the pool for the first time and did things that would be blunders in the dolphin's system of rules, the strangers were rarely punished. But if Roberta ever made a wrong move, the dolphins let her know instantly that she had done something beyond the bounds of etiquette.

In other words, the dolphins had levels or grades of expertise in their social conduct. They expected less of beginners than of more trained humans.

I was thinking that it took a very astute mind like Roberta's to notice those subtle things; things that would have evaded most trainers' eyes. The dolphins were testing and training her as much as she was trying to train them.

Roberta had to perform tests to see how well dolphins can understand and use a bilateral communication system. She held a card in the water at the edge of the pool and Terry, the dolphin, was given twenty trials to see if, upon the command to touch the card in order to receive a fish, she could complete the task. On the first try the dolphin did the right thing. She touched her nose to the card and ate her fish. On the next trial she came close to the card and squirted water onto it instead of making physical contact. Then Terry waited with her mouth open, to accept her reward. Instead Roberta had to back off and give her a time out. For the next eighteen tries she *almost* touched the card in eighteen different ways, all in a creative way, but all of them were marked as wrong on the scorecard that Roberta had to fill out for the test.

Waving her flukes at the card was not a correct answer. Neither was swimming by and nearly touching the card with her pectoral fin. Was the dolphin testing her ability to notice the slight difference between touching the card and almost touching the card? The dolphin was creating variations on the theme of simply touching the target with her beak. Roberta was laughing at her audacity. Was she so intelligent that she altered the game, making it less monotonous? How could we understand what they were saying?

Roberta concluded that while she (Roberta) was a good image sender, she was not such a good receiver, since she couldn't hear what the dolphins were saying with words in her mind. There were others who could do that.

She told us about a time when Terry, the dolphin, precisely positioned Roberta's hands. Then Terry used them as a sort of marker. She would swim in a circle around the pool and brush one of Roberta's hands with her dorsal fin, and brush the other hand with one of the other fins, either the pectoral fin or the tail. The dolphin had a map of the position of Roberta's hands in relation to her moving body. Terry remembered the location exactly where she had positioned Roberta's hands, and then had proven her dexterity by deftly passing her various fins across the hands that were frozen into that position.

Communication was a give and take game. Roberta had to figure out what Terry wanted when she gently used her dolphin teeth to put Roberta's hands into specific positions in the air. Terry had also pressed Roberta's hands against the concrete wall, and once again Roberta had to understand that Terry wanted her to hold them there.

The dolphin knew exactly where she wanted Roberta's hands so that she could precisely stroke them with her fins and body parts. I don't think any human could do that.

One other story was about the dolphins testing Roberta's hearing range. Roberta blindfolded herself and threw fish to the dolphins wherever she could hear and locate them. Soon she heard their whistles getting softer and higher until she couldn't hear them anymore and therefore could not throw them any more fish. Roberta tested the dolphins understanding of her blindness and wondered how they would get her to throw fish. But were they also testing her range of hearing?

A researcher, by the name of Eldon Byrd, performed tests on the range of frequencies in which dolphins vocalize. Previous tests found that they have a hearing range of 150 HZ up to 150,000 HZ and it has been thought that they make sounds in the range of 7000 HZ to 120,000

HZ. Yet Byrd, a government researcher who had specialized in acoustic research, found they have a range that goes far beyond that, reaching up to 1 Giga Hertz, which was the highest frequency the equipment could measure at that time. Ultrasound equipment measures that range, which is probably why dolphins can see into humans and know if they have tumors, or when a woman is pregnant.

It appears also that the sonar, or vocalization by dolphins, even beyond our hearing range, is the reason that humans report healing in the presence of dolphins. In comparison, our human hearing is from 20 Hz to 20,000 HZ. And our normal vocal range is from 85 HZ to 1100 HZ.

The experiment Roberta was doing by throwing fish to the place she heard the dolphins make a sound was simultaneously a test that the dolphins used to see how much she could hear and what her hearing range was.

From that moment on, it appeared to Roberta that the dolphins would vocalize much more in her specific hearing range when she was near them. The dolphins were interactively figuring out Roberta, as she was trying to figure them out.

Of course there were the sad stories too, of how dolphins were used in a petting pool, how groups of dolphins were kept separated, and how they were such sexual beings that they got totally frustrated because of limited outlets for their energy. The males used inner tubes or the backs of the trainer's legs to rub their penises on. The backs of Roberta's legs were almost constantly bruised in her work with dolphins. In captivity, separated from their families and buddies, they were not too happy, and needed all the affection they could get.

Then there was the story of Gordo, one of three dolphins that had been used in a petting pool. He was left without touch and contact after a research team needed to work with the other two dolphins. Gordo was simply left alone. Although he had been a chubby dolphin that loved to eat fish, he suddenly refused to eat any. And within forty days he had starved himself to death. Was this a possible suicide due to the abrupt lack of love and touch?

I was ever more determined not to support any captive situations, where dolphins are simply fed fish as a reward for swimming past a human, or for letting the humans touch them. In the wild, the dolphins can determine if they want contact with us or not. From their perspective we are like little corks bobbing on the ceiling of the ocean.

One day Roberta thought she was hallucinating. She had observed a dolphin staring at a ball that was being pulled away by the suction force of a water drain in an adjacent pool basin. The dolphin seemed very intent on her ball toy, and it suddenly started moving against the pull of the water, back into the dolphin's reach. How could the toy flow against the suction of the water drain back toward the dolphin, Roberta wondered? Was the dolphin using some kind of telekinesis?

Roberta told us another amazing story about their ability to communicate in abstract form. Two dolphins were separated from each other by a trap door that separated two pools. In one pool the first dolphin was shown how to perform a specific task. It took a certain amount of time to learn. When it was time to teach the second dolphin, although he had been separated by the wooden trap door, he already knew the same behavior. Roberta concluded that they had somehow communicated with each other. This required abstract language, abstract understanding, as well as communication through closed doors. Had they used telepathy?

If one takes all of Roberta's stories seriously, one would have to accept the notion of communication outside of ordinary time and space. Telepathy is a reality, and the only thing that keeps us from being as good at it as dolphins is a lot of practice and some years of evolution.

We were very moved by the stories, and I was more determined than ever to continue my telepathy experiments with dolphins in the wild. I could hardly wait for the next day to arrive, when after an imagery class we hoped we would be lucky enough to swim with them.

The Personal Purpose of Life

The next morning we took a trip into the beautiful nature of Hawaii. We hiked through lush tropical forests, gazed at several huge waterfalls, sat under a Banyan tree, daydreamed and snorkeled at some tide pools.

In the afternoon we met again in our circle to dive into the higher purpose of our lives. Many of us felt there was more to life than making enough money to live and then dying.

Once we begin to get in touch with our souls, we realize that the universe is more mystical because we start seeing how our thoughts interact with the world around us, and our dreams start to manifest. Today we were going to be taken on a guided imagery journey to discover our purpose in life.

I like to start that imagery by talking about what children report when they do their "purpose in life" guided imagery.

Children say almost unanimously that they are here on Earth to love more, and to shine lots of light onto everyone. That sums up our responsibility here on Earth very well.

Children don't usually want fame, wealth or reputation. They get right down to the basic purpose of our existence: Being love and shining light. How easy!

I like to preface the exercise that way, because many people want to do something special with their lives and they feel funny when they too come back from the guided imagery and report that we are here on Earth to love and be light-filled.

In looking for a purpose, we usually think of doing meaningful work. We may want to be healers, teachers, builders, writers or artists. What we desire is to fill our working hours with something that is in harmony with our souls.

When I was a flight attendant with Lufthansa at age 20 in Germany, I felt very out of place. I cried about having to live a life of luxury even though I had chosen that work in order to save money to study. The tension within me was hard to take at times since my outside work did not match my inner essence. It took some time to arrive at doing the kind of work I am now doing in my life. It took time to find and practice my skills in speaking, teaching, writing and inspiring others. For me, these activities are much more in alignment with my soul than working as a flight attendant. But those years took up only a part of my life and I was in the process of becoming more of the real me.

Incidentally, many seminar participants have reported that they feel the most purposeful when they are in a heightened state of consciousness while doing whatever they are doing. The heightened state of consciousness *is* what gives us the feeling of being on purpose.

It is not the action or the kind of work we do that matters, it is *the state of consciousness we are in while we do what we do, that matters*.

We may or may not earn money, but when we go into a higher state of consciousness and do whatever we do, we come closest to fulfilling our sense of purpose. Our purpose becomes a multi-layered experience; not a job or profession, but an inner state.

If you want to really know what the lessons in your life are and what skills you may need to develop, I suggest Dan Millman's book, *The Life You Were Born to Live*. It describes life's purpose breathtakingly well through numerology. I only wish I had read it when I was twenty.

It seems that we come into this life as a pattern, much like a geometric design. Our birth date gives us a clue as to our skills and challenges. Over millennia these geometric patterns have been studied in the form of astrology and numerology. What most of us want to know is HOW to express our essence. It is this personality profile that, if we fulfill it, will give us the feeling of living our purpose.

For example: My quintessential number is 3, derived from the sum of all my birthday numbers, which adds up to the number 30. In Dan Millman's book, the number 30/3 is described as sensitive, artistic, and good at writing and speaking. And by using those talents I need to inspire others. This explanation pertains to the pattern of my personality. However it is our soul's capacity, the depth of evolution of our soul, which will determine how well we express our life's purpose.

Overall, most people feel that when they are in touch with their soul and experience heightened states of awareness, they feel they are closest to fulfillment.

Slowly, we all relaxed to the gentle music that started to play. I sat on the floor, again as a participant in the group, and let myself be guided by a teacher in training. Deeper and deeper I went, rising far above planets and galaxies, seeing the beauty of our universe. Guided to rise to such heights, I became just a point of consciousness, a point of light, moving into a deeper matrix, into a lighter bubble of another kind of universe.

Suddenly I broke through with a whoosh. Only stillness and a brilliant silence surrounded me. Out of the mist appeared my innermost masterful being: Gopal Das. Radiant, he looked at me deeply with love. I knew him well and as we looked into each other's eyes, I felt a rush of energy rising within my body. As if we were the most intimate lovers, we became one column of light. A deep wave of erotic energy rushed through me. It was as if this current shot like lightning from the bottom of my pelvis to the top of my head, and then out the top of my head. Dazzling light filled my inner vision. I was so very one with this being. I brought my question with me: my quest for a deeper understanding of my life's purpose for this segment of my life.

Having unified my energy with Gopal Das, the answer came to me in the form of an abstract image. It was a vibrant, colorful, geometric mandala, which expressed my purpose. I etched it into my memory. It didn't spell out what to be or do, but rather felt like a pattern of energy that carried within it all the information I needed to know at a deeper level.

The depth of union with my beloved inner guide, Gopal Das, was very intense. Filled with aliveness, I felt myself open up completely to the higher power of the universe. I realized that I truly have an existence in that dimension, which is the source of my aliveness. Being in that heightened form was not just a dream. From there I could direct all the strings of my physical life. From that place an energy-matrix emanates into my physical world. I had risen to a higher level of vibration and from there I could co-orchestrate the events in the 3-D world.

Coincidences, connections and synchronicities that are baffling to the mind all happen because we activate our energies at that higher dimension. Up there we are the dream-weavers; we are the light that designs and co-designs with the power of thought and awareness, in collaboration with the life energy that pulses through the entire universe.

That heightened state of consciousness is a higher place of co-creation than laboring at our lives in the 3-D world alone. Being situated up there in our identity, gives us a higher vantage point, a higher pivotal point from which light rays can radiate out into our physical reality.

My consciousness emanated like strings of light into time and space, spinning the field of energy into my life more effectively, and I watched how those energies changed the structure of my daily life. There I had access to the time-space matrix, which is much vaster than my human self can understand. When we work from there we are more effective in our "real" lives, and events line up much more effortlessly.

My message was: If I wanted to live my purpose more clearly, I was to become that light more often and let it shine daily into my physical life. As a result, my daily life would express more miracles because I was accessing higher dimensions. I would also touch others and uplift them more effectively, and more love would emanate from my core, turning into compassion, care, respect and help for others.

Lulled into a feeling of deep gratitude for my life, I turned to the center of the universe. It was as if I looked into a huge eye. The eye of God was absorbing me into it and my love for this center of the universe

121

engulfed my heart. We are all given the gift of life as a unit of consciousness, and we can return the gift by remembering the source.

The love and gratitude for life I felt swept through my heart. We are the extensions of this grand source in action. We are the dreamer come alive. The plants do their job by photosynthesis of the light. We as humans do our job by being conscious dreamers and returning our gaze to the eye of the beholder. Touching the face of God, we become grander beings. That is the journey home.

I was bedazzled to have that journey and I wished I could have stayed there forever. Slowly, our teacher called us to come back to a more normal state of consciousness. Slowly, I collected myself into a denser form of awareness and took on my human identity again. It was hard in some ways but also natural to come back, since my body was my guardian, waiting for me to bring the wisdom into form on this plane of reality.

We were asked to gently begin breathing more deeply, and to wiggle our toes and fingers. I started to feel the warm air in the room and noticed the sunlight filtering through the leaves of the nearby palms.

I took some time to write my impressions in my journal and recalled the mandala-like geometric design that represented the image of my life's purpose. How this image would help me with my purpose in life, I didn't know. Perhaps it had nothing to do with a cognitive understanding or with a specific task. At that point in my life I was living my purpose. What I did in the form of daily work and in my relationships were totally in alignment with what I felt my essence to be.

As the sound of the conch shell called us for dinner, I realized how timeless I had felt in my inner reverie. We ended the night by gathering in the Jacuzzi, next to the swaying palm trees; and we talked underneath the brilliant stars. Tomorrow morning we would go to the beach to see if we would be lucky enough once again to swim with the dolphins.

Swimming with Dolphins

The five of us – Don, I, Merlin, Aimee and Irmi – were very much like a little pod of dolphins staying at our home. It had been my desire to experiment with living in a human pod. What does it take to be a harmonious group? Sure, we were together for only a couple of weeks, and yet so many subtleties can be learned from an experiment.

I had observed a number of things about dolphin behavior. There is of course the tendency to humanize them and they have been idealized. They are thought never to be aggressive. Not so. They protect themselves, they defend their playmates and they make sure strangers don't get too close to their babies.

They can fight just like teenagers, rake each other with their teeth, and they can get annoyed. But they seem to induce a more coherent energy field that promotes higher vibrations in humans when we swim with them. Being around dolphins is very similar to being in a cathedral, or around masters. They generate a field-effect that moves our human hearts to feel more love. It is safe to assume that they too feel those feelings.

Breakfast was a communal event with our little sub-group of seminar helpers. While the other seminar participants ate most of their breakfasts at their own time, the five of us shared breakfast at home. All the work seemed to get done without much talk. One of us would set the table, while another made fruit smoothies and someone else brought flowers for each of us from the garden. We lit a candle and all held hands before starting to eat. With eyes closed, we took time to be still, to feel ourselves as energy beings, and to greet each other inwardly in an energy of high consciousness. In my mind I went around the circle at our little table and contacted each person at a higher level.

I saw Aimee playfully laughing, and in my mind she had a fairylike stature. Irmi was queen-like and radiated a strong beam of light. Don was a high priest, a wise, ancient master. He was situated high above the cosmos, waiting for me to join him. Merlin was an angel and together we touched each other's hearts. I was moved to tears as I beheld his beauty inside. It was as if we had known each other forever. But there was something immensely sad between us. Tears filled my eyes and my heart wept about the fact that we could not be together.

Just as easily as we made breakfast we also cleaned up. We squeezed by each other in the kitchen, which was very small and gave us plenty of excuses to slide by each other. I reminisced about how dolphins live in a pod. They are very much "in touch" with each other by touching with their fins, caressing often, slipping by each other and even stimulating each other with their mouths. Maybe touching like that was part of a harmonious life in a group.

No one sexualized our touch in the kitchen and we didn't make any "moves" on anyone in our little pod. But we all loved the smooth flow of our group. We let ourselves hug each other, hold hands, take time to really feel each other, look into each other's eyes and be very close in our souls with each other.

We didn't take our sacred moments into a little corner and hide the love we felt. We felt equally moved by either man or woman. This was a little like being in Heaven on Earth. No agendas, just honest sharing. Honesty gives us innocence in so many ways.

As soon as we had put our food away and collected our swim gear, we jumped into the cars to pick up the other group-members from Kalani Honua. Everyone was ready. The sun was bright and the sky was brilliant blue. We had lots of positive energy.

The opening to the beach lay hidden within some trees just off the Red Road. It was the most beautiful road in all of Hawaii. Along that stretch one can see the water rolling onto shore in huge waves, glimmering translucent turquoise and white foam frothing at the wave's crest, smashing into the black lava rocks in the sunlight. From December to April one can see humpback whales and turtles swimming near the shore. This little beach was the only one on the south-east side of the Big Island of Hawaii where one can swim with dolphins.

Again we went slowly down the steps which had been worn into the lava rock, stopping here and there on an outcropping to behold the breathtaking view of the ocean before us.

From our high vantage point we checked to see if any dolphins were already in the bay. Since they swim underwater most of the time, we waited to see if any came up for air, revealing their dorsal fins on the surface of the water. Some of the waves made it look like there were fins, but they were just shadows of the waves playing with our minds.

Suddenly we saw a whole group of fins surface, signaling us that they were in the bay. This was what I had hoped for. We got very excited and quickly sped down to the beach. My heart started racing, my breath came faster and I wished I knew how to better control my body. But I was excited knowing that soon I would be swimming with dolphins.

This was a special day. With hardly any waves in this protected cove, it would be easy for us to get into the water. I put my basket down in the sand under the shade of a tree, and we all agreed to join in a circle for a few minutes, and then go into the water. It was hard for us to sit in silent meditation while the dolphins were right there next to us in the bay. It was not the time to draw out our meditation, but we wanted to get into a higher state, one that allowed us to mind-link with the dolphins. We wanted to meet them not only with our bodies but to join with their higher essence as well.

Quickly we changed into our bathing suits and I put on a wet suit. My three millimeter suit would help me stay warm in what might turn into a one hour swim. Another participant just wanted to get into the water as quickly as he could. He was thin and I knew that although the first minutes would not be cold, after about twenty minutes of swimming he would freeze.

Into the ocean we went, one after another. Don brought his underwater video camera and I was grateful that the waves weren't too large. I took the plunge and put my face under water.

The world immediately changed. No sounds, but a certain stillness surrounded me. My flippers were still in my hands and I swam quickly though the waves to the other side where I could safely put on my flippers. It takes coordination to swim, snorkel, pull the fins onto your feet and keep an eye on the dolphins. Most of the group seemed comfortable doing all these tasks at once, and soon we were swimming out toward the dolphins, one after the other.

Don was ahead. He was going to signal us as soon as he saw dolphins underwater. There were about 70 of them in the bay, in several subgroups. I started to enter into a deeper state of mind and re-entered the inner feeling of my image from the previous afternoon. My purpose-of-life image had been in the shape of a mandala, a circular geometric design, and it was as if a higher energy pattern and meaning was encoded in it.

I recalled it as best I could and felt it transport me into a higher energy. Just then I suddenly heard the familiar sonar of dolphins touching me. It meant they were very near and were "looking at me" under water. I turned toward the sonar and looked around to locate them. And there they were. A number of them were swimming in the same direction toward me. Two of them veered off, swimming closer to me so that I could see them eye to eye.

They seemed to be interested in me, and I tried to interact with them. Slowly I pulled a little to the side so they could follow me. They swam in a tighter circle with me, which made it easier for me to keep up with them. They were on the outside of the circle and I was on the inside. It was hard to focus my mind because all I wanted to do was look at their eyes and feel our togetherness.

A timeless moment passed and we were communing. There was an intentional desire to swim together. No other wild animal, be it a deer, lion or antelope would have wanted to connect this effortlessly. Since there were so many spinner dolphins it was hard to distinguish one from another. But I felt like I was forming a special bond with these two. I had enough presence of mind to notice that one of them had a white scar on the side and the other one had a nick on his back near the fin. By memorizing their body markings I could recognize them, should we meet again.

After what seemed like five minutes, they dropped away, swam deeper, and I noticed Don. He was all excited because he had been able to film the whole interaction. With all the action I had not even noticed Don swimming behind us. All I could see were the dolphins and our union. Now I noticed all the other participants, each seemingly finding their moments with one, two or more dolphins. Don turned to film another encounter with one of our participants. It took a lot of skill to swim, film and follow the dolphins, since they don't ever stand still.

In my mind I returned to my inner state and decided to replay my life's purpose image. The mandala was clear in my mind as I closed my eyes. Again I attracted that feeling of higher consciousness. When I opened my eyes I was astounded. The same two dolphins were swimming right next to me as I held the mandala-image in my mind. Again, I engaged them but this time I dove down a few feet, to be more interesting than just a cork on the surface of the water. I tried to dive underneath them with my belly up toward them and they again swam in circles with me. This was intentional contact on their part. I realized that it was possible that somehow the energy of my image had called them toward me – both times. But why had they come when I imagined that particular image?

I just looked at the dolphin eyes that were in front of me, trying to understand. Gone were all thoughts of anything other than being in the silent gaze of their eyes, in a state of rapture. The field around dolphins is holy, filled with awe. It is so easy to just be in the moment with a dolphin. It takes a lot of focus to remember to look at their body marking in order to recognize them again.

Don was nearby again and had filmed our interaction a second time. How I wished I could communicate to Don that I was sending the image of the mandala. I ran out of air and in my excitement gasped, swallowing a little water. We are not underwater mermaids. As much as I felt like one, I was still a human.

The water was translucent and the rays of the sun were streaming into the ocean, sending long trails of light into the deep. In the right position, when the sunlight was shining from behind me, it looked as if I had rays flowing from me like wings of light. In this world of water, light and love, it was easy to be in total ecstasy.

The two dolphins had swum off again. "Would I be able to call them back again?" I wondered. I tried. I closed my eyes and recalled the mandala-like image. Filling myself with the same feeling of grandness that this image provoked in me, I must have radiated something that was specifically attracting those two dolphins. Indeed, the same two dolphins came by, as if out of nowhere again! Don was nearby and filmed us again. How miraculous! What was it? Did they think I was calling them? And did they happen to like the feeling I sent out?

Dolphins give off a whistle when swimming in the vicinity of other dolphins. They have been recorded as each having their own sound, called a sound signature. They call each other by name so to speak. Did my image sound or look like my name to their inner, more sensitive vision?

Maybe they liked my feeling. They came back each time I used that specific image. Maybe they wanted to tell me that my image was creating a definite energy field, and they wanted to reward me. Who knows?

We have so many realms to explore in interspecies communication! I wished I could have been certain. It was certain that they were able to tell when I imagined the specific image of the mandala, my life's purpose image. And they left when I dropped that image-energy. So they seemed to know when I was in it and when I wasn't.

We were all so high from swimming with the dolphins that no one noticed how far we were drifting into the other bay to the left. Bruce, who had not put on a wet suit, started to shiver badly and had to go to shore earlier. When I saw him again, he was back for a second time. Don had shot wonderful video footage of several of us. But only the most physical images were captured on film. None of the feelings and images I had held in my mind were able to be captured on film. How shallow film is compared with our complexities as human beings.

We only use 10% of our brains as far as we know, and yet we receive so many subtle nuances far richer than what can be shown on film. When we learn to activate more of the brain's capacity, practice telepathy and have feelings of a higher nature, we can become so much richer in our perception of reality.

We do have to train ourselves to interpret and listen to those signals. Dolphins seem to have made that leap in evolution already. It's my understanding that dolphin brains have already evolved past our human ones. It is just that humans have not recognized such evolution as useful. Feelings of harmony, love, higher states of consciousness and telepathy are not so obvious to our human perception, especially since we as a human species in general seem to place more value on material achievements, buildings, and bombs to protect ourselves.

After a long hour of swimming with us, the dolphins left and went out to sea. We all got the message that we needed to get back to shore. Don had filmed everyone and we were filled with ecstasy. For one last moment before swimming back to shore, we gathered in a circle, bobbing in the water. Everyone was talking about some exciting moment they had shared with a dolphin. I had asked if they had seen the many sexual moments, pointing out how small their penises are. They're hard to notice, if one doesn't know what to look for.

We swam back and made it safely out of the waves. We collapsed onto our towels from sheer joy and exhaustion after the hour-long swim.

How intentional were their interactions with us, someone asked? Did they want to engage with us specifically or did we just manage to swim around them for a while, calling that a communion in our own fantasy world?

That question was laid to rest in the story of the leaf game I had played with a dolphin on the other side of the island a few years back.

The Leaf Game with a Dolphin

One early morning Don and I had gone to the west side of the Big Island to our favorite dolphin beach at Kealakekua Bay. Looking over the large bay from the parking lot, we scanned the surface of the water for fins. After a short while our eyes made out a large group of far away dolphins. If they stayed where they were, we figured it would take us about twenty minutes of swimming to reach them. Quickly, Don got our snorkel gear, wet suits and towels out of the car, and we looked for a place in the shade in a small sandy area near the beach.

Dressed like pros, Don and I entered the water and I tucked a leaf into my wetsuit. I had heard that the dolphins liked to play the game "catch" with a leaf. Off we swam with excitement, knowing that in a short time we would meet them.

Peering into the vast ocean through my mask, I opened myself to the deep underwater silence. Sunlight was breaking on the surface of the water and reflected wavy patterns of light on the sand below us. My eyes scanned the bottom of the bay where soft white sandy waves showed me how fast we were moving. The patterns of that light mesmerized my mind. As the sand below us dropped deeper we oriented ourselves on the rocks near the beach.

The dolphins seemed to stay in the same spot, just out from the "pyramid rocks," as we called them. Sometimes they swam in large figure eights from one side of the bay to the other, especially when they were resting. Today they were jumping and staying in the same area, which made them easier to find.

Soon the ocean floor dropped to a depth of eighty feet beneath us and the vastness of deep water surrounded me. I had not been a natural swimmer, as you might recall from my book "Journey to the Center of Creation," but I had gained a lot of confidence in swimming over time. Dolphins had been the carrot to my courage. We swam for about twenty minutes using steady strokes, and with the grace of our huge fins we finally got close to the pod of dolphins.

Spinner baby-dolphins were jumping, which made it easy to find them. That is not always the case. Sometimes underwater visibility is very low. At times, rain makes the water murky and we couldn't always see the dolphins clearly underwater, even when they were within ten feet of us.

Today was miraculous. We had brilliant, light filled water and it was easy to spot dolphins. Whoever made the twenty minute swim out to them surely had earned the contact, if the dolphins wanted to grant it.

Since we can never out swim dolphins with our own muscle power, it was never a question in my mind if we were harassing them. They could just kick their tails a little harder, or dive down a few feet deeper and they would be out of our reach and touch. Contact is on dolphin terms for the un-motorized human.

I was looking forward to the adventure of swimming with them. I had heard that in this bay some swimmers had been successful at placing a leaf in the water, so a dolphin could try to catch it before the human could. Naturally, dolphins are the better swimmers, so the game is sort of unfair. The amazing part however, is that dolphins are interested in playing this game with a human.

The closer we got to the pod of jumping spinner dolphins, the more the ocean looked as if it was made of a golden substance. I felt a special feeling in the water which I get in advance of the dolphins' presence.

Just as I was fully enraptured by the light surrounding us, dolphins appeared underneath us. Don turned on his camera and we swam in the same direction as them. Swimming above them about seven to ten feet, we felt as if we were being pulled by an envelope of energy, a sort of mantle which was holding us together.

I felt the closeness energetically as they pulled us along. Touching them was not needed in order to feel close. This closeness was on a more etheric level, which was closer in fact than any touch could produce. In our minds we joined the group of dolphins in their altered state. I felt no separation, and so much love poured into my heart that I forgot the world around me.

I took a deep breath and dove down to join them, so I wouldn't appear to just hang on the surface of the water. Swimming in the silence, I entered into an energy slip with about five dolphins. Here, the deep ocean world was even more silent and nothing but beingness surrounded me.

"Let this moment go on forever,' I prayed. "Let me live here in this stillness, this vastness forever." I never wanted to forget it.

Suddenly there were other swimmers around us. Another person was diving deeper than I was, as I came up for air. He had a leaf in his hands and was trying to entice the dolphins to play with him.

He was a young man, muscular, well built, blond and bold. I was awed at the grace he had under water, swimming as if he was a dancer. The visibility today was stunning. He looked like a Greek god, spinning in the sparking blue water. He came up for air and turned to see if a dolphin was catching on. He had hoped to entice one to play with him by dropping a leaf deeper in the water. But the way he was swimming, I could tell that he was pushing the communication. He was trying to interest a dolphin in his game, but he was not actually connecting with them or using his energy body under water.

Soon, another small pod of dolphins headed toward us from further away. In the form of an energy ball, I sent a feeling of play and curiosity toward them. I dove down as deeply as I could, maybe twenty feet and dropped off the leaf that I had tucked into my wetsuit. The leaf started to float up slowly and I had to rush up for air. The dolphins came closer. One of the dolphins caught my intention. I headed toward him and boosted my energy into excitement and I made it feel like I was going to try to catch the leaf before he could get it.

I dove down with all my intent on getting that leaf but also trying to intice the dolphin feel like catching it before I could. I tried to engage the energy cocoon of both of us into a competition of sorts. It worked! I was so excited when the dolphin came rushing toward the leaf that I had to gasp for air. He had tried to get the leaf but didn't. After coughing a little at the surface, I quickly dove down again. The dolphin had stayed with the leaf and now circled around me and the leaf. Since the leaf was closer to me, I made a dash to catch it and lo and behold I did! I couldn't believe it. I held the leaf on my right index finger like a trophy.

Had I been swimming faster than the dolphin? Well, probably not. The dolphin may have been polite, to let me catch the leaf. But now as I held it on my finger he kept circling around me, and I realized that I had to let go of it in order for the dolphin to be able to catch it.

He was not going to take it away from me. I had learned that from Roberta's tales. She had taught us that only that which is in "free" space could be taken, so I dropped the leaf back into the water and backed off to give the dolphin space. But unfortunately, because of the suction, when I backed away toward Don, the leaf kept floating with me, and was now floating around Don, who had been filming the scenario the whole time.

"How lucky we were to catch that moment on film!" I thought. Later, we watched on film how the leaf had been floating just in front of Don's chest, looking like a heart, and how the dolphin came ever so close to his chest but didn't quite take the leaf away.

Just as Don managed to swim a little further away, the dolphin returned, to try his luck in catching the leaf again. This time, the dolphin and I both dashed for the leaf, and the dolphin caught it with his fluke. At first he aimed to catch it with his nose but then he caught it with his left fluke. His joy was as real to me as my own. Maybe it was my own? We were playing with a toy, which he had caught instead of me. It was playing with a wild being, not domesticated, that made the interaction special. Nobody had taught the dolphin any tricks, and he was voluntarily playing with a human. No fish were given to him in payment for a trick well performed. It was a true and free interaction between two members of different species.

Next, in an acrobatic move the dolphin quickly let go of the leaf and re-caught it with his tail. Dolphins have such acute body awareness that I was now sure he had allowed me to catch the leaf the first time. And Don had caught the entire event on video!

Meanwhile, other swimmers had gathered around us. One of the swimmers, Doug, had practiced making underwater air rings, just like the ones dolphins have been observed to make. He dove down to try to make a large air hoop. He stopped about twenty feet below us and slowly formed a bubble of air in his mouth, which turned into a large hoop of air as he slowly let it out. As the ring ascended, it got larger and larger. Dolphins have been observed making that kind of ring, and then taking turns swimming through it. We wanted to see if we could make them do that today as well.

I dove underneath the big hoop of air that Doug had formed, slipped through it gently and gracefully, and came back up for air. But none of the dolphins followed us in the game. Don had filmed the making of the air hoop and my dive through it. We were having so much fun that we started dancing together in formations, like underwater ballet. Our spirits were high and we were feeling happy about everyone in the water. We felt like a pod of beings. Strangers and old friends merged into one harmonious unit by simply swimming with dolphins. How easy it was to feel peace in that moment. Under the tutelage of dolphins, humans united.

Peace has to do with the ability to be in the same space. It is known that no two objects can occupy the same physical space. "That is true for physical objects only," I thought. "But when two or more souls connect to the same space, they in fact become ONE."

That kind of overlapping and all-inclusive energy was prevalent around dolphins. They promote a space where we increasingly expand our energy field, and when we do expand, we are able to enter into a space of eventually becoming one unit. When we become beings of lights, of inter-penetrable spaciousness, we can merge more effortlessly with others. When we become spacious in our energy field, we can interlace with others effortlessly and feel ourselves to be part of a larger whole. If we so choose, we can form a cocoon of light that interpenetrates each other, and we feel closer than when we touch with just our bodies. This can be true even at a distance. Merging into one space is what we call love.

In a more luminous expanded energy form we can share one single space; humans and humans, dolphins and humans, humans and angels, humans and trees – all can do this. The more love we feel, the vaster we become in our spaciousness. In this vastness, our consciousness starts to span all time and space in the cosmos, and peace is not just a word but a prerequisite and result of such expansion within us.

No rules are needed to keep peace. Respecting each other's boundaries in the physical world is part of this expanded understanding of life. The pain we inflict on others is pain we feel ourselves, since we are part of a larger whole that feels all parts of itself.

The dolphin we had swum with, though vastly superior in his swimming skills, was able to honor my swimming inabilities and let me catch a leaf too. If we have superior skills, it is our responsibility to care for those who are lesser able than we are. We need to let them win at their level.

We were very happy in the world of water, play and dolphins. We had spent a long time in the water and after becoming a group of new and old friends, we all started the long swim back to shore. After about twenty to thirty minutes we arrived back at the beach. Being hungry from the long swim, we decided to make some food together. While eating avocado dip, chips, some bread and cheese, I heard a message in my mind, "Take what you experienced with us and duplicate it amongst yourselves. Do not become dependent on us to create this state!"

I realized deeply that we need to transfer what we feel with dolphins to our human community, and we need to share more love with our human peers, without using dolphin swims as a crutch to get us to an expanded state.

Don's inspiration flowed through his guitar as he sat on the beach in ecstasy. A new piece of music came effortlessly which he named, Kealakekua Bay in honor of the dolphins and this special place. When we recorded the piece for our CD, In One We Are, he added some of the sounds of the birds and waves from the bay that morning, immortalizing the moment.

Don and I were in bliss. We felt that special energy between us that we get after swimming with dolphins. It is like swimming in waves of love, and we floated into an unspoken dance of inner contact of our souls. It was easy to do when dolphins were around us, but could we transfer what we had learned with the dolphins to our human lives?

Destiny, Fate and Freewill

We were sad that our seminar was coming to an end tomorrow. The dolphins and our inner work with our visions had moved us to a higher place. We were all getting very close to one another and were starting to feel like old friends, glad to have found a family of like-minded spirits. It was good to permit ourselves to be seen for who we really were: radiant, loving beings, now much vaster than we usually let ourselves be seen.

Some of the women in the seminar were asking Merlin for a massage that afternoon to top off the Hawaiian experience, and I noticed I felt a twinge of jealousy. I felt that some of the women wanted a little more from him and although he had not shown any real interest in me, it was hard to keep my cool.

How strange we are! We can be so advanced and angelic at one moment and at another we can be very human or even rather primal. I had not really let Merlin know that I had feelings for him anymore. Since Mexico he seemed like another person, and I still had to deal with my feelings of attraction. As much as I really tried to let go of them, something was pulling strongly on me.

It felt like I was playing a tug-of-war with a sense of destiny. Destiny and freewill, dream time and reality were playing against one another in my heart. I was very happy and in love with Don, and we loved being together. We worked hand-in-glove together in our work, and in our daily lives we were ecstatic. I had no desire to change this, yet the energy for Merlin was pulling on my heart and soul. Fortunately, it appeared that Merlin was being reasonable and responsible and didn't want to interrupt my life either.

The last evening we invited a Hawaiian woman to teach us to make the beautiful flower lei wreaths that newcomers to the Hawaiian Islands are greeted with. She was also going to teach us some Hula dances at the night's end. Sitting in a large circle around a huge cluster of flowers and tea leaves, we started to follow her instructions of twisting and twirling the leaves, intertwining them with flowers, making our leis.

Silently, we floated in the sea of colorful flowers. Irmi made a head lei for Aimee and I. Don and Merlin wanted pictures taken with the women draped around them like flower girls. All of us looked fabulous in the riches of flowers and in the tropical setting of palm trees and warm winds.

Going home to the "normal world" was going to be a little challenging for most of us. We had created a cocoon of love together that was not only a vacation for our bodies but also for our souls. For a moment in time, we had lived in a world of higher vibrations as a group. We had laughed, hugged, played and risen high in our hearts and spirits together.

At home we would have to individually remember to call upon the images which we had practiced with during this week. If we wanted to produce miracles in our lives we needed to keep practicing, daily. We all knew that it was not enough to work on ourselves at a seminar. Walking between the worlds really needs to become second nature, by daily practice. For Don and me, it is so much easier to remember to do the daily exercises by listening to our CDs from the *Living From Vision* course. We have been using that five-week course since 1989. Each week, the exercises – 15 minutes in the morning, and 15 minutes in the evenings –help to practice a different set of skills.

I need to remind myself daily. Going up in higher vibrations by moving our attention to our seat of our soul, we automatically enter into the higher stratospheres and literally start feeling as if we live in accordance with higher laws. We can make changes much more easily in the blueprints of our daily lives when we choose soul as our residence. It is as if we live beyond the level of identity, having a larger self and from there, personally or at times transpersonal, even globally, we have a much greater impact upon the physical world.

Entering these higher dimensional spaces is the only way that releases us from the bonds of destiny. Fate is usually thought of as insurmountable, a solid path that we must walk. There are people who think that all life is fated and predestined, whereas others see only freewill. The truth as I see it, is that we are dreamers that weave the input of both fate and freewill together.

There are energy waves which are set into action from another dimension, affecting our lives in the three dimensional world. These waves, which create an effect in our visible lives, can come from many "spaces" or "times." They may come into our lives from older times or from the future. They may come from our subconscious or from our higher soul aspects, to which we don't usually have conscious access in our human consciousness.

We operate simultaneously on so many layers of reality and not all of them are under the volition of our conscious minds. That is what we usually mean by fate: Energies that come from a place that is outside of our reach.

The love we feel for another being can come from our past or future, where we love that soul very deeply. This may have happened, or may still happen in other times or dimensions. But somehow we have a resonant line of energy with those who touch us deeply from another space. As souls, we are connecting outside of time and space even when our conscious mind is not aware that we are doing this.

We are rather like a large tapestry of love and creative energy that sways in the wind of time. Such feelings appear as destiny. Yet the higher we are able to rise in our inner awakening of our souls, the more we seem to enter the realm of co-creation.

When we first learn to live multi-dimensionally, we learn to create small things, like parking spaces, and soon we co-create miracles. It all just depends on where we identify ourselves. Jesus identified himself with God. He said, "The Father and I are One." The higher our vantage point, our assembly point, as Carlos Castaneda puts it, or our Seat of the Soul, a la Gary Zukav, the vaster our reach into time and space.

We are the weavers that weave freewill and destiny together, ever changing creation. We are not only one static self, because we are growing, changing and creating. Our seat of soul determines how much we are the effect of higher causes, or how much we are the cause, ourselves. It is easier to makes favorable effects happen in our daily lives from higher spaces.

The way to bring more beauty into our lives is by rising to these heights, to see the blueprints, good or bad, and transform them into even higher expressions. In tracking and doing the Holographic Imagery work we had learned from Dr. Vern Woolf, our time traveler, we realized how true it is that a positive potential is inherent in all things.

Evolution results from the embedded yet undefined potential, and it awaits our awakening so we may become creators within the sea of possibilities.

On one hand we have the freewill to do as we please, and on the other hand we are led by potentials that are beyond our conscious perception. Freewill allows us to create millions of possible pathways that may never be manifested, were it not for our free and creative choice.

The path of evolution utilizes the feedback of pain and pleasure as a tool to help us learn to navigate closer to the Center of Creation. If we close down from this path towards the Center of Creation by contracting or being self-centered, we experience pain. As a result we may be out of sync with evolution for a time until the pain is no longer fun and we discover that we do have an effect on life with our minds and souls through opening to that higher force called God. That moment in our evolution is the point when we start to cooperate with life, when we enter conscious evolution and leave mechanical evolution behind us.

Mechanical evolution utilizes pain as the great teacher, whereas conscious evolution allows us to choose freely to rise in our vibrations, and to experience pleasurable feelings as our reward. The light becomes our inner teacher, the only real teacher there is. That inner mysterious field of energy and light within us is connected to a larger field. As we follow that energy toward the infinite center, it takes us towards the ONENESS. This path takes us to our larger Self and will lead us toward expressing our inborn possibilities, our potential destinies. We may become Angels. We may become Master beings. We can be the Enlightened Ones or whatever step we choose in-between.

It is possible to access the space of a future fulfilled now. Once we are able to enter higher spaces in our consciousness, we can skip through the dimensions of time and have greater freewill by cooperating with the larger energy field. Things in our lives can start working out easily, and we show up at the right time and place, where we seem to be working with guidance from a higher place.

The slow evolution via pain and suffering starts to be bypassed. *Once we want to cooperate with the laws of higher evolution, we are free. We can go directly to where we want to go. We can bypass time.*

All we need to do is realize that the darkness that traps our feelings at times is just one of the many possible ways to get us to a better future. Think about it. At times we get angry because we are hurt. We really feel anger only because deep within us we actually want something else. This something else might be that we want to be heard, to be loved, to be understood, or to have a fair outcome.

By delving into the truly desired outcome, by entering the fulfilled future through the use of imagery and emotion, we skip the process of learning from pain. Instead of feeling negative we can instantly pre-create the kind of future we want, and enter directly into the desired future. By thanking the old energy and letting it transform itself into the imaginary new future, we mold time into the future we want. However, we do need to get in touch with the old, often painful feeling, be truly thankful and ask it for its deeper intent. It almost always willingly transforms itself into its own, more fulfilling, future.

The faster we vibrate in our soul's core, the faster this kind of transformation can manifest. At times it can happen instantly, depending on our beliefs. We simply need to move into the future-time-coordinate we desire, and by completely feeling that fulfilled reality "in our bones," it will manifest. We can move from pain into conscious, pleasurable co-evolution, into a world where we experience what we really want. It works.

Through this method, children have become better in schools, and therapists get healing results when all else has failed. One such miracle story is of a seminar participant who helped a young girl recover from Anorexia. The seminar participant was a naturopathic doctor. She was all excited when she returned home from a Holographic Imaging seminar in Germany and was eager to try these new techniques on a new client.

A teenage girl, who had refused to eat, and was losing weight by the minute, had been introduced to the doctor by the girl's parents. The girl had become so thin that the parents were about to admit her to the hospital, to be force-fed. They were afraid that she might starve herself to death. Just before she was admitted to the hospital, they found the naturopath doctor, who agreed to give the girl a Tracking-session. In three Tracking-sessions, the naturopath was able to transform the anorexia, which is a deep form of addiction.

It came to light that this teenage girl had developed a friendship with a girl from Bosnia. And her weight loss and inability to keep food in her body was an unconscious empathic response. She had not wanted to eat, out of solidarity with the Bosnian girl. In the three imagery sessions with the naturopath, she was able to trace her subconscious desire to be a real friend to her Bosnian girlfriend.

Through the tracking sessions she created a more fulfilling image. In her imagination she went to a future where they were both close friends, had deep love for each other, and most importantly, where they both lived healthily. Instead of not eating, like her Bosnian girl friend, she was able to come to a more effective solution of solidarity.

She was still admitted to the hospital to supervise her progress. But what had not happened previously for months, happened in a few days! Slowly but surely, in increments of 200 grams a day, she started to gain weight and was returning to life without being force-fed.

Many therapies had been tried on her and failed. It was the appreciation of her deep subconscious mind, the ruler of most human decisions, that had been tracked to its deepest core desire of love and friendship. That made the change. Tracking allowed her access to the inner programs of her subconscious mind, so she was able to let her higher wisdom find a solution to her deepest desire in a more life supportive way. In a time jump to a fulfilled future, she was able to change her inner reality, and that allowed her to have a better reality now, so she could heal.

When we operate at a subtler level and enter a dimension where we have access to the blueprint of our minds, we start to move out of the hands of mechanical evolution into conscious co-evolution. Until we open to our higher centers, we are subject to the laws of time and space as we know them. Pain is our teacher. Once we are able to enter these higher states of consciousness at will, by knowing the map of evolution, we can steer our lives via conscious co-creation. Pleasure starts to be our teacher. What makes us happy becomes our carrot.

When I started to learn how to shift reality so easily, I was perplexed. I felt like I was cheating myself out of the pain. Sometime later I realized that I had the choice to choose to live in either pain or pleasure. It didn't matter to anyone but me.

Within a short time I realized that I could not only change my internal feelings and my personal psychology, but that most events in my life were tied into my inner holographic matrix. And I had learned a way to access the matrix!

It takes a readiness to do this. And daily practice. It is not for everyone. We need to remain alert and truly want to live in such a high state to make it real. Not everyone can sustain that state. It takes continuous desire to rise above the noise of ordinary consciousness. It takes a deep desire to open to the next phase of one's soul's evolution. Comfort, laziness and preferring to play the victim role appear much easier at first. But when we realize that it keeps us unhappy, and we realize that we can actually change reality in the blink of an eye, we then desire to put out the extra energy that it takes to make that change.

It seems to me that most people who are interested in dolphins are already interested in higher living. And I was aware that everyone leaving our seminar in Hawaii had to practice co-creation in order to make the changes real. Sometimes life can be so hard on us that we nearly forget the fact that we co-create reality.

During the week in Hawaii, some of us had just started to manifest the first signs of our choices, and we needed more proof of our ability. Some already knew how to manifest well and were now working on their next step of evolution, to teach others. Some of the participants had practiced teaching the Living From Vision course, while others took it for their personal evolution. But each of us was going to have to remind ourselves, back at home, to rise high and touch that space called heaven.

The next day we wore our flower leis and head-leis for our last lunch together on the lanai. After lunch all the participants left. Merlin had been offered a house-sitting job about forty minutes away from our house. He had been asked to watch the house of a friend of mine, a Living from Vision teacher on Hawaii, who was leaving for the Mainland for six weeks.

Since Merlin had been offered a free place to stay on the Big Island, he postponed his Australian trip! And I was thrilled we still had some time to share together. But for now I was looking forward to some quiet time alone with Don.

Rising Through the Thousand Pedaled Lotus

Don and I were happy to have had a very special time with our group and now that we were alone we wanted to celebrate each other. Hawaii is not the place to have much time alone. People have time to visit, to meditate, to watch the sun rise, to connect. And of course, a lot of friends and family want to visit Hawaii too.

But today Don and I had time to ourselves and we took the afternoon off. We drove to some hot springs where we were looking forward to swimming in the warm water of a naturally heated pool. The big rocks that separated the ocean from the warm ponds were covered with white frothing foam. Sometimes whales could be seen swimming by, as well as turtles and dolphins .

We lay down near the rocks in the warm late-afternoon sun. Don had brought a floating tube about 6 inches in diameter and about six feet long. As we entered the warm water, Don and I snuggled closely together onto this noodle, which acted like a floating seat in the water. The buoyancy of the noodle held our heads and shoulders above the water level. We hugged each other as if we had not seen one another for a long time. Just to feel Don's body so close to mine filled me with energy and refreshed my whole system.

We played like kids, made each other laugh and eventually lay in each other's arms like lovers. Warm water and sunlight shining through palms makes a great paradise for lovers. Golden beams of light touched our faces and made our eyes twinkle like stars.

Don became still and looked deeply into my eyes. We had just finished a week of teaching a seminar, working back to back. We had given of our hearts and souls to everyone else; now there was time for us to be together.

The light in Don's eyes suddenly grew more brilliant, and the kind of focus he held pulled me into a higher space. He looked steadily into my eyes and it was as if he pulled me into another world. By looking into his eyes, I no longer looked at just his eyes but started to expand into another world.

I caught on to where Don was going and pulled myself up into a "star," just above my head. I felt Don meet me there. After years of practice, we have mapped the inner vibrational terrain. Don was meeting me in a star space where he was no longer Don with his body but a being of his pure presence. His energy was more intense to behold there and we entered into a deeper sense of connection and intimacy. Taking turns, we pulled each other into yet higher spaces. His gift of love flooded my heart, and tears welled up in my eyes. I started to soar higher again into an even more brilliant space and felt Don follow me.

Whenever he or I had risen to a yet finer space, Don or I clicked into that same radiant space of union. Great love flowed through our hearts; a love nearly bigger than my human heart could contain. Immense gratitude and tears filled me to be with Don, and I felt us unify in the vastness of the universe.

I moved my star closer into oneness with Don. It felt as if I was rising on a brilliant beam of light, up and up. We started to spiral around each other, much like a DNA coil, until I rose through the center of a thousand pedaled Lotus flower. We both burst forth into a space of Allness, vast silence and full brilliance. As we hit the zero-point of merging together, any sense of separateness totally faded and I was suddenly immersed in a world that I call God.

No longer could I tell myself apart from anything. There was just Allness, total vastness that was in me, and I in it. Ecstasy filled my heart, and tears filled my eyes. In my soul I felt a total surrender into God with Don. It was impossible to measure the love I felt as large, huge waves of utter speechlessness engulfed me. I was in awe at the miracle of our union, and I was taken fully into the sense of Isness. Again and again I re-entered the moment of "two into one" and re-experienced the ecstatic moment of fusion and Allness.

I wanted the moment to go on forever, but of course it ends. Somehow I find a point where I don't really have the energy to keep going or sustain focus and energy. And then, slowly, I need to come back to my human self. Don and I have practiced letting this state last as long as we can. Depending on how much energy we each have, we can ride that wave of ecstatic oneness for a long time. It has become longer with practice, since ecstatic states require a sort of spiritual endurance training. Yet we have not managed to remain in this state forever. Not yet.

Don started swaying with me in the water. There was love in his eyes and a deep smile and love engulfed me as he held me like an angel. As he turned me slowly to face the sun, the long evening rays were sparkling like a million stars in the water. It was as if we floated in the ether of the cosmos. It was a miracle and gift to be able to share such high cosmic love with the man I had married, loved, and lived with.

After the sun went down we went out to dinner to *Paolo's*, our favorite Italian restaurant in Pahoa. It is a tiny town on the edge of the living volcano. Many of the dropouts and the Hippies have moved there. It is a colorful town with people as varied as one can imagine. Some wore their hair in dreadlocks, like Rastafarians. Others were dressed like Gypsies. Still others were dropout millionaires, or devoted young people who want to live a life "off the grid," using the least amount of resources from Mother Earth. There was even an ex-professor from a German university. Some of our friends live under tarps; others live in very creative, alternative, large open wooden villas. Pahoa and the Puna district is a collage of creative people. We loved living here.

Tonight we sat across from each other at our favorite little round table in the corner. The cook, who helped the eccentric Italian owner and gourmet chef Paolo, was a Krishna devotee. He blessed the food as he cooked it. As Don and I sat in silence waiting for our food, we again rose to heights of immense love and brilliance in our minds and souls. It was not just a dinner. It was making love in our Souls with God.

I love our dinners at Paolo's. They are our Heaven on Earth.

Holding Hands with a Married Man

Roger, a Krishna devotee had called me a few days before the seminar began and asked to visit. I missed him and agreed to see him the soonest I could after the seminar was over.

Roger allowed himself to be friends with me, even though I wasn't a Krishna devotee and didn't follow any particular path. I've always found it a sign of higher evolution if one can include the beliefs of another path. A religion or teaching that declares itself to be higher and exclusive to the rest of the teachings on Earth is going to have trouble in Heaven. It reminds me of a joke.

A man who has just died comes to the Golden Gates of Heaven, where an angel meets him. "Let me take you around Heaven," the angel says, "so you can choose where you want to go." Soon, they come to a group of wailing people. "Who are they?" asks the newcomer. "Those are the Jewish people," the angel answers.

Next they pass an encampment that has people singing and dancing. "Those are Hindus, they love to go to Heaven," the angel says, unasked.

Then they come to a high wall and the angel asks the newcomer to be very quiet as they tiptoe past it. "Why do we have to be so quiet?" asks the man.

"Well," the angel answers, "this is where the Christians have their heaven. They think they are the only ones up here." God can include all of life. It is only humans that harbor a limited view.

You can substitute any religion in place of the Christians in the joke, as most paths usually teach that they are the only true one. How often do we think of ourselves as the best, the chosen ones, better than the rest? In our attitudes toward heaven we can see how inclusive we are.

I appreciated that Roger, though a devout Krishna follower, let me enter into his deeper spiritual world, even though I was not part of his religious beliefs.

When Roger arrived we took time to be alone in the garden. We slowly meandered through the flowering pink oleanders and yellow white plumerias, breathing their scents in deeply and speaking as slowly as we were walking. Soon we rested on a bench that overlooked a small pond under the shade of some banana leaves.

He and I had practiced not needing to chit-chat. Roger often just naturally fell into silence due to his meditation practice, and it was all right for us to simply sit quietly together for a moment, and to gaze into each other's eyes. I cherished his worlds that started to become visible when we shared silence.

As I looked at his eyes, he tilted his head back just a little as if to listen to an inner sound, while he still looked at my eyes. But layered within his gaze were images of other worlds. As if a bit of Heaven descended upon us I started to feel as if we were in the garden of Krishna. It felt holy, light-filled and sacred around us. We sat in this golden silence for a long time.

"What a friendship," I marveled. In this golden silence we felt love for the divine plan of life. This was not the kind of love as in "falling in love." It was blissful, deep, grateful knowing that we can live in a higher octave in communion with another, if we so choose.

I loved to look at his eyes and receive glimpses into his shimmering inner world that he had learned to access through his adherent meditations. I felt his inner world come alive when we sat in silence together. With Roger's love surrounding me it was easy to feel as if we were sitting in the garden of Krishna or some heavenly world. This nectar of the gods was feeding my soul. How tangible these inner vibrations are when we practice sensing the subtle dimensions.

We truly are like library keys to each other's cosmos. It was as if Roger's immense focus on Krishna created a tangible sweetness in his energy field that showered me, and I could literally see the deities and symbols he meditated upon when we closed our eyes. His polished inner worlds were immensely uplifting to partake of. I shared my nuances of heavenly consciousness with him without a word being spoken, and he shared his with me.

Then he reached out to touch my hand. I felt a gentle shiver go through my body and I took his hand in mine. It was as if our hearts extended through our hands and we felt a great flow of love between us, and we were deeply grateful. At first it felt totally innocent. But then, almost imperceptibly and then more clearly, Roger started to slowly caress my fingers with his thumb. It was wonderful. I was so open, and then it started to feel like a man touching a woman. I felt torn. Was this behavior wrong? I was almost in a trance and it was hard to get my mind to kick into gear.

Something in me began to worry. I knew that his wife would not approve of us holding hands. He was a man, I was a woman, and we were human after all. As soon as we started talking again I asked him if his wife would approve of us holding hands. Upon thinking about it he decided that she probably wouldn't. Slowly, with difficulty, I pulled my hand away. We were not engaging in any overt sexual act, nothing and nobody would really judge me; not yet.

But everything starts as a seed, small and invisible at first. I needed to be clear, and make it clear that it was best to be sure we weren't heading in the direction of personal fire and attraction.

High love can be enchanting. It starts innocently and then the fire of higher love slowly starts to ignite all of our chakras. Even if I didn't want to become sexual, perhaps his fire was lighting up his lower chakras. It was a clarity we both needed to deal with. If I didn't bring up the subject because it would be too embarrassing, I would have to deal with all kinds of difficult questions sooner or later anyhow. A desire might develop in him, or even both of us, and soon a love would develop and likely a sexual attraction would start to rise.

He and I were married and not really free to send our energy anywhere we wanted to. It was best to stop the seed while it was small. I personally didn't see any harm in holding hands in friendship, even with deep loving feelings while we were in our soul-to-soul contact, but he was in a committed relationship where his partner would feel hurt if she felt his energy going into another direction.

Married or deeply bonded people are often very sensitive to the presence of intimacy their partner might share with another being. Unspoken, partners build a cocoon of energy together which nurtures both of them. They are able to open more deeply in that committed cocoon to each other. The love-field which they build together is indeed in need of daily care and nurturance. If one partner starts to significantly share his or her energy with another being, or starts to draw sustenance from that new relationship, the primary partner will find himself or herself, often without knowing it, increasingly devoid of love. They will feel as if they live in an increasingly dry garden.

Together they have been living in an energy cocoon and neither party wants to suddenly find themselves without that energy supply. If one person starts to create a cocoon with another person, small as it may be at first, they will unconsciously withdraw that amount of energy from the primary cocoon.

Usually we do this when we don't get our major needs met from our primary partner. As a matter of fact, we don't usually get all of our needs met from one person. We do have various relationships simultaneously, in such diverse realms as with children, work colleagues, etc. And we don't normally feel any competition. But when the kind of depth and primary love is supplied from another source, we start to experience a conflict of priorities in mind and heart.

At times we simply seek new stimulation; we want to grow in a new direction. Roger was able to share with me in a way that allowed him to grow spiritually and vice versa. At other times we are simply driven by our biological program to procreate, and we seek new biological partners, even if we don't want to create children. The drive is still the same.

If the secondary exchange is similar or stronger than our primary relationship, we will usually find our energy traveling more and more toward that new being. The person from the primary relationship who is left at home and who has not yet set up another source of love and nurturance will feel pain from the loss. Naturally we want to keep our supply of love going.

Our threads of love and our feelings of heart-opening are very precious. They are very sensitive and I was aware now that at this stage of the game in my life it would be a crime to step over the boundary of another couple's agreements. In our human primitive brains, no woman really wants to share her mate. Nor do many men want to share their wives. But in keeping such boundaries clear, it was not only the man, but the other woman – in this case me – who shared the responsibility.

However, sometimes partners feel sufficiently secure, and well nourished, that they don't mind their mate sharing energy with others. In the long run, most people will desire other kinds of input and stimulation for growth and will often leave a partner in order to find it.

Don and I had chosen to stay together and include other soulful relationships, along with our own, just as my dream had asked of me. Other people can be a very fertile enrichment to the relationship *if* it based on honesty.

Even if I didn't feel I would do any harm by holding Roger's hands, I wanted to abide by the agreement he had with his wife. If he didn't care for their agreement, he was free to ask her for a different one. But knowing that she would not agree to give him more freedom, he never asked. Simply wanting another agreement but not asking for it doesn't make the original agreement any less real. He was free to renegotiate a new boundary with his wife if he really wanted it.

Yet Roger and I needed to be honest with ourselves. Were other feelings starting to bud? Were sexual feelings rising in him, which would undoubtedly rock his spiritual and married life?

As long as he had an agreement with his wife, we both needed to abide by it and what felt right for the kind of relationship we wanted. For now, that meant not holding hands. If I were to break that, I would eventually have to live by denser rules. As I set an example myself, my life would be denser as well.

Miracles happen because we are able to enter finer vibrating realms. Lies, cheating, hate, anger, disregard for others, can only exist at slower vibrational rates. When we enter those, which we tend to do at times, we need to work at reaching upward again.

I prefer to live in truth. So I don't need to hide what I know, what I have seen, and what I do. Honesty also keeps our lives cleaner. Our friends or family members don't have to cover for us, compromising their integrity for us. Or should we be in the reverse situation, we don't have to start lying because we want to cover for our friends.

In my choice to honor the vows of unity that Roger was sharing with his wife, I was moving from feeding myself, to feeding the larger whole. I moved from selfishness to generosity, even with my personal loss. In the end I needed to live by my own rules.

As we sat together on the bench in deep communion, we swayed in bliss under the banana tree. We wanted to share love of a higher kind, to touch the borders of heaven and live in a world of Shangri-La.

Ethics of Soulful Connections and Jealousy

Karma, the law of cause and effect, makes sure that whatever we send out flies back to us like a boomerang. The higher our own vibrational rate is, the swifter the return of the boomerang. Our actions have reactions, and what we send out is what we get back. It simply works faster for those who live at a higher vibration. The less conscious one is, and the lower one is vibrating, the slower the response time of the boomerang. This lag-time is also true for manifesting wishes. The faster or higher we are vibrating, the faster any manifestation that we focus on can occur. This is true of conscious and unconscious intentions. When we practice living as a focused being with our attention gathered at a higher point, such as in our "soul state," the faster our thoughts and visions will manifest. I rather like living in a magical world of speedy manifestation.

Am I my brother's or sister's keeper? Yes! Imagine how great it would feel if you could trust others to look out for your well being! Although I have suffered great loss by letting go of my closeness to some of my male friends, since their partners still lived with old fear, I still prefer to be clear in my interactions. Because I am also responsible for any break in an agreement between mates.

Many women feel that it is up to a potential lover to be honest in their relationships with their own partners. They reason the issue is between the husband and the wife. I feel differently. Their clarity is part of my life as well. I will set up subtle karma for myself if I go against the inner wish of any one of the participants. If I don't like the kind of company that likes to lie, I can simply attract the kind of people who already live with a higher set of laws. As long as the person I interact with lives in the domain of fear of loss, and God knows I still have those feelings myself, I need to abide by the same rules of the game.

We are still dealing with the primitive parts of the brain in most of our human interactions. Our evolution is slow. I understood the part of the brain that was very protective and territorial. Don has seen me very jealous at times, shaking from fear of loss. Often it was all in my head, and usually, as Don says, I am most jealous when there is no reason. When I feel real love between him and another person, I'm often not jealous.

It is important to understand that it is the primitive part of the brain that makes us feel so territorial. The feeling is there to ensure the survival of our species and it has been around a long time. To ignore that part of the brain is to pretend we are not in a human body. By pretending we are superhuman, we either disconnect from our feelings to avoid pain, or we run into more problems. It's better to face the fact that we still have territorial chemicals ruling our behavior from time to time.

In her book *Why We Love*, Helen Fisher explains how the brain chemistry in animals, as well as in humans, sets up predictable emotions. Lust turns into romantic feelings and finally attachment. It ensures the survival of our species. Territorialism is a part of that. Our mating behavior, our being "in love," is designed to ensure the survival of the species whether we actually procreate or not. Also, we still want to keep the cocoon of energy, love and care intact, whether we have offspring together or not.

Similar hormones and chemicals are triggered even when we engage in higher feelings of love, such as in soul to soul union. The ability to attach ourselves ensures our safety and survival, and allows for the long term care of the young. Without it, we would be very selfish and only able to bond for moments of sexual pleasure.

Nowadays many humans suffer from lack of bonding. Our lives would be simple, superficial and barren of the deeper, selfless qualities of love and care if we didn't attach ourselves.

Each culture has developed mechanisms to ensure the survival of the species. One very good comment in an article I once read stated that the environment determines our form of relationships. We allow the type of relations that ensure the biological continuation of our species. In Tibetan society, women have married several husbands and vice versa, to this day.

Eskimos have shared their wives with visitors. Perhaps to avoid being killed, they shared a rare commodity, or maybe this type of exchange kept the gene pool alive. The environment might have produced too many females or males during some time period. All of these different environments set the stage for different mating behavior.

Hormones, as they come and go in a woman during her monthly cycle, also determine the intensity of such protective mechanisms as jealousy. During the days when a woman has her ovulation, she is more apt to be promiscuous. She needs less foreplay, is hotter, sexier and easier.

Conversely she is likely to be more protective and fearful of loss during the time before her period starts. She is usually less interested in sex, more emotionally needy and more fickle. The day just before a period starts, many women experience a sharp incline in sexual desire. And usually their testosterone levels take a sharp jump upward.

The night before my period starts I will have sexual dreams and I start feeling more available sexually. Exactly when the different hormones start to change depends on each woman. But if a man would study the cycle of his partner at any given time, he would know when to hold her, when to let her cry, when to ask for that extra little bit of space or when she is likely to be easily aroused. A woman's mood and mind changes with her cycle. A man just needs to know when to be bold and when to accept her weak moments. Such is biology.

Similarly, men have their cycles but they are less pronounced. And both the cycles of men and women change with age. Biology doesn't waste energy.

Throughout history, women have had to function very differently than men. Men hunted, while women have nurtured the young. Male and female differences also show up in the different neurological connections between the right and left side of our brains.

To get a man to talk about feelings is very difficult, as most women know. It is biology. Men, in general, have less neurological pathways that connect the left and right side of the brain. On the left side we have our speaking center; on the right side we find the ability to feel. Now imagine a person with less neural pathways connecting the feelings to the language center and you can understand why men talk less about their feelings, and why women gab.

It seems best to learn to understand and cooperate with our biology and make the best of it.

There may be no way around our biology. We love our hormones when they serve us, allowing us to feel love and sensuality. We will do better in life if we learn to work with our biology as we move onward in our soul's evolution.

Bit by bit we train our biology to be kinder, wiser and more able to sustain higher frequencies in our bodies. By being more forgiving and understanding of our natural biological tendencies, instead of ignoring what so blatantly is staring all of us in the face, we will gain more freedom.

Don and I have found that by gently nudging our limits to greater capacity, we install new habits. SLOWLY, we expand the envelope. When we were younger we wanted to change both ourselves and the world overnight. We were headstrong. If we felt limits in our psyches, we pushed. But then we were thrown back.

It is like a rubber band. If you pull in one direction, you get thrown back into the opposite direction. There is no rush. Proceed gently and make sure you have fun in all stages of growth.

All stages are valid. When Don or I get jealous, we know what to do. It doesn't last forever. No feelings do. We remember that we enjoy the freedom of soul's love more than the prison of safety. BUT sometimes we need to feel like there is a safe haven around us, since we carry both the need for safety as well as adventure in our paradoxical human hearts.

Collectively we create new genetic memories and morphogenetic fields for generations to come. Quite possibly we may be doing it for all humans around us. If not, we do it for our own evolution.

We are in fact creating new neurological pathways in our human systems by expanding soul's capacity to enter into conscious union with others. We all long for freedom and love. And we need to work at developing our neurological capacities to sustain such a goal.

With time and exposure, and by pushing past the boundaries of our comfort zones, a neural network will evolve in our bodies to allow for more love and more electric charge. In connection with others, we will allow our partners and ourselves to live with more electric energy charge. In expanding our capacities we will increase our abilities to have cosmic connections. We will learn to tolerate more pleasure. Ecstasy is a new frequency, as the book title by Chris Griscom tells us.

We need to be aware as we enter into deeper communion of soul, that some of the reactions between ourselves and others are based on the older, more primitive limbic brain and hormonal activity. This is true both within our own marriages and in our deep friendships.

Women who have guarded their men from me were often not really worried about sex. They were worried about the degree of intimacy and pleasure their mates were experiencing by letting our souls commune. The kind of bliss that results from entering subtler dimensions and experiencing such union can produce ecstatic states far greater and more satisfying than sexuality.

Don and I created the Soul Seminars as a result of years of our joint experiences in meditation and dolphin contacts. Human heart connections thrive in the field around dolphins. To share our hearts with dolphins seems less threatening than sharing ourselves with humans. Don and I wanted to create a sacred space where people could learn how to access higher states of awareness that allow us to feel greater love with our mates; to navigate our lives far more profoundly and live more fulfilling lives. To that end we created the "Soul Seminars."

In those seminars we first practice connecting with our own soul awareness, and awakening to the various levels of awareness of our Souls. It is like learning to see after we have climbed out of the cave, as described in Plato's cave allegory. We also learn to differentiate the many levels of meetings with others as we encounter each other soul to soul. As we do, a door magically opens into a higher center of awareness, a higher octave. That is the door that remains open long after we have gone home.

The more Don and I lived in soul connection in our own relationship, the more we realized that we also yearned to share that space with others who could join us at those levels.

We are all made of the same light. Many people have told me that they would love to connect in this soulful way with all beings. We do not really ever live in isolation. We are not islands unto ourselves. Nothing in the universe lives independently of anything else. All is interconnected.

Can you imagine how angels commune? As angels, we would all share a higher form of communion than as humans. Some of the ET movies depict that kind of higher functioning of union and telepathy. Usually, a being of a higher order is not tied to the limits of the three dimensional body but is often depicted as living in an energy body that has the ability to fly, to merge with another in space, to share telepathy and to move instantly into pure light forms of existence. As such, they would most likely not have sex as we do in physical bodies. They would not let their hormones run wild, since they live in higher space-time bodies.

As we enter into union we feel love. It is something we can do in our daily lives. By expanding our vibrations while still inhabiting our bodies, we become capable of being in the same space with others, in pure ecstasy. One or more of us can merge in consciousness into the Oneness. When we enter into states of sublime bliss, we usually want to offer such energy to the service of a greater whole.

When we enter into a state of oneness and union at the center of creation, we feel totally unified with all that is. That is the ultimate experience of love.

At first, this may stimulate the mating drive. So at times, in our human bodies we need to hold back our hormonal drives. For example when we feel a desire of sexual union arising within us simply by unifying our souls, unless we have green lights on all levels, of course.

If we wish to engage in soul to soul contact outside of our partnerships, we need to understand that this feeling of union can register in our limbic brains as a desire to merge and unify sexually. Even though stimulated from a higher vibration, we need to realize that we are entering into states of feelings while using parts of our brains that we ordinarily only use when we wish to merge in the physical.

When we connect our hearts and souls, our chakras tend to open toward each other. As the lower chakras open, we can feel this heightened surge of electric charge create strong feelings, each one pertaining to each of the chakras. This can be confusing in the beginning since such an increase of energy can turn on all of our centers. And this can result in wanting to love, wanting to make love, wanting to create projects together and on and on. But we don't need to give in to all those feelings, unless the conditions are right.

Once we get used to having more energy flow through us, we don't mistake the feeling of soul love for the need to unify sexually. Of course we all would love that freedom, but in reality most people who are attached to their bodies would fry their emotional nerves if they gave or took that freedom while in a bonded and committed relationship.

Not all people are wired that way and it is possible to un-train some of our habitual chemical pathways, but it is not an easy path. It is a road that takes years and dedication on everyone's part.

Bonding is a sacred act and we will give our entire life energy to those that we bond deeply with. With a deep bond often comes an unconscious desire to protect that bond. To let another being enter into a bond with our beloved partner, we open the possibility for us to get kicked out. Most people tend to manage only one deep bond to one mate. Truthfully, not too many people have enough energy to keep more than one deep bond alive at one time. People that have more than ample energy are the ones who engage in the luxury of multiple partners. Most mortals don't have the energy or need for that.

It seems that once we enter the union state with one soul, we also often desire to take that union to its transcendence point, into full union.

Yet, I also know that we can go into high states of God-consciousness and simply acknowledge the feelings of erotic attraction, if and when it comes up, without the need to do more. The feeling of sexual energy is part of our makeup and part of the chemistry of being human. We may get aroused getting a massage as well, but we don't want or need to go to bed with the massage therapist.

We can certainly share a heightened state of consciousness and not go into full union with other beings. There are many stages of love. With time we simply learn to be more fluid, more loving, more embracing. And more souls can share one space in harmony in love.

We can certainly love more than one soul. Each one has a different intensity or grade. Yet for most of us mortal humans, it is enough of a challenge to be in one committed intimate relationship. Most people manage to build walls instead of keeping the doors to their souls open. To allow our mates to have deeper eye-to-eye contact or a deeper energy contact with a being other than ourselves could be unimaginable.

Many times people feel jealous about small levels of contact. However, this is exactly what they really wish to change, because they would like to be able to connect deeply, and connect soul-to-soul with more than one person. It feels natural, and we would like to have that without jealousy.

In years past I had to stop deeply soulful relations with some men because it caused jealousy in their mates. But upon review, after many experiences, most of the men said they should have continued with our soulful connection because they felt that this higher communion and stimulation of soul was the true purpose of why they were living here on Earth.

We want to have the kind of connection that takes us home to God. Home! That is the word used by almost everyone. And looking into each other's souls or doing so on the phone in silence is the fastest way "home."

In retrospect, those male friends now feel that inhibiting their soul connections was almost a crime against their souls. They had experienced becoming a vaster, faster vibrating being, but chose to stop sharing such states of consciousness with another only because their mates felt threatened. However, having chosen a partner who could not understand or tolerate such higher states was also part of their lessons and needed to be addressed. In the end, those men had to come to realize that they were not really looking to have an affair but truly wanted to live on higher ground.

Sometimes it takes years to arrive at such wisdom, and sometimes it takes a long time of living in a vacuum to realize the immensity of the meaning of meeting soul to soul. Connections that generate a field of enlightenment are like doorways to Heaven on Earth.

The day I was in communion with Roger, I made sure we would stay within the boundaries of what he and his wife could tolerate. And I also avoided taking this energy into the sexual realm.

We are the creators of our lives and we are going to experience the effects of our actions, sooner or later. When we truly realize that "what goes around comes around," we behave much more responsibly.

We all want to share more love and kindness, more than our normal lives usually allow. Yet we need to dance within the boundaries of unspoken ethics and at the same time deal with the conflicting desires we have as humans.

With Roger it was easy for me to keep my head straight. He was married. But Merlin was another matter. How would I handle the lingering feelings of attraction that danced across my mind? I knew better, yet I felt like there were two voices inside me.

Talking with Rain Clouds

We had ordered a Balinese bed to be delivered to our house. But the first time we could take delivery was the week after the seminar. The couch-bed was meticulously carved with Asian craftsmanship. I had dreamed of owning a Bali bed for a long time and we finally found one in Hilo. It was going to serve us as a large couch as well as a guest bed. It was so big that it needed to be delivered to our house by truck and the delivery date was set for the coming Friday.

The nice weather we had had the week before had turned to rain. By Thursday a tropical storm had begun its downpour and we were looking at a very wet week, and a very wet delivery.

During tropical storms in Hawaii it doesn't just rain, it pours buckets. Once we had thirty-six inches of rain in twenty-four hours. Since our Balinese bed was made of heavy teakwood it would need to be carried upstairs in several pieces, on slippery steps.

Friday evening had arrived and it was now thirty minutes before delivery. I was getting nervous. We had hoped the rains would at least slow down, but there was no sign of a reprieve.

As I stood on our balcony in the open doorway, I looked at the rain laden clouds. I remembered when I was twenty I had read in the book *Autobiography of a Yogi*, that Paramahansa Yogananda had managed to talk to the clouds to make them rain. On a very clear blue-sky day he had formed a cloud above himself and asked it to rain.

As I was reading the story, I was sitting on a green grassy golf course in Baltimore, Maryland in America. In my youthfulness I was totally inspired, and wondered if I could make something like that happen too. Something in Paramahansa Yogananda's book had deeply affected me. His stories of miracles had slowly seeped into my heart and mind, and altered me in such a way that I was inspired to believe in the miraculous. I had been studying philosophy at the time, attempting to crack the cosmic code. On the golf course, beneath an absolutely clear blue sky in a large open field, I was moved into a heightened state. Yogananda told of humans who could talk to the clouds and make it rain on a clear day.

"Maybe," I thought, "just maybe I can do it too."

Something had changed in me as I had read his story. It was as if I had allowed myself to be transported to an expanded space, letting myself become part of a mysterious larger whole where I could communicate with all of life. Yogananda had written of many miracles in such a way that felt totally believable. His innocence and truth were palpable. His open heart and his own transformation were visible in each word of his book. His stories transported me into a new universe in which we can appear to others at a distance, where we can talk to beings in other dimensions and talk to the clouds and the wind.

As I sat on my picnic blanket on the golf course, I decided to try my communication skills with these ephemeral friends. Closing my eyes, I sent a prayer to the sky. It was as if I rose into the area of the sky where clouds would be. When I felt that I was really inside the level of the conscious sky, and felt I was making "contact," I asked the sky as though it could really hear and feel me, if it was at all possible, to please let a small cloud appear above my head and let rain fall upon me. I really wanted to know if the sky could hear me, even though there was no sign of any clouds. It would be a true miracle since the sky had been absolutely blue. So I transferred the message in images and feelings.

When we are able to travel into the realms of pure energy, we reach a place of co-creation. In our minds we move about in the realm of energy patterns, which precede physical manifestation. To make changes, we use our imaginations. This realm, and higher ones, are supersensitive to our consciousness. We navigate realms via inner feeling and inner seeing and are able to make sense, as well as effect changes in these ephemeral dimensions through the use of our subtler mind. At these levels of reality we act as designers, working outside of time-space as we know it.

Finer layers of reality are stacked within each other much like an onion with its many layers; it is just that they are not really physically separated. By making a change within the less dense dimensions, we can see the effects that start reaching into the more dense world, the world of form. And we can witness miracles taking shape in the world "outside" of us.

As I sat on the golf course pondering the story of Yogananda, in a heightened state myself, I felt light raindrops fall upon me. I looked up, and right above me a small cloud had formed. I marveled at such an impossibility, and was moved to tears when I realized what was really happening. The sky and the clouds had heard me! From that moment on I've felt a special connection with clouds.

Yogananda's book, his stories of miracles, and my willingness to suspend my old beliefs, had opened a new horizon for me. The experiment with the clouds offered me a true crack in the cosmic egg. I trusted Yogananda, and by believing in new possibilities I allowed for new boundaries in my own mind to take shape. I understood that by allowing for the impossible I had opened the window to another more magical world.

Tonight, on the balcony facing the pouring rain, I thought I would try to talk to the clouds, to see if they could possibly stop raining. We really wanted a dry delivery.

I reached up high into the dimension where I could talk to the clouds. It was as if I could feel the entire "mind" of the clouds surrounding me. When I felt that I had made contact, I asked them if they wouldn't mind stopping the rain during the delivery of the Bali bed, which was about to arrive. As if they were a little upset, I heard the clouds reply in my mind, "You should have contacted us sooner. We are big and heavy now and we won't be able to just stop raining within seconds."

"Rightfully so," I thought. They had indeed accumulated a lot of water, and for me to just snap my fingers and say: "'Stop now," was asking a bit much.

"Ah," I realized, "they would have liked me to have asked them earlier."

I knew that time-space is just dimensional vibration. In my mind, right then and there, I knew that all I had to do was go "up," as in lifting off, and go to a higher space-time continuum. It is hard to put into words but it feels like going up beyond the clouds and imaginarily reaching into the past. I went back in time by speeding up, by going to a higher layer in the matrix of time. I knew when to stop, when I got to the right "time." Once there, I asked the clouds again, now back in current time, if they could possibly stop raining by the time our truck delivered the Bali bed.

"Sure," they replied, "we will try!"

It *felt* to me as if they could now make it happen. An inner feeling in my spine is an important feedback tool. It helps me to know if something is likely to become "real" or remain a fantasy.

At seven o' clock it was still raining buckets. The truck rolled into our driveway and the driver got out. I moaned, and dreaded having to help him in the pouring rain. We would get soaked through and through. I didn't want to walk up the wooden steps, which were very slippery in the heavy rain.

Just as the driver slammed his door shut and walked around the truck to pull the blue tarp off the wooden bed, the miracle happened.

The rain stopped!

What?

"They have kept their promise!" I thought. "I heard them right!"

Don, the driver and I quickly untied the ropes and carried the bed, piece by piece up the stairs. We set up the couch-bed on the turquoise carpet in our living room. The beautifully carved Bali-bed was Don's present to me. The daybed would serve as our couch, be a meeting place for friends and Don and I to snuggle together on rainy days, where we could have tea and cookies and read books. The bed looked fabulous.

Finished with the delivery, the driver stepped outside onto the balcony to put on his shoes. The moment he did, the rain started pouring down in buckets.

"How was that possible?" I wondered. The moment the driver had stepped outside the door, when he had finished his job, the rain began falling as if it had never stopped. That was truly a moment to remember!

It was Yogananda's gracious sharing of miracle stories that had inspired me to believe in the miraculous. Life was a living miracle. It was grand to be alive and grow!

For years I told no one about my experience. I was well aware that most of our culture does not believe in the ability to talk with inanimate objects or animals. Not only are dolphins telepathic but so are clouds, and in fact all of life is nothing but a sea of alive co-creative energy.

Nothing is solid as we think of it. But it takes the ability to tune into higher states to affect levels of reality in ways that we consider out of the ordinary. It is my hope that by sharing this story now, it will open the doors for you as well, to do your own miracles.

Don and I enjoyed our moments of alone time. We snuggled on the new Bali bed in our home and just held each other for a long time. Nothing had prepared me though for what was coming next.

Home Alone with another Man

Merlin had offered Don and I each a massage as a "thank you" for having given him the opportunity to make some money by giving massages to our participants during our seminar. Soon after the seminar had ended I drove over to his new house to meet him. Merlin was house-sitting for Carl, who was back on the Mainland to make money, as so many people who live in this remoter part of Hawaii need to do. Merlin was making sure the house was safe and was feeding the dog. Carl, an artist, had outstanding creative art pieces adorning the whole house.

I had taken Merlin up on his offer for a free massage. My sacrum ached, I felt weak, and I was looking forward to a treat, especially from Merlin.

As I entered the open house, Merlin was still setting up the massage table. He invited me in and we cordially sat together, sharing some tea. I told him about my discomfort in my lower back and soon Merlin started his massage in a special loft. The room was warm, light-filled and open. The tall peaked roof made space for my spirit to expand. Soft music lifted me into a dreamlike space. As Merlin massaged me very slowly, focusing his energy deeply into my body, I felt an increasing desire for him to touch me more personally, more intimately. Though feeling weak, I was very aware of feeling aroused, wishing for more. I couldn't believe myself. I had studied massage and I knew all about keeping clean boundaries. I knew that one should never mix massage with erotic energy and that good ethics keep the massage trade on a clear path. But I had to admit, as I was lying on the massage table, I wished for something else. Married and in love with Don, I was nevertheless very aroused by this other man. My heart beat faster and my breath betrayed my desire. But nothing happened.

The massage was over and Merlin quietly gave me space to return to my normal state of consciousness. I had been agonizing over my feeling of desire during the massage. Maybe I should have thanked my angels that they hadn't fulfilled all my wishes. What would I have said to Don? Unthinkable! I couldn't and wouldn't keep any secrets. One way or another, I would have come clean with Don and told him the truth, and it was best that nothing more had happened.

Back home, Don greeted me and asked how the session had gone. I had nothing to hide! I was relieved. But I noticed that I had gotten the flu and needed to go to bed. The next day, I was out of commission and unable to get up.

That is when we got bad news. Our secretary in Washington had stopped coming to work. We were scheduled to return to our office in the Northwest within a few days but we couldn't figure out what had happened, why she hadn't called us and why she wasn't at work. When we tried to call her at home we only got her answering machine. Had something bad happened? Our office depended on her and while we were away in Hawaii, we were especially dependant on her. Luckily we were scheduled to fly back home in a few days but we were puzzled at her sudden disappearance.

The next evening I was able to reach her husband. He didn't say much; just that she was not coming back to work! What had happened? I didn't know. She had been with us for just under one year and it had all seemed to go well. We had been gone a lot during that year, teaching seminars and traveling, and just weeks before we went to Hawaii to teach the seminar we seemed to get along so very well. I couldn't figure it out. Without her we would be stranded in our office, and one thing was clear – we needed to fly back as soon as possible. But since I was seriously ill, I was unable to fly. Indeed, I needed to delay my flight. Don, however, would be able to fly back on time and get home to the office to check on everything.

Don and I are hardly ever apart. We seem to spend 24 hours a day, seven days a week together. Now he had to leave, and by nature's design I was stranded in Hawaii. Merlin offered to take Don to the airport and soon Don was on his way home.

Meanwhile I lay in bed, exhausted from the flu and tired. I used the time to heal. On one of the days I called my girl friend Betty. She is a tremendously spiritual woman, world-renowned flautist, teacher and writer. I still remember the moment when she asked me during that phone conversation as I was laying in bed: "Ilona, are you thinking of getting pregnant?"

It had been over eight weeks since Mother Mary had appeared to me in my vision. I had not seen any sign that Merlin, the father who Mother

Mary had in mind for the baby, desired me, and I had forgotten the story. But Betty asked me point blank. She was highly sensitive and intuitive and I was a bit perplexed.

Instantly, I realized that I was in Hawaii without Don. My return flight had been scheduled ten days later, so I was about to have time alone with Merlin. I caught my breath for a moment. I told Betty the entire story of Mother Mary and the vision of the baby, and she told me to watch out.

As soon as I hung up the phone with Betty, I called Don. Don had his own confessions to make. He had found a letter from our secretary to both of us, explaining the whole situation. The secretary had let Don give her a massage on her shoulders just weeks before we left for Hawaii. While giving her a shoulder massage she had felt that she had let him come too close. Truth came to light that it was not just her shoulders that he had massaged but that they had let the touch wander just a tiny bit more.

I didn't know what to say. Should I have screamed and shouted? Should I have spoken of ethics? Should I have understood? Not much had happened, but when our secretary had told her husband that Don had massaged her and then touched her some more, they felt it was best for her to stop working for us.

I understood her point. I could have kicked Don. He should have known better. Although she could have protested, it was his place to watch the boundaries. But not too many days ago, I had also felt the desire to be touched by someone else!

Next it was my turn, and I made my confession to Don. I also told him of my vision of Mother Mary and of Betty's sensitive perception, and Don had already known how Merlin and I had kissed in Mexico.

Don was in such a vulnerable state that he could not be angry with me. He had made a faux pas himself and was just happy that I hadn't left him right then and there. He was sweet in his agony. His betrayal tormented him. It seemed like a small transgression to me but in essence it had been a lie. Don was only hoping I wouldn't kick him out. He had endangered our office and now it had come to light.

Both of us had felt openings toward other people in the last couple months, even if the seeds had been very small. I recalled, as I spoke with Don, how just weeks ago in our office I had talked to our secretary about massages, and how one thing can lead to another. Don had felt bad for her since her husband had been very attentive to another woman, who happened to be my music teacher. Innocent in his mind, Don had felt that our secretary was being neglected and he wanted to make up for it.

"How selfless of you," I joked when I talked to Don.

But I also recalled one morning how I had felt some strange twinges in my body. In the past I had experienced those twinges when my partner had been engaged with another woman erotically or sexually. Although I had been upstairs in my office and Don had been downstairs with our secretary, the feelings had reached me through the walls. I had asked Don if something was happening between him and our secretary and at the time he denied it. Now, in retrospect, I swore that I would listen to my intuition more often!

But here we were. Don was alone at home, crying at his confession, small as it seemed to me. And here I was, wanting to be more sexual with Merlin, and stuck alone in Hawaii.

Don had the wisdom not to condemn me but to suggest we take time to think about the undertaking of having a baby with another male. Since he trusted my visions, he didn't just brush it off. Don had had a vasectomy many years ago, and we didn't want to have children. And my having a baby with another man didn't seem any more inviting to him.

But my subconscious was making different plans. Who had arranged my inability to go to Seattle with Don? Who was the master planner behind it all? Why was it all happening as if choreographed by another hand?

Luckily, it seemed that Merlin had not had any desire. So I planned to visit him as soon as I was healthy enough to drive again.

Merging with Merlin

I had asked a neighbor to make some soup, since Don was not here to cook and take care of me while I was sick. When we are not well, we seem so alone and fragile on this planet. Just like dolphins, we depend on each other to survive. I was grateful to have help in the neighborhood. Merlin couldn't help because he was living forty minutes away from me.

Slowly, I got well enough to get out of the house. It was a beautiful sunny day and Merlin and I made plans to meet. Having had time to be alone and meditate, I was ready to live multi-dimensionally again. It takes a lot of energy to live in higher presence on Earth, and it had taken a lot of attention and energy just to get my crown chakra to spin while I had been sick.

As I drove down the main street toward the ocean, glowing white sunlight reflected off the water and blazed into my eyes. We live rather remotely and at that time didn't yet have electric power in our area. We loved living "off the grid" as they call it, and we opted to keep off the grid even when electricity became available. We had no bills, produced our own electricity, and caught our own rain water, so we were a lighter burden to the environment. The rainwater is heated by the sun on the roof to give us warm showers, and we have a garden of rich fruit-bearing trees.

Driving along the blue, vast ocean I passed the little dolphin beach where we had just had such spectacular dolphin encounters with our group. Soon I turned north toward the house where Merlin was awaiting me. The house was sitting in a farm-like neighborhood with many flowering trees adorning the long driveway. I drove up slowly and got out of the car. In the distance I heard the ocean crashing gently onto the lava shoreline. As I breathed in the ocean breeze I let myself become aware of the paradise surrounding me. The quiet in between the trees opened my heart. With anticipation I walked up to the house. My heart was beating quickly. How would Merlin greet me?

I entered the house, as the door was open. Gently I called out "Aloha." With the sweetness coming from my heart, the sound of my voice must have hung in the air like a poem of love. Merlin was making a special fruit drink in the kitchen but stopped when I walked around the kitchen counter. We hugged for a long time and he held me not only with his body, but also in his heart. His arms wrapped gently around me, not to squeeze me, but to feel me. He was totally different from the weeks before. Why was he so different now? Did he feel he no longer had to share the stage with Don, since Don was on the Mainland? I let his energy enter into me and I breathed deeply.\

Since the day was so like paradise, we decided to have a picnic in the garden and took the fruit juice and some peeled fruit outside. We laid out a blanket on the grass, under the shade of the flowering trees. The fruit, the juice and a flower blessed our blanket like an offering on an altar.

Sunlight lit up Merlin's long golden hair and the moving patterns of light and shade across his face made him look like Krishna. I started to gaze at Merlin with those special eyes, eyes that defocus a little. I looked deeper into his soul as we sat across from each other and we both started breathing more slowly. What happened next can only be described as entering a supernatural world. I literally felt as if we both started to expand. The light took on a glow that I had not seen before. Merlin looked like he was an angel and we both felt as if our energy fields were becoming larger and vaster.

In the imagery that superimposed itself onto my physical vision, we started to merge magically with each other in another space. As I looked into his eyes I saw starlight, which became the doorway to his higher nature. As if entering a tunnel, by looking at the starlight in his eyes and at the same time traveling to the vision that enfolded me, I became a flame of light rising into a higher space within him.

Ever so slowly, our eyes locked onto one another. While gazing at me, he reached out to touch my hands. As if I was offering him a lotus blossom, I opened my palms into his, gifting him with my imaginary offering.

Our hands took on a dance of bliss, tracing subtle spirals of energy in the ether between us. Our fingers touched and together formed what looked like a geometric pattern, much like a mudra, a sacred hand position. More than our bodies, our energies started to dance with each other. We were becoming more and more sensitive to that which was beneath the surface of our bodies and we let ourselves be moved by a force vaster than ourselves.

Our minds started to expand and the light in our Garden of Eden was more beautiful than ever. At one moment I felt like we were morphing into other bodies, becoming bigger beings, godlike in nature, in this still dance of rising fire. As if in slow motion, Merlin reached out to trace the outline of my hair and his hands flowed around my face in a winged-like movement.

I was transfixed, breathing deeper, softer and becoming very open. Gently, he moved his hands under my hair and onto my neck. He rested his hands there for a moment to feel me welcoming him. As I received his touch, he started to gently pull my face closer to his. His breath fanned over my eyes and my breath responded to his. His lips opened more as his breath became a poem in my ears, asking me to meet his lips ever so lightly. I kept my gaze on his eyes and entered a trance-like state. Gone were all concerns and all I felt was the moment. I wanted to open my whole self to him and touch his lips with mine. As if in slow-motion our lips met, gently, with no effort, no plan, no place to go. I was soaking up our communion as I felt our lips melt, our soft waves of breath enter into one another.

Our bodies and lips took on a life of their own and we moved into a greater dance. His mouth was soft, open, large and unpredictable. His

174

mind had surrendered to his body's wisdom and he explored me with the electric touch of his wet lips as he pulled me closer into himself.

We didn't move much, but moved together as if in a slow, unfurling dance of angel wings. Slowly, we were feeling each other, taking time to respond to the movement of our inner energies without planning our next physical moves. We let our energy bodies build a wave of motion first and then followed that pulse of energy with our physical bodies into a depth that went deeper than the skin.

We moved with the wave of ecstasy that took us on an ever-richer ride. I don't know how long we moved like that but I knew that not many men knew the art of dance like this. Merlin could clearly feel me from the inside out and I could feel him. Our breath increased together. Our mouths opened more. My heart was in absolute heaven. Here we were in loving union! Weeks and months later, out of the blue, we were kissing again. In that moment I could not see any harm I was doing to Don or myself. It was a gigantic gift to me, a moment of heaven in time and space.

He moved his hair out of the way as his gaze fell on the fruit that was lying on the plate before us. He slowly picked up a piece of tangerine and knowingly looked at me as he placed the tangerine into his mouth. Provokingly, he started to feed me as he dreamily looked at my eyes. The moment was like a dream come true, a hope I had given up. Yet suddenly it was being resurrected and came into reality like a picture-perfect movie starring two angels.

Holding the fruit with his lips, he moved forward and touched my lips with the sweet tangerine juice. He teased me into wanting to take the fruit from his lips into mine. As I did, he gently pushed the slippery fruit and penetrated my semi-open lips as though he wanted to enter my whole being. My vulnerable mouth was completely open to him now. At one moment when we were most transfixed, he bit into the fruit, letting the juice drip onto my lips and we kissed. Mixing the juicy fruit in our mouths, we passed the pieces back and forth and totally surrendered into passionately entering each other in a most primal way. Our instinctual feeding-drive took over.

Feeding, erotic feelings and pretend-penetration all melted into one. My hair flowed like a radiant river of dark ebony over his golden locks which cascaded in waves of golden sunlight into mine. I was getting very aroused and our bodies swayed in a grand, wavelike motion in this world of paradise – a world of sunlight, patterns of shade, flowers and utmost feelings of love.

We opened ourselves deeply to one another. Sensing where we were going, I slowly pulled apart and we looked at each other. My hand in his hand, we sat upright in a semi-lotus position.

"You know," he said, "I had a vision during a meditation a few days ago." His voice trailed off as if he was wondering how to tell me something. I breathed in deeply. Somehow, the way he was saying it, I could feel that something very large and special was about to be revealed.

"I went high up in my meditation," he continued, "and in that very high state I was told to have a child with you!" He paused as if foretelling a prophecy. I was totally and completely mesmerized. At no time during the last few weeks on Hawaii had I imagined that he harbored the kind of feelings for me that would allow him such a vision. He was astounded himself, so he told me, because he had not nurtured the feelings, since I was married.

We both were aware how perfectly funny this could sound to anyone else. "God told me to make love with you!" I smiled, sighed and told him that I understood perfectly. Then I told him of my own vision weeks ago, of Mother Mary and how she too had told me to have a baby with him.

Had we both had true, higher visions? Or had we conveniently transported our personal desires into a more spiritual metaphor? We decided to get up and move our bodies. There was a lot to digest, accept and understand.

Since I was still a bit weak and Merlin had wanted to take a walk, I suggested that he walk for a while by himself as I took a short nap. I knew that he was the kind of man who easily lost himself in another person and that he really needed to regroup himself into his own center to keep feeling empowered. He agreed and I went into the house to lie down on his bed.

Still stunned by our opening, and feeling my heart reeling from the beauty of our encounter, I recalled all the moments of the agonizing desire I had felt for him in the last few weeks. I recalled the words I had heard in my head in Mexico as we had shared our first dinner at the beach with the group. "He is to be your future husband."

I remembered the directive in my dream to allow other men into my life, and finally I recalled how the super-clear, psychic health-reader told me that I needed to allow more partners into my life.

The last eight weeks had led me to believe that this was not going to happen, and yet here we were in a perfectly set-up situation. Merlin and I felt like we were players in a play that we had not written. Up until now we were trying very hard to avoid following the plan.

The Multi-dimensional Art of Making Love

Merlin came back from his walk, refreshed. He looked centered, good and was very open. As he sat with me on the bed, we entered into our ignited fields again and marveled at the coincidence of our visions. We didn't question them, we simply let them be.

Since Merlin had given so many massages during the seminar, I asked him if he wanted to receive one from me. We kept our clothing on, which I thought was a smart move, and Merlin stretched out on the bed. I started to massage his head, slowly rubbing my fingertips along his scalp. In my mind I imagined what I would feel like if I were in his body as I ran my fingers gently over his scalp.

We sensed each other intensely. All my sensors were wide open; my mind felt and traced every subtle millimeter of energy and touch that we shared, tracing the sensations beneath my fingers as I touched his head and face.

In my mind I sent a pulse of energy through my hands to his whole head, allowing Merlin to slow down and enter a deep state of relaxation. We need to be given time to relax and open our energy bodies. When making love, a lot of times we get aroused and then rush into sexual movements, which tend to split us off from our deeper, truer erotic feelings. We need to give our subtler bodies a chance to open deeply and get in touch with this true erotic pulse.

At his core, Merlin deeply opened to himself, and in doing so he was opening to the presence of my fingers and of my penetration of his energy body via my fingertips on his head. I listened intently to his deeper breathing which now was a barometer as to how open he truly was.

In this stillness we were reaching an ocean of lightness and we merged in that light. I ran my fingers through his long hair and Merlin could feel that I could feel him. With both of my hands cupped around his head, I entered the thick of his hair, holding his head in my palms and moving my fingertips to the spots on his head that called out to be touched.

I loved the magic of holding his head as I was feeling his pulse in my hands. Love streamed from my heart. I sensed his head under my fingertips, and waited to sense if the energy in and underneath his skin was responding to me. Silently, I listened with my fingers for the dance of his energy. If I was indeed touching him I would hear his answer to my call, and could touch him along the dreamtime lines of his body. And yes, his energy invited me to move forward, deeper, stronger on his head; and I did.

178

This is a different form of touching than most people are used to. I felt like a cat. I was sensitive to every nuance in him and listened to every response he gave me. His head, scalp and hair talked to me, and he was, in a way, entering me as I was entering him energetically.

My hands moved gently down to his neck, not only touching his skin, but the entire energy inside his body, beneath his skin. Then my fingers came to rest in the cradle of his neck, where the spine entered his skull. Here was a most primal opening and my fingers sent out rays of light down along the spine into his body.

In my imagination I saw, and most importantly of all, I felt how I was traveling as a wave of light down into him. I was entering him like fire, merging our energies. I waited to hear an echo from his subtle bodies, feeling how his energy was responding to my touch. As I penetrated his whole being with my touch, I was also able to feel him interpenetrate my hands with his energy. We didn't just touch, we were making love in a very deep and yet subtle way.

He was not only Merlin, but also transfigured into my inner guide Gopal Das, as he lay on the bed. Spread out like a trusting angel, he glowed in a supernatural light. I was expanding into a being that was at once Ilona, the human, as well as a mythical being, a dakini, a goddess, riding on wings of energy into a dimension where we were able to feel ourselves enter each other like liquid star plasma. We flowed, and our lives were in the hands of our higher dimensions.

After massaging him for a long time in silence, I reached his legs and couldn't help but tantalize him with the same slow movements. In doing so I started entering a dance that was no longer very subtle but awoke a fire that turned from white, to pink, to orange and finally to red. We had started a dance of our innermost essence and now we were feeling the fire of our bodies emerge.

Merlin was moving his body in rhythmic waves, in silence, as if in a dream. With each movement we waited until we felt the resonant echo from deep within each other. We were both letting go of our controls, and were opening on a deep level to one another. His excitement, though we had gone in slow-motion, had mounted, as had mine, and he started to pull me near his face. He breathed more deeply, touching my ears, and began to enter the deeper part of my primal mind.

He gazed at me as he lay there like a God, and slowly started to move into his own action. We were becoming a dance; living, flowing myths together. I had worn a golden outfit in an Arabic-Indian style and in colors that had been inspired by Merlin. Never before had I wanted to wear gold, yellow or orange colors. But he had entered my inner world weeks ago and had infiltrated me long before we had kissed again.

Flowing, as these clothes were, he ever so lightly freed my shoulders to reveal my skin, bronzed from the tropical sun, and now very open to his kiss, heated by my desire for him. It was just like in a perfect movie. In moments I opened my eyes and caught glimpses of the play of the light and shade from the sun as it streamed into the house through the windows, creating a work of art to behold.

Large plants, soft colors of the curtains and our clothes partly on and partly off, were moving in the wind. My dark hair was cascading onto his face and his lips reached to kiss mine. Engulfed by his presence I surrendered to his lips, to his movements as he pulled me into him, and I surrendered to his touch, as his hands came to touch my heart. My body arched toward him, to be in his arms completely.

With time we got bolder in our movements and we wrapped our wings around each other, the full length of our bodies touching, legs curled around each other, entwined, as if to bond eternally. In a moment of deep fire we slowed down and held each other in stillness. With a masterful movement Merlin sat upright in a lotus position, to be able to take me across his lap.

We breathed the energy up our spines to ignite our higher centers. In my imagination I pulled my increasing fire up my spine with my breath, up and out, toward the crown chakra, for our surging energies to meet above our heads.

Looking at each other, we circulated our breath of fire through each other again and again, breathing the light up and out with our imaginations. Receiving the cosmic fertile breath from Merlin, I breathed out again, imagining how my intimate energy flowed down his spine into his loins from where he pulsed his current into me, surging into my womb. From there we pulled the energy up again, with our breaths, into our hearts and then back out of our crown chakras, where we met in the synergy of our starlight, shooting up and out into the vastness of space. Here too, we wrapped ourselves around each other, coiled like a double helix, our energies touching the heavens, where we rose higher until we met each other in an infinitely far point of union, in a momentous rapture of primal star creation.

My body instincts also moved me, and as we kneeled together I began circular movements as if our bodies were also a helix. Somehow I came to rest with my back to his chest and his arms wrapped around me in an embrace, as if I was the tree of life. We swayed in the wind of our passion, our bodies pulsed in rhythm, rushing into each other like ocean waves that pulsed onto the shore. Strong desires fanned our fire and my ethereal wings opened to him as he pulsed his energy from behind me into my core column of light.

But I had a small amount of reason and for a moment tried to pull away. It had helped to be honest with myself and with Don, as well as to have talked with Betty. If I gave in and we went further, I would surely get pregnant, as our visions had shown. Maybe I should have let go of all control in that moment, but I didn't. Was destiny wise? Was I bound by our visions, and did they really come from high sources? Reason is one thing, but feeling is another. Yet in that moment when I took time to gain perspective, it was enough to choose to avoid going down that road.

I closed my eyes and felt us again. We were so very close, so inside each other's energy. My body's currents were electrified and wanted him. Yet refraining from conventional intercourse made us shiver even more.

At times, his breath in my ears came in crashing waves; at other times we held still. I could hear him want me, as he held me in his arms. We did not want to stop. Not now. We were both in the midst of a current of excitement, struggling to keep our human lives in order, as we felt the nudges and pulls from so many levels of our selves. The visions, the dreams, the desire, the enigmatic words I had heard in my mind, the larger feeling of destiny, were all pulsing together in us at that moment.

I pushed my hips ever closer into him; partly dressed, we were keeping that little space that made all the difference. It didn't matter to us, we didn't know anymore if we were inside each other, or just fully feeling our energies. The dance was so intensely real and we were so deeply enmeshed within each other. Touching, dancing, slower and then faster, breathing in primal merging, took us to a moment where I could feel us reach a level of fire that ignited both of us like stars about to explode.

As he pushed himself with more vigor tightly against me, I pulled my entire focus upward. I felt myself rush up inside the central column of my spine and imagined Merlin doing the same. Exploding in ecstasy I breathlessly asked him to raise himself up high into God and to meet me up in the star.

A central light was shooting high out of my head, through the center of my crown chakra, and sought to find his soul up in the vastness of space. I met with his light as we rose higher, and as we touched a point of no return we went into a brilliant explosion of our entire beings, engulfed in the vastness of God.

I offered this union of our energies to this Allness, as if our love, our energy, our explosion was the very gift God had been waiting for. Not holding onto it for my own pleasure, but giving it away, I felt even more the powerful surge shooting through our bodies, hearts and spirits. The further I took this wave to the center of God, the longer and more intense the electrifying shockwave became in my entire system.

Being just energy, or pure consciousness, we met in a space of a brilliant star, igniting with each other into an explosion that was higher than any mortal love could reach. We were one at that moment and high, high, high in the heavens. We both felt the moment of ecstasy and held still, arching our heads higher as if to touch the heavens with our souls.

I was panting and swirling in my mind and body. We had climaxed together in a supernatural way. Stars and the cosmos enfolded us. Love and utter joy were pulsing through my heart. What we had just experienced was beyond my wildest dreams. I was sure we had both had the same kind of experience. His arms were holding me in his loving body; his mind was blown open as wide as mine. Our moans were poetry from another dimension. Our hearts pulsed with ecstatic, wild surrender to the vastness of the sky.

We stayed in this reverie for a long time, slowly letting our bodies, hearts and breaths become a tropical breeze, letting the wings of our souls land softly on the lotus flower of our hearts and minds.

Eventually we got up, and very silently, as if arising from a holy dance with each other, as consorts we walked into the garden, and marveled at the sunlight. The breeze, the flowers and the paradisiacal flames of light touched our souls.

The shower was in the garden, built of lava rock, surrounded by large leaves that gave us shelter and privacy. We undressed slowly and stood as Adam and Eve under the shower, and let the warm water splash onto our bodies. We washed each other using sponges to make lots of foam, and played like children. We sent splashes of water dancing into the air and it reflected the sunlight, making it look like we were surrounded by a million stars. I kneeled in front of Merlin and washed his feet as I kissed his thighs. Flowing freely into our hearts, outside there in the garden, in the sunlight we were in Heaven on Earth. What a blessing had been given to us! And we had managed not to go all the way. Not really.

Don had asked me to take time and think about getting pregnant. We had agreed that I wouldn't have sex. But though I lived by the letter of the word, I was nevertheless fully penetrated by the experience. I was on fire. Merlin and I had been in rapture, in a union of soul and body. Don and I made love like that too. Sometimes it was while being sexual, having intercourse, and sometimes we would make love even more subtly where we didn't move much at all.

I had caught fire and yet I was also really aware that I was a bit like a teacher with a student. I couldn't always tell who was more masterful, but I wondered how much of my inner sharing Merlin had managed to consciously experience. Some of it I knew he had felt, yet whether he saw the cosmic fireworks as I did and as Don knew how to experience with me, I didn't know.

On the other hand, I now had to deal with being on fire myself. Would I want to leave in order to start a new family, which is what most people would fear would happen? I didn't think so. But difficult months were to come and I had a feeling I was being pulled by fate. Where would it take me?

• A **dakini** (Sanskrit: "sky dancer") is a Tantric priestess of ancient India who "carried the souls of the dead to the sky". This Buddhist figure is particularly upheld in Tibetan Buddhism. The dakini is a female being of generally volatile temperament, who acts as a muse for spiritual practice. Dakinis can be likened to elves, angels, or other such supernatural beings, and are symbolically representative of testing one's awareness and adherence to Buddhist tantric sadhana.

The Truth Shall Set You Free

The next few days Merlin and I spent a lot of time together. It was as if a curtain had lifted and we were living in a world that was the total opposite of the previous weeks. We baked bread together, one of Merlin's specialties. We went into nature, swam, took hikes and walked in a dreamlike space. My head was spinning, my heart was pulsing and my body was on fire. I had a few days left before my scheduled flight back home and we lived like lovers.

We discussed how Don had asked me not to get pregnant and to wait, till we had a clearer headspace. I talked with Don on the phone every day and as well as I could, I filled him in on what I was going through. I must admit, I didn't give him all the details and, while I didn't hide what I was going through, I didn't paint the picture quite as glowingly as I was feeling. I agonized about how much to share and knew how bad I would feel if I was to lie. Sooner or later I would tell the truth because I never could live with lies.

If I told him about things later, Don would feel betrayed, and in the future he might not trust me. Breaking trust is harder than telling the truth. What did I want to avoid if I lied? The worst thing I would encounter would be Don's anger and his request for me to change, to stop connecting with Merlin. But it would be kinder and more truthful to Don if I told him the truth. Then if he asked me to change I could choose what was more valuable to me.

If I lied, I would be building a brick wall between me and my Beloved. As Erich Fromm says in his book *The Art of Loving*, each lie, each small truth withheld is a stone, which in time will turn into a brick wall. Such a wall keeps all intimacy and love from flowing. When one keeps a secret, one cannot remember what was shared and what was not. Withholding the energy builds the wall.

Sure, by telling Don about what I was doing and asking him for permission for it, I gave him the power to veto it. But in the end I wanted to give him that right. That is why I was quite truthful with Don asking him, in a way, for his permission.

Since Don and I had gone through the imagery work in Mexico, and since the clairvoyant had told me that I needed to make a change in how I was living in relationship with my partner, we were willing to experiment. I was getting stronger, and the illness I had had the previous year seemed a thing of the past. In a way, I realized that by being so monogamous, I was holding my auric field very tightly together. By doing so, it seemed to constrict my lymphatic system, clamping it down.

I didn't know if my suffering was caused by clamping down sexually or ethereally. My suspicion was that it had to do with my life in the etheric body. I seem to need some time in higher spaces with other like-minded etheric beings. I love to journey inwardly into higher realms. I love pulling myself and anyone who is interested into the higher spaces and into God. Such relationships spur us onward, toward being at once more illumined, loving, dolphin-like and sharing our brilliant light. It allows us to merge with not only one precious person in our lives but makes us available to love many beings, even beings of various species.

When we perceive the subtle realms as real, we are able to merge our own vast reservoir of wisdom with the vast reservoir of wisdom of another's soul. We can touch the realms of God together and take on a mobility that is no longer restricted to the three-dimensional life. We start to become global in our identity and begin to commune with beings of other dimensions such as dolphins, angels and inner Masters. We can span time-space in undreamed of ways.

It seems that so many people I have talked to want the same thing. They want mystical love, a soul-mate with whom they can touch the face of God. And most people would like to feel that love with another, if their Betrothed cannot keep up with them. Such contacts serve as cross-fertilization of our souls and help us establish a network of light beings across the planet.

But our "old" brains seem to have a hard time keeping up with our evolutionary urges. It was not in my nature to be a permissive, sexual being. I was more possessive and protective. My mammalian brain was definitely still working well! But I realized that by living conventionally, in harmony with our western social norms, I was going against my inner nature. Deep down inside I needed to come to terms with my unruly nature. In some way I had known I was not quite so normal, but I really wanted to be accepted. I wanted to be kind, sweet and certainly not branded.

I felt somewhat embarrassed. It had taken many years to understand myself, the larger purpose of my drives, to arrive at accepting the strangeness in myself.

My relief came when I read about Tibetan women. Even now, some of them have two husbands. In Ladhak it is still the custom, as it is in Tibet-China today. A year ago I met a woman on the roadside by her house in North India, where the Dalai Lama lives. As we talked, I found out that she had fled Tibet-China four years previously. She was a daughter of two fathers. Since her mother had been married to two men, she never knew which one was the biological father. She told me her story candidly, without any feeling of it being strange or odd.

Not that I wanted to have two husbands or live with two men, but perhaps I needed to live multiple lives at the same time. Maybe I needed to live a few lifetimes in one? Maybe I needed to understand that love exists beyond the bond with a particular person and is a *state* of being? Maybe I needed to understand that I was interested in union with God, which is the ultimate purpose, and not get lost in the particulars. With some special souls I could go far in that direction. Maybe I was holding my soul back by being more traditional.

The sexual component with Merlin was an addition I had to reckon with. Whatever it was, Don and I were willing to explore life together.

Merlin was not the kind of man I could really run off with, and Don felt that instinctually. Don really wanted to stay with me, and I with him. We wanted to find out what we would become, and who we would become, if we tried to expand beyond the boundaries of our current lives.

Merlin was en route to revisit an old girl friend of his who was now living in Australia. He was looking forward to possibly continuing their relationship.

In a way, neither he nor I were planning on being together past this one week.

The day to fly home had arrived. Merlin drove me to the Kona airport, a three-hour drive. We were listening to Loreena McKennitt singing Irish songs of love as we passed over volcanic mountains shrouded in misty fog. Low growing shrubs that stretched into the hilly landscape of sparsely covered mountains and some occasional trees dotted the hills. My heart was drawn to the music and it made me think of past lives. I envisioned how we might have lived in Ireland and how we could have ridden on horses in the same kind of misty fog. We held hands and caressed each other as we drove, stopped the car, kissed, and held onto each other for a long time. We could not quite fathom that it was already over.

At the airport I realized the immensity of emotions to which I had opened myself. I was shaking and crying as we held each other. As Merlin laid his forehead against mine I saw brilliant fuchsia-red in my inner mind. The color was stronger than ever before. Our auras had had an immense effect on each another.

But I had to leave. That had been the plan all along. Slowly, we let go and I walked toward the gate. I climbed up the ramp, and the wind blew my long hair like a flag. Deep in thought, I gazed out the window and sadness filled my heart. The woman next to me asked when Merlin and I would see each other again. I was shocked. She had seen us at the gate and had become deeply inspired by our love.

"Oh my God," I thought, "she is imagining Merlin and I as a couple!"

That was wrong. She didn't know Don was my husband! I was giving her the wrong impression.

"When are you going to see each other again?" she had asked.

Merlin and I had never even mentioned the thought of it. Never! I didn't even see a future, and I didn't plan on one.

As the plane took off and I left the paradisiacal island of Hawaii below us, I cried. Maybe I had underestimated my emotions. To have "just one moment in time" is a great idea, but emotions have longer time spans. They live on, and even touch us from past lives and affect our future lives. We can care very deeply for another soul and do so for many lives to come. I really love that, and I realized that I wasn't good at a fling.

Here in the world between worlds above the clouds, I tried to focus on my future. Don was going to greet me in Seattle and I was emotionally caught in-between the worlds. Had I done the wrong thing?

As our flight approached Seattle we were given a grand view of the mountains and islands of the Northwest. We flew closely over the Cascade mountain range and the evening sun lit up Mt. Rainer. It is a huge, 14,000 feet volcano, clad in white snow even in June, and it glowed in the orange rays of the setting sun. The ocean meandered between many of the small islands. Dark mounds, which were tree-laden islands, languidly rested in the calm waters of Puget Sound. Seattle is a most beautiful city. We landed, and I placed my feet consciously on the ground.

"I belong here!" I told myself.

I made it to the baggage claim where Don was going to greet me. As I came around the corner I gazed up the stairs to where Don was to wait for me. My eyes searched for him in the crowd and suddenly I saw him! He was waiting for me at the top of the escalators. Dressed in white with a huge bunch of red roses in his arms and glowing blue eyes, he radiated like a master! I fell in love with him right then and there all over again.

His immense blue eyes glistened as if they were made of jewels and he was glowing with a light from another dimension.

Don took me into his arms so lovingly that my heart just flew wide open. No reproach, no regret, no hate, no pain. Not now. Just love! I was grateful that he was so in love with me.

In the days that Don had been alone at home, he had had time to think about what a jewel he had found in me. He was not about to throw our love to the wind. We were a match made in Heaven and he wanted me.

We drove home holding hands, in love and thankful to have each other. It had been over sixteen years since I had met Don. We had jointly grown so much, and had an exquisite life together. We had hammered out all the nuances of our beliefs. Our work revolved around all the things we loved, and now a little fling! It was a small moment in time, compared to the vastness of the energy and life we shared. Not that it was easy, but we looked at our recent relationship experiences compared to the entire life we had shared.

The following weeks I found that my mind still reeled at times, and the feelings for Merlin were still there. In moments of silence I gazed at the clouds and whispered poetry to him in my heart. Or as I picked strawberries, I thought of Merlin in the early morning and the dewdrops on the leaves were like pearls of love still in my heart. At times, when Don and I made love, I had glitches. I missed Merlin and wanted to feel him. It was becoming apparent that it was hard to reconcile two lovers. It was hard even though Merlin was soon leaving for Australia and planning to get together with another woman. I was trying to let go, so I thought. And I did, for moments at a time.

But I was definitely in love with Don and didn't intend to leave him. What for? Even Mother Mary only spoke of Merlin fathering a child, not raising one with me.

June went by quickly and Merlin was off to his new world in Byron Bay, north of Sydney, Australia. I just focused on my life at hand. Our time at home was spent working in our office, catching up with all the work and production that had been left behind. We had to work double duty since our secretary had gone. We answered all the phone calls and had to find and train a new secretary since we were to leave again for Florida, to lead the Dolphin Swim Seminars for a few weeks. We were very much looking forward to swimming with our favorite dolphins, as we had been doing every summer for many years.

Shifting the Time-Space Matrix

The day had arrived for us to leave for Florida. As Don and I got onto the airplane we were grateful to be constantly working together. Three weeks of intense work and fun awaited us. We had become very attached to our dolphin pod in the open waters of Key West.

Our flight was taking us from Seattle to Miami, via Washington, D.C. From Miami we still needed to rent a car and make the three-hour drive south to Key West where we were holding the seminar.

As we were flying above the clouds I was reading a book on "Time Shift" (Timeshift, The Experiment of Dimensional Change by Janet Iris Sussman, ISBN # 0-9643535-0-4).

"Time wobbles, as it learns to select variables from different compartments of the time-space continuum," she wrote. Her book is for those brave souls that already have access to living as time-shape shifters. It is a book that elevated me instantly to a larger perspective as I read the prosaic essays on multi-dimensional living.

Clouds passed below us and I felt suspended in a timeless world on the wings of a machine that carried me through time and space. I pondered what I was reading.

Memory is what holds time-space-matter in a recognizable shape, both in the microscopic as well as macroscopic aspects. If it were not that way we would and could change shape every second of the day. Sometimes it is convenient to change realities very quickly, like when you need a parking place, or a healing, a little miracle, or some rain.

Memory however, is also part of repeating the old story. Memory upholds a timeline which in turn is the glue that holds time-space in form. Without it we would not experience matter, stars or planets. We would switch from one shape of gaseous nothingness to the next, and nothing would coalesce long enough for us to have existence. I imagined that without the bond of memory we would shift from one mate to the next in a matter of seconds, never developing families, care, love or selflessness. And we would never develop the real wisdom that comes with time. Love is, in its most universal form, at once the magical elixir of gravity that glues all quantum foam into shape, and the effervescence that creates the duration of matter-space-time.

As I looked around, I realized that being able to see the quantum foam as the material building block of reality allows one to be free to move within the world of Maya, the illusory world. This understanding grants me the ability to be a co-creator of life. This is true freedom. However, one needs to be able to allow for a sudden letting go of old forms if one wants to shift into a new parallel dimension.

Shifting the time-space continuum requires that one lets go of an old reality arrangement and re-attach oneself to a new reality. If you need a miracle, just remember that your memory holds the key. Shift to a coordinate of a time-space matrix of your liking, enter a desirable future memory, and then if you manage to convince your emotional body/mind to occupy the new space with full presence and interest, you will be there. Voila, a miracle.

The size of the miracle is determined by the intensity of your presence that you can muster up. We need not identify with being a mortal human but fully realize that we are a unit of awareness that helps shape the quantum foam of reality. That is when we are free to be anything we want. If we manage to choose a different time-space-matter matrix and manifest it, we have, in effect, been able to go beyond the identity of being in a certain, inevitable future. Instead of following the inevitable timeline that we are accustomed to project, once we let go, we are allowed the quantum jump of time.

The process of being enlightened, being free of identification with a given past, and therefore a given future, is what our soul's growth seems to need to become fully conscious. Most mystery teachings tell us that we are not the image of our Self but the energy behind it all. Until we are able to see ourselves as the dreamer, until we realize we are the light behind the moving pictures, time serves us as a trainer. Not until we have voluntarily accepted the laws of cause and effect, which teach us true ethics, true compassion and true forgiveness, are we free to go beyond it. Once we can care and give love freely, we are free to choose our realties at a higher level of co-creation because we have understood that we are living these principles ourselves.

Suddenly, as I was in the midst of reading and thinking about the quantum world, I was pulled into the "real" world by an announcement from our captain. We were nearing Dulles airport in Washington, D.C. as we heard the bad news. Due to inclement weather we were to circle Dulles Airport for one hour, and the captain hoped to still land in Washington, D.C. Dulles Airport. If the weather didn't change however, we would eventually have to divert and land in Baltimore, Maryland. Baltimore was one and a half hours north of Washington, D.C. by car.

"That would be very inconvenient," I thought. "It could delay us for one day! We really need to land in D.C. in order to catch our next flight to Miami!"

Our seminar started in two days! That was too inconvenient!" I concluded.

The words of the book I was reading hung in my mind: *Shifting into parallel dimensions, shifting to the time space coordinates of our choice.* Should I bother to shift my field now? I wondered. I could fail.

"What if I have an adventure waiting for me in Baltimore?" I asked myself inwardly. I wanted to wait and see what would happen without any of my prayers.

After an hour of circling Dulles Airport and hoping we would be allowed to land in Washington D.C., we were diverted to Baltimore. The rain had not let up and we had no other choice.

The man sitting next to me was a pediatrician, on his way to give a lecture on the negative effects of sugar in children's diet and the coming epidemic of diabetic children. He was following the airplane's route on the screen in front of us. He traced his fingers over the image of the flight on the screen which was showing our plane still headed to Dulles, D.C. He said emphatically: "Now we will be landing in Baltimore. I have been here before!"

And sure enough, the image on the screen switched and was now showing us flying north, heading toward Baltimore. This had happened to him a number of times before, he told me, as Dulles was famous for its bad weather. He recounted to me all the difficulty that we would face and the time it would take to shuttle us by bus south to Dulles Airport. After that ordeal we would still need to reschedule our flight to Miami! The pediatrician was convinced of his future and tried to convince me too.

I however closed my eyes. How do we surf the many parallel time zones again? Ah, yes, I need to sense them, to feel them and to expect them!

I surrendered my personal will to the greater will. I also asked the greater force that sustains all, to do what was right. At the same time I was imaging that my personal wish was to land at the Dulles, Washington, D.C. airport, provided it was for the Good of the Whole.

In my mind I looked at the whole picture of the detour. Landing in Baltimore would add a very large cost to United Airlines, and they would have to rearrange all of the passenger's flight schedules and tickets.

I went higher in my mind into the realms where I could feel the mind of the clouds and felt them commune with me. In my vision I saw them open up, saw the weather clear, and I sensed the harmony between myself and the clouds. Inwardly I saw and felt our flight return to Washington D.C. and I pre-envisioned our successful landing at Dulles Airport. I felt that special feeling I get when all realities align. To top everything off, I imagined how I would shake Don's hand upon landing successfully in Washington's Dulles Airport.

The sound of the wings signaled to us that we were slowing down, getting ready to land. The landing gear unfolded with its usual noise, as we flew through layers of clouds. Soon we touched down, landing on the long runway. In my mind I kept seeing us happily landing in Dulles Airport, in Washington, D.C., getting to our next plane and then flying onward to Miami.

But I shook Don's hand to confirm that we were landing in Dulles Airport in Washington D.C.

However the screen in front of us still showed us landing in Baltimore.

"Welcome to Baltimore," the flight attendant announced.

"WHAT?!" I nearly shouted out loud. I had fully expected to have landed in Dulles Airport, Washington, D.C. I pondered what I had done wrong. It was hard to understand. In my mind I reviewed my imagery steps. Maybe I had shaken Don's hand too soon. We had congratulated each other at the successful completion of our landing in D.C. Had I done that too soon, before I had heard the announcement?

But I had also received no inner signs that would have told me the quantum shift wasn't possible. Usually one can feel or hear a resonant sound, the echo of the parallel worlds that tell us if we will or will not connect with the new universe of choice. Sometimes the clouds simply cannot cooperate because of the mass of energy involved, the bigger picture, or other reasons. But I had not gotten an echo that said "No."

Just then I heard the flight purser's voice over the loudspeaker.

"Excuse me," he said, perplexed, "I was just informed that we actually landed in Washington's Dulles Airport! Please pardon our mistake!"

"Oh my God!" I thought.

His voice was audibly happy and surprised, and huge applause broke out from all the passengers on the airplane. We really had landed in Dulles Airport in Washington D.C! I was ecstatic.

"Well, that was easy!" I thought, "It's great that I have a belief-system that allows for shifting into parallel time-space zones!"

Don and I got up. We were excited to be living in a magical universe. The force we call God, the big YES force, is working as a co-creative partner with anyone who wants to be awake. The Bible speaks of how to create miracles but we usually put that job off to be fulfilled by a special few.

But didn't Jesus say that we were to do such deeds as he, and even greater ones? Even the texts of the Essenes, as written about by Greg Braden tell us how to pray successfully. The translation of the Essenes' text says: "As you pray, imagine that your prayer has been answered, *without a doubt.* See your prayer fulfilled!"

I packed my precious book that had reminded me to be courageous and to be a conscious time-space navigator, into my bag. It is age-old wisdom, but few of us dare make use of the power to dream. I thanked the universe for the miracle I had just experienced. As I looked at Don's sparkling, we knew that we were co-creating reality guided by a higher force.

We were able to get onto our regular flight to Miami and rented a car as scheduled. Soon we would meet with seminar participants and join the dolphins in the wild.

Captive Versus Free Dolphins

The drive to Key West was magical. We headed south on Highway 1, along long bridges that allowed us to cross shallow turquoise water. White beaches, palms, puffy clouds, balmy air and brilliant sunshine in a blue sky tantalized our senses. The road took us from one island to the next, building a chain down to Key West, which is the very last of the islands.

We had rented an entire Bed & Breakfast house, on one of the quaintest streets in the old part of Key West, to accommodate our whole group. From there we were able to walk almost everywhere we needed to go. The boat and harbor was within a five to ten minute walk, as were all the restaurants.

Many little white houses adorned with decorated balconies and tropical flowering trees, makes Key West a very charming town. The Colonial style homes are what give it its charm. The island is a real vacation gemstone surrounded by the sparkling, turquoise ocean.

A long time ago, Key West had been a pirate's island after Native Americans had lived there. Later it became famous as a home to writers such as Ernest Hemingway. Maybe it was not a coincidence that I had written a large portion my last book *Journey to the Center of Creation* there, while I was near the dolphins.

There were twelve people in our seminar together with both Don and I. We only take five or six people on the boat at any given time –five people on morning trips and the other five in the afternoon – to be with the dolphins.

Other dolphin swim coordinators try to find boats that pack twenty passengers on board, to make a good profit. However we really wanted to ensure that all of us had personal contact with dolphins. Most of all, we didn't want to overload the dolphins.

Our room in our B&B was painted in the bright color of a papaya. Our own little balcony was overlooking the pool and the palm trees in the back yard. I draped purple and magenta scarves over the bed posts, which gave the room an even more tropical flair. On my bed stand I set up candles, postcards of sacred images, my little Buddha statue and my books. This was to be our home for the next few weeks.

Everyone had arrived and we were eager to connect with the dolphins. Most everyone had read *Journey to the Center of Creation*, and seemed to know me better than some of my family members.

On the first day we went to the only public beach on Key West, to practice snorkeling. After a short taxi ride we gathered under the shade of pine trees. Our vacation had begun!

After getting acquainted and sharing our names, I asked everyone to tune into the energy at the beach. We started by looking around us, at the ocean and trees, feeling grateful for all the things that we were experiencing in our lives, large or small. After we fell silent for a few minutes, the chirping of the crickets around us suddenly grew into a loud cacophony. Each time we raised our vibrations the crickets increased their song in the trees. It seemed that nature was in full harmony with our inner vibrations. Even the beauty of the turquoise water today and the sailboats going by, with their white billowy sails which stood out against the brilliantly blue sky became more breathtaking as I felt us raise our vibrations.

How true it is that beauty is in the eye of the beholder. How much beauty we are able to perceive depends on our inner states of mind and less on the outer reality. The same beautiful surroundings seen through the eyes with a foul attitude can make everything seem dull. The higher we raise ourselves the more brilliant the outer world appears. I think this happens because we actually activate higher and finer receptor sites in our brains as we expand our auras. We start picking up signals that are beyond our human norm.

Just increasing our gratitude raises our frequency and we will perceive a higher version of our universe. We are the artists whose eyes are guided by our higher minds.

The interplay of the light and shade from the sun shining through the trees onto our faces created a mesmerizing atmosphere. Deep joy and relaxation started flowing over our faces as we started to breathe slower and deeper.

Again we practiced the expansion of attention that I like to share with groups. We started to focus our attention on all the little sounds around us and began to hear things we had not noticed before.

My sphere of attention grew larger and larger, as if the circle of my energy and even I myself expanded. At first I heard all the obvious noises and sounds, and next I heard sounds that were further away, that were harder to hear. As I did that, I felt myself relax more deeply and I felt as if I became the wave of light that surrounded me.

Next we started to pay attention to all the things we could see. Paying more attention to the field around us is such a great exercise to increase our awareness and to silence the chatter in our minds. All we need to do is to simply become mindful and attentive to all that is around us.

Studies have shown that humans love to be in the flow state. One of the feelings associated with this state is a feeling of floating. We like to go beyond our limited form. We love to float in a bigger space than our ordinary minds and human bodies normally allow. Humans have found all kinds of mind altering methods to achieve that. All the methods, starting from alcohol, to other recreational drugs, to high level sports, all produce a state of being "outside" of our normal bubbles. In noticing all the little things around us, even how the air was touching our bodies, we expand our subtle perceptions which make us feel larger. We simply need to enlarge our sphere of awareness to alter our minds.

Slowly, we all got up to walk around the beach in this altered state and to take in all the beautiful sights that surrounded us. I took gentle breaths as I moved very slowly onto the beach, walking in between the trees, and noticing the energy of the space in-between the trees. When I was a teenager I had discovered that I often felt these spaces in-between the trees, while most people who walked with me just talked and barely took notice of the surrounding energy. We just need to feel "into" the spaces "in-between" things, becoming aware of the energy which is overlaid onto the physical reality, and we enter a magical kingdom.

The turquoise water called to me and I walked up to the ocean's edge to let my feet touch the warm water. Small, tiny waves lapped at my legs as I dug my toes into the white sand that was covered with algae and sea shells. The expanse of the ocean gave me space to feel myself stretch far, far into the horizon. I reached into the sky and started to feel the special feeling of largeness, of belonging mysteriously to the whole of life.

As I walked back to our picnic spot I passed one of our participants. He was walking silently as if listening to the sound of a growing tree and it seemed to me that he had his angel wings wide open. His aura stretched far into the space between spaces and his inner silence resonated strongly. For a moment our eyes locked and we met in a larger space – a universal space.

A woman from our group, who had been standing by the ocean and had let her mind fly far away, came toward me and smiled in a deep stillness.

"It is great to have a vacation with higher minded people!" I thought. "'Together we can build a field of high vibration."

We shared our experiences in the group and ate sandwiches. Then Don practiced snorkeling with everyone and taught a special dolphin swim technique. We dove underwater and moved only our bellies, as if we were one whole body of muscle. That is how dolphins swim. We tried holding our breaths and some of us practiced snorkeling underwater for the first time.

Underwater, we gazed at each other's eyes while pretending to be dolphins. The better we were at snorkeling, the better our chances were at having an encounter with the dolphins. We laughed, spouted water, felt successful and loved being in the warm turquoise water.

The next morning came all too slowly for us. Breakfast was served by the very sweet hosts of the house, who lavished us with omelets, toast and fruit, tea or coffee on the veranda in the back yard next to the pool. Finally the time arrived when Don could take the first group to the boat. My half of the group stayed with me at the B&B, to prepare ourselves with meditation and imagery.

We sat outside in the shade of the palm trees, next to the pool, in a circle. Though it was still morning, the temperature in Key West was already quite warm and the humidity made the air feel balmy. July and August are the best months for dolphin interactions, since fish are plentiful and dolphins don't need to hunt as much as in the winter time, when the water is cold and fish are scarce. We took the warm weather in stride. On the boat, the temperature was heavenly any time of day, and a light breeze kept us feeling very comfortable.

Now in our circle, we prepared our day. In our minds we met with dolphins and we pre-imagined how we wanted to swim with them later on. With sweet music in the background, I imagined five dolphins swimming straight at me. I had an experiment in mind that I wanted to conduct this year. It was built on my experiment of the previous year, where I had imagined a configuration of five dolphins swimming straight toward me, sonaring me, before they parted in front of me.

And indeed, it had manifested exactly as I had imagined it. Normally, one would expect the dolphins to swim side by side with us, or that once they headed toward us, they would "see" us and swim out of the way. But I had really wanted them to face me, sonar me and download information to me that day. And they did.

Today I wanted to see if I could recreate the same experience, by imagining the same image; to see if last year had been just a chance experience or not. If they swam at me again, in the same formation as they had last year, I could keep assuming, as has been our experience, that dolphins read our minds, and that they respond to our thoughts.

Frank Robson, who had written the book, "Pictures in a Dolphin's Mind," had been a dolphin trainer and had experienced that dolphins didn't need to be trained with fish and whistles, but rather that he just needed to imagine what he wanted them to do and they would do it. If he wanted them to jump high and touch a red ball, suspended above the pool, he simply imagined the end-result and voila, they performed it.

He rewarded the dolphins with love instead of fish. And they kept performing and reading his mind. He also discovered that other trainers, who thought dolphins were dumb animals that needed to be trained with fish, whistles and punishment, were equally rewarded. Those trainers also got what they were expecting. Only they never got to see the intelligence of the dolphins but simply a reflection of their own expectations.

How often we are like that in our daily lives! We often focus on what our partner or our children are doing wrong. Instead, we could expect the best of them and let ourselves be surprised over and over again. Don certainly was more of an angel if I was willing to see him as such.

Each one of us in our little group had imagined how we wanted to swim with dolphins. Today I was going to try my experiment a second time.

The sun soon climbed higher and it was time for us to go. We gathered our bags, meandered to the Waterfront Market by the harbor, picked up our custom-made sandwiches and greeted Don and the other group members as they climbed off the boat.

Glee in their eyes, they were excited! Dolphins had been with them all morning, and they had had a number of chances to swim with them. Don told me of how Grandy had been there to greet him, with her baby dolphin under her, and, as it had happened many years now, she took Don on a long swim with her, away from the others. She seemed to remember Don from year to year and favored him. She was Don's favorite female dolphin, and had been swimming in the same region year after year since 1993 when we had first come to Key West.

Each person had an exciting story to tell us, and we were very happy to listen. Indeed we were a pod ourselves, and if some of us had a good time, in effect we could be happy for them, as if it had been us. Of course we were wondering if we would be that lucky today too.

It was time for us to set foot on board the catamaran. We climbed over the small railing, took off our shoes, and settled into the cabin below to change into our swimsuits. The boat took off and we helped each other put sun screen lotion on our backs. The sun was brilliant and we were in a great mood. After about twenty minutes the boat slowed. The blue turquoise color of the water that surrounded us was out of this world. Looking out over the vast open water, we helped our captain, look for dolphins. The water was so shallow that we could see the banks of sand and the occasional patches of algae just six feet below us. The captain scanned the horizon with his binoculars and we wondered if the dolphins had had enough play for the day and had gone.

I started to play soft music over the loudspeakers and we gathered together for a meditation. The lapping sounds of the water against the boat and the soft rocking motion were lulling our senses. We joined hands and let our hearts open. Together we formed a circle outwardly as well as in our hearts, and as we rose up higher in our minds we formed a circle in the heavens. It seemed to me that we were pearls, strung together on a necklace made of stars.

How high we can get together! It had been less than ten minutes when we suddenly heard: "Pfaaaaa," the sound of a dolphin's breath, coming up next to the boat. Everyone looked overboard, and we were instantly taken by the presence of the dolphins. Our meditation was over without question and we jumped up to watch them.

It was picture perfect –a mom with a baby. They had come close to the boat and the captain told us that it was Lea and her baby Mark.

Those two seemed to love to be near humans. We leaned over the railing, walking here and there to watch as the dolphins swam around the boat. It seemed as though they were traveling in one direction and he slowly throttled up the speed to keep following them, but also kept a respectful distance.

"Maybe they're taking us to their bigger pod?" I thought.

We enjoyed watching the two zigzag across the water in front of us, next to us, and behind us. We ooed and ahhed, loving our first contact.

Swimming with dolphins was a touchy subject. Though there were no rules that denied contact, the Marine Fishery Department had guidelines, such as you should not be closer than fifty feet or chase after them, which could be construed as harassment. But we were not chasing after these two. They had come to us, and as if they were as curious about us as we were about them, they turned on their sides, eyeing us as we bent over the railing to be close to them.

The sound of breath they took through their nose holes came in short bursts. Dolphins have to breathe consciously, and as such they are not able to fall asleep as we do. They turn off half their brains at a time and close their eyes only in a semi-sleep mode. Sometimes we would watch an entire pod swim in a sleep mode. As dolphins in Key West swim next to each other in close formation, they swim close to the surface. This was different from how the Spinner dolphins rested in Hawaii.

When we found dolphins in their resting mode, the captain made sure the boat was far enough away to let them have their space. After all, we wouldn't want anyone sitting in our bedrooms, pulling on our bed covers while we slept.

But today Lea and Mark were staying near the boat. Were they studying us as well?

I took the opportunity as we were watching Lea and Mark to explain underwater etiquette. No matter how close dolphins swam with us, even within inches, we never touched them. For one thing, that way we never scared them, or accidentally scratched their very sensitive skin. But for sure we also didn't want to disturb the trust we had built over a long time.

"Just imagine," I said to everyone, "if you occasionally went to a market in a foreign country and mingled there. It would be fine for you to watch closely as everyone shopped, but think of how offensive it would be if you started touching a stranger here or there on their body, maybe even in areas that would be forbidden? You wouldn't know the rules of social conduct, and no one likes to be grabbed by a stranger!"

That usually got the message across. We typically think of closeness in terms of touching. But we were here to practice a closeness that would go beyond the ordinary five senses. We were going to practice a closeness that was larger and more fulfilling, so we could go home and start living in our relationships within a much larger context of unity and union.

Our body's touch is very immediate but it reaches only a small portion of ourselves. We can feel closeness, union and communion much more intensely in our subtler bodies. That is what we wanted to practice with dolphins and it seems to me that this is what most people really want: to feel really connected.

It was very exciting to watch dolphins in all aspects of their normal lives. Just to be close to them was rewarding. There was something magical when I gazed upon them. Lea was lying on her side at times, so she could see us hanging over the railing. Dolphins usually swim in small groups, and their daily activity cycles and moods can shift almost every half hour.

At times they want to rest. Or one can observe how suddenly one dolphin after another dashes off into the distance following the hidden call of another dolphin who had spotted fish far away. As if on cue, they would swim off to fetch fish.

In moments of leisure they are often very sensual together. We have watched groups of dolphins be sexual together within a few yards of our boat, at times even underwater within arm's reach.

Dolphins, contrary to some hopes, are not monogamous, but rather group bonded. It makes sense, since they depend on each other for survival as a group. So they make love as a group too. They don't even seem to mind mingling with humans in their midst at times as they are sexual with each other or frisky. However, when we are in the water and they want to be alone, they swim past us to check us out, and off they go.

The contact we can make with them is clearly on their own terms. This is what I like so much. Because dolphins are superb swimmers, superior to us by far, with one kick of the tail they can go as fast as boats. We can't force them to make contact with us when we are only swimming with fins and snorkels. The contact we have with them is based on freedom, on respect, and on real interest.

Many of the captive dolphin camps feed fish to the dolphins in order to make them perform required tricks. To swim past a human they get a fish, to jump through a hoop that a child may hold, they get a fish. If they sonar us, touch us or let us touch them, they get a fish. If they don't perform then they go hungry. Not every captive organization treats dolphins that way, but I have seen it numerous times.

That kind of dolphin contact is like prostitution in my mind. Humans in that case are like pimps using prostitutes to make money. There is no love involved, no true respect, and anyone who pays high dollars to have an experience in such an environment supports dolphin imprisonment.

Paying money to such an institution, one is supporting usury and slavery. Though I have seen pictures of people who are smiling from ear to ear, looking very happy at the once-in-a lifetime chance to touch a dolphin, sadly it's an embrace they bought with tainted money, using captive dolphins. We need to know that behind that smile of the captive dolphin lies a suffering being that is no longer free: not free to love, to learn, to swim, or to live in freedom on their own terms.

Big companies who fund captive dolphins have been trying to pass regulations to forbid swimming with wild dolphins. Here in Key West we were still lucky enough to have the option to swim near wild dolphins. Today we were hoping that Lea, the mom, and her baby dolphin Mark were taking us to a few more of her pod members, so that we might all have a chance to get into the water. And I was excited to see if my experiment would work!

Telepathic Experiments with Dolphins

Still in my reverie about finding a larger pod, I heard the captain suddenly call out for us to pay attention. He pointed a little to the right, a hundred yards away from the front of the boat. He had found the dolphins again!

"A group of three or four dolphins at two o'clock," he said as he was referring to the approximate location of the fins in the water. Since dolphins live in shallow waters around Key West, we can usually see them easily. They can hold their breath up to eight minutes but they often come to the surface more frequently, depending on their activity. In deeper water, such as in Hawaii, dolphins can stay underwater longer and they can be harder to find.

We were riveted. Indeed, soon we all saw the fins break the clear water and we got excited. Then someone shouted "A few more at eleven o'clock." We had been standing on the deck scanning the large body of shimmering turquoise water.

Sensuous, rhythmic sounds full of longing filled the air. The captain had chosen a CD from the B-Tribe, called "Sensuous." Curiously, it seemed to me that whenever he put on that particular CD, we would soon find dolphins. Maybe it was due to the fact that the music put all of us into a sensuous mood, moving us gently into a quiet inward dance, getting us in touch with our deeper longings. It made me feel like I was very open, and I loved being lulled by the soft rocking water, the grand view of the majestic water surrounding us and experiencing a dream come true.

We rushed to the railing and leaned over the edge to be as close to the water as possible. Soon more dolphins came right under the front of the boat, riding along and staring up at us occasionally. What do they think when they see us? We were squeaking like children for joy.

The dolphins started to lag behind the boat near the motor, right where the dive platform was. I couldn't help but feel that they were saying, "Come into the water!"

It was not just my impression. The captain too felt like it was a good time to get ready, and he maneuvered the boat ahead of the dolphins, which made it look like he was trying to lose them. Meanwhile he asked us to get our snorkel gear ready. What we didn't know was that we had to get farther away from the dolphins to comply with the suggested respect zone for marine mammals. But no one can keep dolphins from swimming after humans.

One by one we got into the water and formed a circle behind the boat. Breathing through our snorkels, we floated on the surface of the water like corks on a string. After a few minutes of meditating, I dove underwater to listen to the sound of the dolphin's sonar, which would indicate that they were coming closer.

What a different world it was underwater in the silence. I had learned to hold my breath quite well with years of practice and I loved to stay under the vast blue blanket of the ocean. From the depth of my heart I sent a ray of love to the dolphins and slipped into a feeling of being light. Instantly I dropped my sense of body and simply felt this ray of love coming from the center of my crystalline-like self.

Pure silence surrounded me, a stillness that is so different from our terrestrial norm. Water moves our entire body in rhythmic waves and alters our consciousness instantly. In this stillness time stood still and my thoughts subsided. The white sand beneath me soothed my feeling of aloneness in the vast watery space. Although the water was less than two meters deep, it was a silent world and as alien as the moon.

As I came up for air I got word that fins had been sighted swimming toward us. Still in this altered state I decided to focus on the image I wanted to re-experience today –five dolphins swimming toward me, sonaring and treating me like they had exactly one year ago.

"They are coming!" exclaimed one of the participants next to me. Several of us took deep breaths and dove down where we became more interesting to the dolphins. I heard the sonar before the dolphins came into view. Suddenly five dolphins appeared right in front of me. The moment stood still and all I could do was stare at them. It was unbelievable. They headed straight toward me and I felt their sonar scan my entire body. Although I am sure it was only a few seconds, it seemed to last for a very long time. The sonar was multiplied by five. This was exactly what I had imagined earlier that morning, just like I did one year ago!

My heart flew wide open. As fast as I could, I turned to swim in the same direction as them. Excitement filled my whole body. They were so very close, swimming right under me as my thoughts stood still. As I watched the waves of sunlight on their backs, there was only that moment – of the dolphins swimming brilliantly underneath me. I spread my arms and sent blessing energy toward them. An eternal stillness embraced us as a whole unit: humans and dolphins. I swam as long as I could with the group. I no longer felt any fear of being alone in the vast water; I was filled only with the desire to stay with these dolphins forever. As I dove down one more time, I was able to look into the eye of one dolphin and felt his knowing eyes touch my soul.

I had totally lost track of where I was, where everyone else was, and how far I had swum away from the boat. It didn't matter to me anymore. Dolphins move us into a state of total presence, joy and love. Gone are thoughts of yesterday or the future.

Seeing how far I had strayed, I quickly swam over to the group to find out what they had experienced. Each person had a different story to tell.

One of our participants had not been able to swim that well so she just stayed close to the boat. She simply radiated love from her heart and waited. A single dolphin had come over to swim in circles underneath her. She had not been underprivileged despite the fact that she couldn't swim well. She was jubilant.

This was my second time I had experimented with sending the same image. Five dolphins had come again in the same formation and sonared me again. This proved to me how accurately dolphins can read our minds. Life, just like dolphin contact, seems to work best when we, in advance, hold the image in our minds of how we want our experience to be. To manifest our wishes, we always need to *feel* in advance how *we would feel if* we experienced what we really want to experience. Dolphins seem to respond instantly to this kind of telepathy.

Swimming with dolphins, I found that I had better results meeting them when I embodied a higher energy within myself. When I left my meetings up to chance, nothing much happened. And yes, there were days when I felt too tired to focus or I was too exhausted to want more as well.

This inner state of awareness is not permanent and it requires our daily awakening. All states of consciousness are in flux. Love, soul and life are in flux, and whether we walk in Heaven on Earth or not depends on the state of our vibration at any given time.

As a matter of fact we seem to be able to walk in and out of heavenly worlds within seconds. As soon as we raise our vibrations and hold our energy-fields in heaven, we find ourselves in that space again. This happens more easily, if we have learned to rise intentionally to a higher assembly point above the crown chakra and have solidly established a higher seat of soul.

We can always tell what frequency world we are in by observing the amount of light we see around us. Do the trees shimmer with diamond-like rainbows? Does the sunlight shine forth as if from another

210

dimension? Most likely it does when we walk in heavenly states. We think of the sun existing only in one dimension, called the physical universe. But we have octaves of universes to choose from.

Heaven is not a location, it is a state. We can move into higher planes and still think it is one and the same Earth. But it isn't. The best model I can currently provide is that we have parallel worlds that interlace. The moment we are high, everything works together as if orchestrated by a higher hand. Though just a model, we can work with it. When we vibrate higher ourselves, higher laws apply. When we are in a higher space we are able to work from there, affecting the physical world more effectively. The body appears to be in one place but we as soul can be in any dimension we focus on. That alone makes a huge difference in how well we are able to manifest.

Today the water was super-luminal and I was in another world. I had met the dolphins on another plane but everything still looked like the same planet Earth. I felt utter awe at their impeccable timing to coincide with my vision.

How are they able to do this? Are they truly living at a higher world space, higher than we, as humans, ordinarily live? Do they have abilities that we can't even measure because our scientists, who are believed to know the truth, have not figured out how to measure which dimension we occupy at any given time?

Mathematically it has been established that parallel worlds exist. But we can't imagine that we shimmer in and out of them seamlessly. Our linear mind has a hard time understanding simultaneousness. I may look at a person and if we both know the feeling of occupying higher grounds together at the same time, then we both know it when we look at each other. We can both tell we are really meeting together "up there." Yet we still have no scientifically accepted equipment that can tell when we are ignited at higher dimensions.

But luckily, we need no equipment to feel that we are walking in Heaven.

Slowly, we all swam back to the boat and climbed up the ladder. One by one we took off our masks, snorkels and fins and hugged each other, wet as we were.

Beyond the Seven Chakras

Back on board we danced and jumped for joy. It was easy to see how being with dolphins had opened our hearts. We began to feel like one group mind and we were happy for each other's experiences. This encounter had been our highlight today and after drying off, we gathered in a circle on the front of the catamaran to tell each other of our exiting encounters with the wild dolphins. We were like a pod of humans, a circle of joy and happiness.

Soon we calmed down and just lay in the sun, basking in the silence surrounding us. I loved the brilliant turquoise water and the great surrounding expanse. Transfixed by the supernatural light we were all very high in our spirits.

Many times I have observed how we become very open and loving with each other in a group after we have been sonared by dolphins. I realized how much we need to practice being this loving without the dolphins serving us as a crutch. Even just imagining dolphins can create this inner state of harmony and heal us, as many therapists have found. In our seminars we have practiced some of those methods and found that they really do open the power of our higher minds. Imagery tools can allow us to be master creators, move into higher frequencies and allow us to enter states of enlightenment.

It is good to learn great tools and master them. One thing was clear to me in this life: I did not want to encourage people to depend on me as a teacher. That has happened in the past. In other times we might have needed a very tight student-teacher relationship to grow, but not now. For me this is an era to encourage independence, autonomy so we can learn to tap the wisdom within. Tools can offer us methods to reach the light within.

I also acknowledge that some people do need the steady strength of one teacher. Some even need a religion with strong rules and a very serious image of a God. Not all of us are at the same level of evolution, willing to be self-responsible.

For myself however, I no longer wanted to be part of that body of teachers. I love to see everyone stand on their own feet, to be able to master the art of living in an enlightened way, as often as possible.

My mother had been a great example to me. She taught me to listen to my own inner voice and not to depend on an outside authority to figure out what was true and what wasn't. Now I wanted to be that kind of teacher too.

We truly just need to get in touch with the inner light, which is our ultimate teacher. Once we can tap this current we are taken on the high road to the center of creation.

It seems that we live in a dreaming, self-tutoring universe, which responds to our mental blueprint of our future visions and expectations, and we truly are interactive co-creators with the larger universe. It also seems that we have greater freewill as soon as we understand the basics and power of our imagery mind.

The secret key to manifestation is learning to shift inwardly into that state of fulfillment. However, at times it is easier to keep imagining our emotional pains, inventing negative reactions, fantasizing about revenge or making excuses for our failures.

Taking the leap to shift from a negative feeling into a feeling of the future fulfilled takes an extra portion of energy. It is a feeling of shifting, of jumping from one space into another. Inside of me I first have to feel the energy of the end result before the universe replies in kind. Usually, it feels as if I have to move into a brighter space, a bigger more vibrant universe.

It does seem that the theory of parallel universes applies. Once we know that we really do influence the kind of world we live in, we are more interested to extend that extra energy and pre-experience the future positively. As we feel the wish fully realized, we become the time traveler within the time-space matrix.

One reason why some people can manifest better than others has to do with the degree of focus they can hold, as well as the position of their **"Seat of their Soul,"** a term that Gary Zukav made popular. The seat of the soul is the assembly point of our consciousness. The closer we place our seat to God as soul, the more brilliant we become and the more potency we carry.

Many people are here on this planet, which I prefer to call a plane, in a diffused state. The attention gets pulled here and there without much overview, without much "presence." In this state one can be likened to an ordinary light bulb. Over incarnations we manage to pull our attention together, to focus, to be present and we become like a laser light.

Upon this beam of laser light we ride back home to God. We usually speak of it in terms of time-space movement. Such is the limit of our 3D minds. Indeed, it appears to be more accurate to say: When we go beyond the speed of light, we eventually start to vibrate so finely that ultimately we vibrate in All-space and All-time simultaneously. We don't travel to a distant God.

The amount of presence determines how alive we feel and how potently our life energy is able to penetrate the physical matrix. Our intensity can be seen in our eyes, can be felt in how alive we feel and in how alive the world seems to us. It can shift from day to day, from year to year.

In becoming more alive and focused, we start to occupy an increasingly vaster space. Imagine above your head innumerable chakras stacked upon each other. Most of us know of the seven general chakras in our bodies and are familiar with the seven major centers of energy that link the physical body to the astral body and beyond.

214

Each center can spin more or less vibrantly, depending on how active we are in any given area. When our third eye spins strongly, we find visions pouring into us.

We each have stronger and weaker chakras. As we mature in our soul's evolution, we learn to rise higher and activate chakras at will, as well as develop perceptions in those chakras above our head, which represent much subtler dimensions. We practice holding higher points of assembly in these higher dimensions with increased awareness.

Think of it as dimensions stacked upon each other. Our linear mind has an easier time to think of it as layers upon layers, ascending upward into space and onward into the cosmos. That is how a visual type of person will perceive it.

Another way is to think of it as layers within each other, becoming finer and finer or going deeper and deeper as kinesthetic types prefer.

Since we walk upright, the image of going upward works best for our human, spatial mind. In the finest and fastest vibration we move beyond the speed of light and are the beginning and the end, the alpha and the omega, of the same light. Then we find ourselves occupying the entirety of Is-ness where we are the vastness all at once. We start to enter a space beyond being an identity. Such states are called states of enlightenment, Satori, where we are no longer the small self but merge with the whole.

However, in my experience so far, I also still have a bodily vehicle and my ego state still carries on. The more I practice merging with oneness, the vaster my perspective becomes and the more I can embrace others. I also have the freedom to know that "I" am not the body, the emotions, the self, but free to be one and all. That is what we truly are. We are the source and at the same time we are the form too. We are the living paradox, the living form of God's dance.

When we are both the self and the all, we are the happiest. We see the dance of the universe coming alive in our return of our attention upon the oneness, upon the source. Dancing the individual dance of ascension and enlightenment to become the One we always were, our individual experience is nevertheless real to us and has real consequences. It matters in our personal lives if we are high or low in our vibrations, in our understanding and beingness of our localized attention.

As individuals we can gather our spirit increasingly at higher velocities. Imagine yourself gathered up into one point maybe 30 centimeters or one foot above your head. Move your entire attention to that star point, to the space that is already in the cosmic space. Move to a world that no longer has form, but is just a collection of your consciousness. You need only to pop into such a gathering point. Move up, become that space of your attention being just a single point.

Pop. Out you are.

As we do that, we learn to gather our mana, as Hawaiians call the energy of life. We need to gather our presence, our full attention into these higher collection points. Over longer periods of time we can learn to become fully present at increasingly higher gathering points. As we do, we become an umbrella of energy over the spheres below us. A person who has gathered themselves up high and can hold the view of life as a vast display of light beneath themselves, can work from this higher vantage point beyond the ordinary time-space configurations.

Time and space are increasingly finer as we rise within the dimensional fabric into finer spaces. Normal time and space as we think of it has particular laws. When I talked to the clouds in Hawaii, they told me I had to have made my request to them earlier in time. I rose higher, into another time-space matrix and was able to talk to the clouds in the past, if you will; giving enough time for them to reassemble to the wish I needed urgently fulfilled.

It was my understanding and my image of how time and space are not static as we think of it in our ordinary minds, that allowed me to make such a request. Having a concept of reality allows us to navigate and get results. The limits of the concept determine how much we will experience.

When we thought our Earth to be flat, we never ventured around the planet. Each culture and each religion, each scientific teaching comes up with a different roadmap of the universe. Depending on how far each system has explored the universe, it can provide us with a larger or a smaller map. It can tell us part of the story, give us the map of just one region, or show the whole planet. Some systems may even show us the map of the entire cosmos.

"Was my communication with the clouds real, or did I just have a vivid imagination?" I wondered.

I can only say that the results speak for themselves. Did things happen in alignment with my inner visions back in Hawaii? The answer was yes!

It is most important to keep alive the feedback loop which tells us if we are actually in touch with reality or if we are mind-tripping. It can be easy to have all sorts of visions, but they may be just pipedreams. We need to repeatedly check how to make real changes, how to really interact with the larger universe.

Are we really making changes? Are miracles happening? Is our inner visioning reflected in the outer world?

Life is a co-creation of the life-force and the dreaming minds. Did aborigines talk with animals at a distance? Did a waterhole give out a specific call? Do we really have the ability to interact, as shamans do, with life?

YES. And we don't have to travel far. We just need to rise in our minds to a place of greater and greater light. Gathering our attention in an assembly point above the head gives us that higher vantage point. Once we know one of these stations well, we can keep going up to the next assembly point until we enter the center of the universe.

Some people like to take side trips. They go sideways, into the expansive worlds of light. They explore the many options of light patterns, and it is said they can get so mesmerized that they forget to keep going up toward the center. Well, I believe that we all keep going to the center when we are ready. What does it matter if we spend one more lifetime in an astral heaven? Time seems to matter only to us.

But as we are able to gather our attention in high cosmic gathering points, we have more potency. Not only do we hope for a dream come true. Up high, when we reconfigure a dream into the matrix, we have much more power, more focus and more potency. And those dreams come true. And with it comes responsibility.

As I spanned the horizon and listened to music on our way back to our dock, I thought of Merlin. Visions of him filled my soul. I was yearning for him in my heart and soul. "If I could just share this world and this moment with him. But he is in Australia," I thought.

I had tried to let go of him over and over in the last few months. I had kept my daily life so full that I didn't have time to think of him. Merlin was attempting to get together with an old lover of his anyhow and he didn't need my attention. I had only spoken with him a few times as he was getting acquainted with Byron Bay, a little north of Sydney, Australia. All I could do was to try to let go, again and again. This seemed to be my mantra for Merlin.

Reaching Beyond the Zero Point

I could hardly wait to get home and tell Don about my experiment. As soon as we docked in the marina and were greeted by solid ground under our feet, we skipped home to shower and get ready for dinner.

Brilliant blue eyes greeted me as I opened the door. Don had already showered and was dressed for dinner as I walked into our room. He was resting from the afternoon's teaching.

I was so very grateful to live with this masterful being. It was great for us to have some time for each other, since we had been apart nearly all day to be with the seminar participants.

I glided onto the large bed to sit with Don. My purple and pink scarves decorated the papaya room and soft music was playing. As I made myself comfortable in a semi-lotus position in front of Don, I gently placed my hands into his and we looked deeply at each other. As our gaze met, we instantly moved into a deep state of consciousness. His inner spaces were visible to me and pulled me into his current of light.

Don had been my teacher in Baltimore when I was 21, when I sought to learn the methods of the Light and Sound from him, methods based on teachings from India. Don showed me how to jump beyond the void in my awareness, beyond the state of Nothingness into pure soul states of awareness.

The void is a state often sought after by various schools of thought, yet Don had taught me how to become aware of existences beyond it. He had followed the teachings of the Light and Sound, which taught how to move beyond the etheric, the astral, and the mental realms. I learned how to locate my entire awareness in a singular point, the zero point, and go beyond the void. These methods teach one how to move beyond the dual awareness, jumping through the black hole, beyond the nothingness into a brilliant state of singularity. There, we are pure consciousness.

As we shift the core of our attention through the finer dimensions, upward from the physical dimension, we move from being a particle with a distinct form and become a wave function. This wave becomes increasingly finer and finer until it becomes so fast in its frequency that it is simultaneously everywhere. This transition happens to light for example at the junction from the physical to the energy world, where light is both a wave and a particle.

Scientists are puzzled how light can behave in experiments as both a particle and a wave. Seeing life from an energy point of view it is easier to understand this paradox: Life is rather a continuum of vibration.

The Big Bang began with the fastest vibration in its core. From then onward this energy cooled down, slowed down and became increasingly more solid. This solidification can be imagined as a column of vibration, as a column of light, running from pure white to absolute black, with all the gradations in-between. Along this scale of vibration, any position chosen will have either more light or less light relative to itself. This in turn will give a sense of a relative higher truth or lower truth, higher vibration and lower vibration. What appears higher to me at one position may appear to be lower to someone at a higher position than mine. What is seen as good to one may appear as evil to another.

We perceive our movement through dimensions as changing our form, moving from one form to the next higher form, but really all we do is move through the dimensions of the same Isness. As we move beyond being a particle, a body in time-space, we become a wave and we supersede the usual linearity and confines of time-space. In the astral realm we are angelic. We have a Higher Self. It has a shape, color, attributes, abilities and tendencies. We can travel forward and backward in time to some degree. However, the different realms are not clearly defined as they are rather like the column of vibrations.

The astral vibration turns into the frequency of the mental realm. At the mental realm we might experience ourselves to be more like a crystalline structure, a geometric form. In this space we "become the object" instead of just looking at the object from the outside. At this mental dimension, at this frequency, we become a field of light lines and intricate designs of geometry.

We are then the landscape made of sheaths of light of cognitive undulations. Words make no sense when we go into the beingness of knowing. When we become fields, we are no longer just a body-mind, isolated from the rest of the universe by our five senses. Instead we become one with the known.

Beyond the mental realm is yet another world. It is impalpable but one can train the inner mind to perceive subtle nuances and develop mental footholds. The higher we rise, the less we can say that we have a distinct form as we know it. We can enter into the space of superstrings or become the quantum field.

Eventually one arrives at a space that lies outside of these undulations. It requires that we move through the center of a tunnel that narrows increasingly into a singularity, much like the center tube of the toroid or a black hole. This is the space of the void. Since the black hole is a never-ending suction into zero, it appears as the everlasting stillness. This can be the nirvana, the void, the no-thingness. If one lands there, one can be convinced that there is nothing more. Yet when we focus completely on another reality, beyond that singular state of consciousness, we suddenly pop beyond this zero point domain. It is hard to even say that one is a singular point but that is what it feels like if one moves into just a singular point of awareness. In the many other subtle levels of dual reality we still take on form of some kind, yet here we are simply awareness.

After practice one can go there directly. I call it the pure soul realms. That is what I had learned from Don. It is easier to get there when one knows someone who can enter this state. As they hold this space like a lighthouse, we can find the way more easily within the many possible landing spots in creation.

This is the first state that Don and I entered today. It was our starting point as we rose up in ourselves. It had taken me years of practice to reliably find that state. It was located above my head, if I had to give it a place. A feeling of grand cosmic space surrounded me, although I didn't move there. I simply shifted there; showed up there.

Don had held that space for me when I first met him and he taught me how to find that space. Our love was my rocket ship to heaven. I loved to find that space and when I was particularly high, I would see little blue or white stars blink in mid-air, even with my eyes open. Blue stars usually tell me that I am descending in my vibration or that serious trouble is ahead. If I see white sparkling stars appearing suddenly in mid-air, I know I am in the company of masters. The first night I sat across from Don in the teaching center in Baltimore I was star struck, as I saw stars blinking up above his head.

Today as we sat across from each other I couldn't believe my luck. He beamed love to me as if we had just traveled a million light-years to see each other.

As I moved myself to that brilliant singular space, I simultaneously tuned into Don. I was, in a way, in a dual and non-dual state of awareness at the same time. There is an art to be able to hold the focus and concentration in this singular state of mind, yet simultaneously keep the mind gently going enough to take notice of the other person also entering this same state of singularity at the same time. All the while we must keep ourselves from drifting into the usual mind chatter.

Words to describe this make absolutely no sense to our normal minds. How can one be aware of anything if one is in singularity? That is a paradox. Words can't even begin to hint at what this feels like. But everyone has this innate ability within themselves.

We all know that this state exists. We are soul, which exists beyond the mind. We just need to know what signs to look for as we move into the subtler dimensions. We only need to be reminded that this state exists and we can experience it. If we have the sincere desire to find our way to God we will be pulled by the very matrix of creation as soon as we ask for it. It works that way. Once we want to go somewhere, we practically have set foot on the road. The road shows up. The signs appear.

Today it was easy for me to focus. I found Don's soul signature, his star, in an instant since he had warmed up the field by meditating. As we met in this singular state of consciousness I felt a light flood through us. We were inside each other and love filled all spaces. This union of soul is the best intimacy method I know.

Soon we rose to a yet higher space, into a higher point of assembly. It was as if we were dancing around each other in an upward moving spiral, much like a DNA spiral helix. I imagined our stars converging in an ever closer space of purity, where time and space converged over and over into yet another zero point.

222

Each of us rose to the next junction point where the spiral merged again. We did this as we held our eyes open. As soon as we landed in the next higher state of union, we knew it. It was easy to know when we reached the next level. We could tell by our feelings. It was as if an echo in space was instantaneously transmitted to both of us.

Eventually we overlapped into total oneness as we simultaneously entered into this union. It catapulted us into the purest state of consciousness.

As I stared at Don's eyes, with the distinct feeling that we were One, the love and gratitude I felt was overwhelming. It was as if we had just popped into another existence. Time stood still here and there was no more movement. My mind ceased to work. We were touching the core of the universe and we both knew it. We could track each other and tell if either of us was there or not.

Just for this split moment the Allness was all-pervading, and then my mind, having awareness of all this, came into view to witness the event. Something had to report on this and if not my mind, what else?

Tears streamed down my face as Don and I entered over and over again into this state of union. By now, I no longer expected such moments to last more than a second but I knew that I could reignite this state over and over again.

Enlightenment is gained over and over again. Because we have bodies we have a mind, and we live in dual awareness. Yet without a body of perception there is no awareness at all. I guess duality is a great trade off for God to perceive its creation.

All it took was refocusing and within a split second Don and I could gather ourselves again in that Oneness. But as soon as awareness set in again we were two. As we rotated between those states, oneness and duality, and kept our focus upward, it was as if we repeatedly cycled between self-awareness and Oneness.

This is the Great Dance. The Oneness seems to look back at itself through our eyes, being at once the observer and the observed. This is the in-breath and out-breath of God, the eternal dance. It is our gift to the Oneness to return our attention to It, to let It see Itself through our eyes. We are the self-awareness and in our surrender of our self into that which birthed us, we are given the greatest gift of all: A moment in eternity, being All that is.

Peace came over Don and me. Our love was so powerful in this stillness, a kind of love that supersedes all human notions. The emotions I felt were immense. If I filtered all the perceptions through my heart, I was overwhelmed with love. If I stayed more in the filter of my mind, this experience took on a magnitude of abstract light and movements on our journey upward.

This was the secret to our love. We chose to use our love as our high road to God. By merging our souls, making love at the soul's core level we were growing in our enlightenment. Don and I felt like we were truly inside each other, as there was nothing but the brilliant state of light.

Don's eyes were filled to the brim with love, and tears were forming too. We squeezed hands and were both speechless at the immense spiritual experience we were able to share, and we were at awe at the depth of love we felt for each other. What a rare gift this was on this planet! Don and I hugged each other. We were so in love. This is the way to have a multidimensional soul relationship.

We built a triangle with God. We found our mutual union in the third point, which left us not fixated on each other as humans, but rather in the hands of higher guidance, of higher dimensions, of our soul and Spirit. Instead of focusing on our partner alone, something which often leads us to see human shortcomings and to feel trapped in the human cage, we focus on a higher form of union in heaven. This forms a triangle with God. It requires the surrender of our love to a higher force but it infuses us with a love that is sublime. Sitting in this cocoon of light with Don was immensely fulfilling. We had practiced it for so many years that by now we could do it in quick moments across the dinner table without anyone else really noticing.

I became aware that I still had to shower and dress before leaving so I had to pull myself away and get up. Full of bliss and joy in my heart, I danced into the bathroom. Everything was so small down here in the 3D world by comparison. The dark wood on the bathroom walls had withered through the ages and bugs had left intricate designs on them.

The warm water felt filled with love. Just like the shower running over me now, I imagined that I was standing in the center of the cosmic fountain I had just shared with Don. I let the descending cosmic energy filter down into my human sphere, and let this energy gather at my feet. Then I pulled my attention upward again through my central column, up through my torso, allowing the energy to rise back up through my spine and out of my crown chakra, beyond it, until I reached into the heavens. From there I let the light descend again, falling down upon me like the warm water that was flowing over me in the shower.

It was still warm in the evenings so all of us liked to dress in the loftiest of clothing. I loved to let my creative self dance in a myriad of colors. I could have lived as a fashion designer in another alternate life. But since I had chosen to teach instead, I found fulfillment in dressing myself creatively. After all, flowers and beauty adorn all of nature, so we humans can surely be beautiful too.

Tonight we were going to eat at a restaurant called "Blue Heaven." What a great name! It was a creative-looking, Caribbean styled restaurant where we would sit under large trees with roosters walking in-between the tables on dirt floors. This was Key West at its best.

The carrot-curry papaya chutney soup was a hit with all of us. Our waiter was a black man, who was very funny, with sensual food descriptions. When he described the "Banana Heaven" desert all the women want to be served by him only. We all had fun and were in a magical mood.

Healing a Dolphin with Energy

The next day came quickly, awakening me with sunlight caressing my body. Rose and orange-colored light came flooding in through the window, painting the room in a soft, celestial mood. The room was a very daring, papaya color and it tantalized my senses. Silently I got out of bed to sit in the morning sun on the balcony and meditate.

One of my favorite moments of the year was to sit on the balcony in the morning sun, basking in the tropical air and letting the world of wonder touch all of my cells. Silently, I sat in a white reed chair and gazed at the gently swaying palm leaves that overlooked the blue pool below. The magical light of the sun touched my skin and colored the white balcony in orange hues.

Breathing slowly, I let the presence of the air around me touch my core and I dove deeper into myself. Again, I concentrated on just feeling the presence of life, not paying attention to the form but letting my mind and attention feel the waves between all the forms. As I did this, the light started to touch my heart.

It is an art to be awake to this aliveness of life. Every moment we are surrounded by the amazing mystery of the universe. The energy that lies beneath the majestic formation of gigantic galaxies is also right here – all around us. As I let my mind embrace this presence, I shifted from using my mind as a logical observer to an instrument of noticing the greater feeling that was beyond the mind that names objects. For now, I let my mind be in touch with the silence between the palm trees and between all the things that surrounded me. This feeling lifted my soul.

This was my simple way to become aware. I let my feelings receive the fullness of the mystery that surrounded me, As if I were opening the barriers in my body, opening my blood cells. And in my oxygen intake I was feeling a flooding of aliveness touch my core.

God is alive in all Isness and as if I had just realized it for the first time, I breathed deeper, letting that understanding enter me. It is an age-old method of becoming a Tantrica.

In the truest sense the Tantricas of old made love with life. They felt the essence of God in all that surrounded them, allowing them to feel the ecstasy at any moment. Especially when one has mastered centering that receptive awareness of being in touch with the essence of life in every moment, one is in the state of ecstasy independent of circumstances, independent of how much love one is getting from a Lover or Beloved.

After I felt this aliveness I was ready to pre-envision my day. Sitting on the balcony with my eyes closed, I made my request for a perfect day via imagery. I imagined being taken into the middle of a pod of dolphins as they made love and caressed each other and letting myself be closer than ever. I had swum within inches of one or two dolphins before, but I had been too scared to be surrounded by a group of them in the midst of their frenzied foreplay. The respect I showed by not swimming closer was really a fear that I felt about being too close to dolphins. Reading my energy well, the dolphins paid me the same respect by meeting me on my terms.

As soon as we had eaten breakfast my group headed out to our boat. The captain greeted us with a hug and we were ready for a great day. I stood by the railing on the boat and let the dolphins know that I was ready for very close contact with them. We watched the dolphins as they swam all around the boat. In my mind and heart I recreated the energy I had felt in my morning meditation.

I felt the pod of dolphins touch my heart. That is what I wanted: a sense of aliveness which made me feel as if I was in Heaven on Earth. As I breathed deeply I expanded my sense of self and started to identify more with the energy field around me instead of my body and my ego. I was feeling the ocean, the air and the dolphins as part of the Us-ness, the Is-ness, the aliveness.

In that state I reached out to their resonant echo in the time-space-energy matrix and felt it interlock with mine. Today was a good day to connect deeply.

Soon our captain let us know that it was a good moment to get into the water. Gently we slid into the blue ocean from the back of the boat. All seven of us gathered within a few feet of the boat, held hands and made a human star shape in the water. We didn't get to spend much time in this group mind since some dolphins made it a point to swim toward us and circle around us pretty quickly. As soon as we saw them we let go of each other's hands and dove under water. Holding my breath, I swam alongside of several of them.

I felt as if I was being pulled along effortlessly. Either the current of the water was in my favor today or the dolphins were willing to take me into their pod, just as I had imagined. I didn't have to kick my fins hard at all. Pushing gently with my legs, I stayed right in their midst, holding my arms behind my back so as to not appear threatening. Their mood soon shifted to an erotic one and suddenly I found myself in the middle of a pool of throbbing dolphins. They were so very CLOSE; I had to suppress my natural anxiety at the size of their large bodies. Underwater, the almost nine foot long dolphins appeared even bigger. As they were caressing one another and even rolling over top of each other, I hoped that they wouldn't want to touch me.

One dolphin was love-biting another. Another, which was right below me, was running his tail along the body of the other dolphin. Another dolphin turned his face toward me and sonared my body. Next he turned to caress another dolphin right next to him with his fin as if wanting to hold hands.

They actually looked like they were holding hands. Then they became a bit friskier, diving over the top of each other and I became even more concerned about them rolling on top of me.

I really had to work with my trust. I swam slowly next to them as they didn't seem to be in any hurry and we stayed together for what seemed like an eternity. They really took me into their pod and let me look in on their love-life at a very intimate moment. It was exactly what I had wished for in my imaging session earlier that morning.

Years of swimming with dolphins has taught me that they either choose to swim with us or they don't. They don't pretend to be interested and don't come very close to us unless they want to. There is no way we could ever swim fast enough to keep up with them when they don't us want to, even when it looks like they hardly move.

If they feel like having humans around, they make it a point to swim very slowly so that it feels as if one is being pulled into their midst like a magnet. They also have incredible command over their bodies. They seem to know where every inch of a swimmer is located and they never accidentally touch us or strike us when they allow us to swim in their midst. They know how close to come to each other but leave us humans alone. As I watched every movement they made my heart was as vast as the ocean.

Today's experience had been another sign to me that they can read our minds. I have realized though that I have to deeply want the experience. There were days when I felt like I was too tired to draw in the desired result. On some days I was not able to muster up the Chi needed for an intense desire. So when I didn't project that joy or that energy from within myself, nothing much happened. Other people would have great swims that day but I was not in the right places and it didn't matter to me since I had no energy that day anyhow.

It is the same with life. When we just follow the daily schedule and are in the humdrum of life, we often fail to pre-create a matrix of new energy around us. Being the same every day takes less energy but is also less rewarding. To dream anew, to expand our expectations and to start spanning a larger energy field in the universe takes extra energy and focus at first but is much more satisfying.

It had been a great day. But to make sure that the dolphins weren't just accidentally fulfilling the wishes I had imagined that morning, I tried the same experiment the next day as well. This time I asked the dolphins in my mind if they would swim a little more gently around me. I had been scared the previous day by the intensity of their play and it had been hard to fight my fears. Today I wanted to be in their midst again as they were in their love-play but I wanted to feel more at ease. I was concerned that they would be too rambunctious and that they might mistake me for a dolphin!

As if they could read my mind, they took us into their midst again. I was with the same group of women as the previous day but the mood of the dolphins was different as we swam within inches of them. Again they were very interactive with each other but much more gentle. It was superbly magical to swim with them in the midst of their love play and I could breathe easier. Their click and sonar touched my body. Michelle had been swimming right next to me, holding her hands behind her back to appear non-threatening. Both of us felt deep respect for their permission to swim so close to them and we felt total honor for the dolphins and each other. Gone were any selfish feelings and I felt Michelle and I swim as ambassadors of the human race amongst the pod of wild dolphins. I was taken by the immense closeness they allowed, as we were truly taken into the midst of their pod. Today was a sure sign that they had read my mind again and fulfilled another deep wish of mine.

It was important to me to experiment with telepathy, to see if they would repeat certain behaviors. It was all too easy to say that dolphins read minds. Who could prove otherwise? Repeating some of my imagery experiments showed me to some degree that the likelihood of thought exchange was based on reality.

Michelle hugged me with utter joy as we left the pod after a long miraculous swim with them. She had felt one with them and me, as I had with her.

Most of us were speechless after we let the dolphins swim off. While we swim with them, we are moved into a total sense of NOW and only pure presence and joy pervades us.

We swam slowly to the back of the boat, took off our fins and masks and climbed up the little ladder. It was time for a snack and we had been filled to the brim with feelings of love and joy and were celebrating being together.

Our captain took the boat further out to the sandbank, leaving the dolphins behind us to play and make love. Dolphins are so very sensual and sexual. Making love as a group, they still seem to have favorites. This had been a group bonding experience for all of us and we were in love with life.

Suddenly the captain called out for us to come to the front of the boat, to take a look at a dolphin that had been severely bitten by a shark. He had heard about it over the radio from other boats and now we were sighting the dolphin that was swimming off to the side of the other dolphins.

Instantly the mood changed from joy to compassion. The group members had practiced Reiki before coming on this trip, and it was as if we all knew what to do. We lined up at the front of the boat and spread our hands as if giving a blessing. The hurt dolphin was now ahead of us, about 60 feet to the right of the boat. Each of us beamed a ray of light into the water to where he was. A shark had tried to get a meal in the deeper water further out past the channel where the dolphins sometimes go to feed. In the shallow waters by the sandbank, the dolphins were quite safe from sharks. Their sonar easily detects any intruders and they can warn each other through sonar underwater. In the shallow water, a predator wouldn't have much chance against a pod of dolphins. This is why the dolphins must like shallows.

Nevertheless this dolphin had been bitten rather severely and although he had not lost any blubber it was only slightly hanging on. At first the injured dolphin swam off to the side, away from other companions. But then the dolphin seemed to notice that we were pouring energy into him through our hands. Within a short while he positioned himself in front of the boat, right underneath our hands. He seemed to notice the energy. The air became quiet as we sent healing energy as one group mind. Each of us sent a beam of light. Collectively we felt as one unit. The air around us took on a mystical glow and the light on the ocean grew even more magical. We were no longer just on a boat; we were in a cocoon of light together.

This experience was even more magical to one of our participants than swimming with dolphins in the water was, as she told us later. While on the boat she had the presence of mind to be multidimensional, since she was in her own element. She did not have to pay attention to the water, swimming, or breathing at the right moment. Although this was a sad moment, in some ways it showed us how real the healing energy was to the injured dolphin. This dolphin confirmed to all of us that he or she was able to feel our energy. It was another sign of how interspecies, multi-dimensional interaction can really happen. As Don was with the other group on land, we included them in our prayer of our hands.

Later, when the sun was getting low and we were heading back to shore I sat by myself and leaned against the captain's console. The CD "Adiemus" was playing and Merlin popped into my mind and heart. On the wings of that music that I had heard while Merlin was with us in Hawaii, I felt my spirit soar up high into the clouds to meet Merlin's spirit in the sky. Our energies were so vast together that I marveled at our purpose.

My heart had been so opened by the encounter with the dolphins that now all my truths, including the ones that I had wanted to ignore surfaced in my heart. My love for Merlin burst forth from my heart in a giant, sudden starburst. I really missed him. Letting go was apparently not easy for me. It felt to me as if I was in the cathedral of the universe and he and I were in truth much larger beings than we ordinarily imagined ourselves to be. In my mind we were large swirls of light much like galaxies, intertwined eternally at the most celestial level.

It became obvious how much I had suppressed my deeper feelings, and yet in this quiet moment the deeper truth surfaced again. Feelings rule our hearts. Our minds may have one kind of wisdom and our hearts may have another. This was challenging. Back in Mexico, Don and I had intentionally opened the doors to another, but it still required a lot of maturity on both our parts, to handle the fire of the heart, body, mind and soul that ensued. The kind of expanded feeling I had with Merlin right now bordered fully on the feeling of destiny in my heart.

"Will I see him ever again? Is there a destiny for us, or is it just my passionate heart gone wild?" I wondered, looking at the clouds.

I was soon to find out!

It was so beautiful to see the sailboats approaching the small marina. Our captain docked the boat gently and we collected our bags and hugged him good-bye until the next day. In deep bliss we walked back to our tropical island home, adoring the beauty all around us. At the B&B we joined the other half of the group for dinner, and that night we explored another outdoor restaurant: Mango's. We were treated as if we were angels from another star. It must have been the love we all radiated from our experiences today. Tonight I wanted to call Merlin in Australia and see if he still harbored feelings for me.

Through the Center of the Lotus

I could hear my heartbeat with every step I took on our way home from the restaurant. My stomach was filled with butterflies as I thought of calling Merlin tonight. Everywhere I looked, as we walked home from dinner, I was reminded of Merlin. The starlit night became a poem to match my inner feelings of being in love. How could it be that one moment I could feel like I was a million miles away in my heart, happy that Merlin was in the hands of another woman and the next moment I could feel so infatuated?

Was it right to feel this way while being in love with Don? How could I be in love with both men? Here in Florida, Don and I were very busy with everyone else and it didn't matter very much if I was away in my thoughts with another man. But how ethical was it? And how could I sustain my love for Don and at the same time feel love for another? That was not how our culture viewed true love. True love was only felt for one person, and one only.

Yet again and again I thought of Merlin. While looking at the sky I felt the vastness of my spirit reaching out into the cosmos, remembering a vaster world where our beingness knows no human limitations. Does our soul have multiple soul mates? Could we love multiple souls? Wouldn't it stand to reason that another mate of mine from another lifetime was out there in the heavens or incarnated here on Earth, possibly even as a woman now? How small we believe ourselves to be! All too often I fall prey to thinking of myself as a mere human. But my spirit remembers again and again that I am something bigger. Maybe in truth, our essence is more like a galaxy, or a vast nebula.

When I dive into the center of my highest consciousness I become the vast stillness and simultaneously the light that is beyond any forms. Tonight I felt my spirit drawn into such a higher space and I wanted to feel the merging of Merlin's energy with mine.

I took a moment to walk alone. Under the star-filled sky I expanded into silence until I spread my wings across the cosmos, searching for Merlin's soul. In my mind I went up higher and higher until I was no longer human but rather just a star of consciousness. Then suddenly I felt that I made contact with Merlin's ethereal essence.

I was sure he too was calling me in. I had not talked with him for a while but I wanted to feel him. In this serene inner stillness the world around me took on a deeper sense of meaning. By opening to the light that surrounds us we truly enter a higher version of reality. This time I was using my deep desire to get in touch with another being that was far away. I used my desire to meet Merlin on a higher plateau of vibration as a carrot to enter a finer state of consciousness. My eyes were now seeing through the love in my heart. Some of the palm trees we passed were lit up by spotlights. Shining columns of light raced up the tree trunks and created a very artistic look. The palms swayed gently in the wind and reflected the cascading light back to our group, caressing our eyes and glowing with a special light in the warmth of the night.

In a moment that lasted for an eternity, I stood still by one of the trees and gazed into the night sky. My heart and spirit were so open. I longed to be with Merlin this very moment and I let my soul touch his and merge our cores. The wisdom of lifetimes fanned into this one single moment and as if the contact I made with Merlin in this way ignited in me a deep inner remembrance, I received his wisdom and made it my own. We are truly keys to each other's cosmic libraries when we unite our souls, hearts and minds with one another. By connecting with Merlin at that level I was ignited by his vast field of knowledge, wisdom, energy and memories.

Maybe that is really what love is all about. When we join with others in friendship or in love, we both expand further in our own and collective wisdom. In effect, we expand the intricacy of our soul's design by merging our souls. If this were made visible in the form of light lines, it would be seen as a new matrix which we were creating in our merging. We would indeed be creating a new design in the tapestry of our souls. Sex was really not even necessary.

As soon as we got to our B&B, I asked Don if it was all right if I called Merlin. Don said yes. Since Australia was nine hours behind our time zone on the East coast it was now afternoon where Merlin was. He told me things had not gone as he had wanted them to. He was visiting with his old lover north of Sydney, and the timing had been off. I felt his aloneness and reached out to him. What a miracle phones are. His voice was soft and I could tell he was very open to me.

I had already felt very connected in my stillness earlier while walking alone in silence. I wanted to share this deeper type of connecting and I suggested to Merlin that we try to be silent together on the phone so we could feel each other more clearly.

As I held the phone to my ear I imagined that we were beaming energy to each other. A very warm feeling surrounded me as Merlin had a very unique energy about him. With a sudden sense that he had locked onto me, I felt our energies actually touch. It felt as if Merlin had found me. But as soon as he had, he faded out again.

He had found me for sure, and I had felt that. After some more silence, where I tried to send him a homing beam to find me again, I felt him lock onto me more clearly. I knew that he knew, and that he had "found" me again. And indeed, he told me in a soft voice that he "felt" me. We can tell when we meet, even over the phone in silence.

As Merlin is more the feeling/kinesthetic type, inner seeing was more challenging for him and he had to learn to feel his way around. Since I am more visual, it is easier for me to develop an inner map. Also, Merlin had a strong rational mind and he was not sure at first if he was really "there," so he doubted his inner perceptions.

Doubt is a fantastic blocker of intuition. But it is just as easy to let the doubt fade, simply by paying attention to the inner feeling and seeing that the left brain is tuned out.

Perhaps because Merlin was such a kinesthetic type, I was overwhelmed by his presence. I felt as if I was magnetized into a vast energy vortex and I didn't want to come out of it. We touched each other in that tangible silence for a long time. I was truly *with* him. His presence was as real to me as the dolphins had been earlier today. This experience was as real as any physical touch to me. Merlin was breathing deeply and we felt an intense communion. My heart was wide open.

I suggested that we try to move up a notch in our merging. I would move up first, as if I was moving up within the frequency of the universe and he would try to find me again on the next rung of this imaginary ladder.

I soon found the next rung in my inner journey. I held my focus steady and beamed my feeling and presence back to Merlin, reaching across time and space for him to find me. I could tell when he started to rise to the same vibrational presence where I was located. Soon his focus found my location and when he locked on, our light became more intense. It was not like finding a specific form but rather a feeling, like a buzzing sensation in my mind that let me know when we connected with each other. In the core of my awareness, I could tell that we were ascending higher and higher to yet finer vibrations from where we had started. Unlike astral projection, which would give me more a "double" of a humanoid version of Merlin, I met him more like a star meeting a star.

In my mind I saw visions unfolding. I saw us unfurling our lights into each other, rising up higher through a tunnel of what looked like a toroid to me. We got closer and closer and it felt like the spiral dance of our soul's DNA. Then we became fields of light and passed through the center of what appeared to me to be a lotus flower.

Together, we started to merge into one singular light and when our awareness gathered into one point, I felt like I was entering the center of all creation. In one magical moment of union, I totally lost my sense of self. Bright light engulfed us and I felt like we were in the center of God. In this breathless moment I surrendered all of what I was, all I wanted, and all that we were to be to the cosmic center of Isness. Intense waves of expansion penetrated my body and my heart. Visions of celestial bodies surrounded me and I felt that we were HOME!

Merlin and I stayed in this stillness for a while until I slowly felt my endurance wind down. I wanted to come down from this high vibration. It took a lot of energy and I was not able to sustain the silence much longer. I wanted to know if he was feeling and experiencing the same things as me. Slowly I came down the cascading fountain of vibration, back into form and into feeling my body. As I descended, I tried to feel if Merlin was doing the same. I coalesced back into feeling.

I heard Merlin breathe audibly and I was sure that he too was coming back.

"Hi," I said softly, just in case he was still out there.

"Hi," he echoed back with equal softness.

We were both speechless and our encounter had taken our hearts to another level. This was true intimacy. At the same time it felt like a true Homecoming for both of us. We had come home to God. What could possibly be wrong in this? Is it that we humans are just not used to so much love?

I had to admit that I was falling in love even more. Now I was sure that I wanted to see him again. I had shared this state with others, with my niece, with my women friends and with other men. I had known that this closeness could make one feel more love than ever before. After all, when we move into a state of union we feel love. Love is the result of two or more being in a state union of soul. That is the secret. But with Merlin my love was colored by a very tangible attraction as well, and we were merging our souls in a way that was akin to being lovers. Was it the destiny of our souls that stimulated our attraction or was it purely human to feel it? I didn't know.

My body was tingling, that was for sure. Merlin had entered my core light and it was as if we were making love in a most intense but very sublime way. His light was pulsing my inner core flame and I kept rising up with it, taking him into this ephemeral Allness that felt like entering the One.

Merlin had indeed felt similar things as I had. We shared in words with each other what we had felt and seen on our silent journey. This was my training. By getting feedback and listening to another person's story and visions, I learned to decipher if I was lost in my own fantasy or if my images were matching those of my counterpart. Merlin and I were indeed overlapping and he knew it.

In the old Buddhist teachings, what we were doing was called the path of the White Lotus Tantra. I like to call it the Tantra of the Soul. It is said that by merging our individual state of consciousness with another or a group into a singular point, the singularity will take us over, which is the fastest way to God.

This method, when taken to its highest form, will catapult us into the highest experience of God. It is utilizing our innate drive to merge. We love to merge our essences with another. All of nature is set up to do that. In doing so, we surpass the paradox of separation. We move the two back into the One. Within us is a natural desire to surrender ourselves to the core of another. As we purposely superimpose the climactic focus of our soul's locus onto the very core locus of another, by being annihilated we make the return journey into Oneness possible.

What started out as a Big Bang now calls us back once again into the folds of Oneness, and we are fulfilling the call of our destinies. As we become part and parcel of the entire circular motion of existence and call multiplicity into singularity, we complete the cycle of the Big Bang. All returns home again.

The Big Bang creates complexity which then desires again to return to the Oneness and be swallowed whole into It. We derive the largest form of joy and ecstasy when we surrender ourselves, when we lose our sense of separation and move from dual awareness into singular awareness.

In lovemaking, in orgasm, in intense involvement of art, music or work that stems from the depth of our souls, we enter states of this ecstatic loss of self and become absorbed into a larger unit. Even galaxies have now been found to have at their very core their own black hole. Each galaxy will be completely swallowed into this chamber of singularity. No one knows what happens past the entry in a black hole but I imagine it would be very similar to what we experience in our deepest meditation when we surrender ourselves to the core of what looks like a toroid. We get spewed back out into another dimension, into a heightened form of Isness. Perhaps it is a parallel universe or maybe it is the next layer of the never ending journey into God, into the Center of Creation. However, it seems to me that God in its singularity wants our conscious return to Oneness as a witness to itself, as an ever more complex "I" of the eye of God.

We are not here to obliterate our locus of perception, our body, or soul. Nature, as the expression of the creation force has worked too long to manifest very complex structures that can house this awareness. What we are here for is to be the observer of the creator force, to be in awe of it and to complete the feedback loop, that allows the One to become aware of Itself.

We are the self that wants to return to Oneness. As a gift, in return, we retain our seat of the soul throughout time until we start to merge with larger seedpods of consciousness along the way of our ascension.

In visions I have seen beings piling into mountains of light, each surrendering their individual identity to the larger whole. Other times I have seen the units of individual soul awareness ascend into a larger seed-pod much like the stems of dandelion seeds, which are each facets on a diamond, collectively birthing a new and greater unit of awareness. I felt that Merlin was part of my most sublime seed pod and that we were essential to each other.

The merging of our souls on the phone had been deeply fulfilling and in a way I knew it had to be. Can love exist in multiple forms beyond the conventional ones like love for our mate, children and parents? Many cultures have explored varied versions of union in the physical realm. What seems to determine the choices are economic needs and socio-political power structures.

What a day this had been! Swimming with dolphins had opened my heart so much that I was swept into a larger ability to love. How would I be able to keep my balance? On the phone, Merlin and I had briefly talked about the idea of seeing each other again. "But how could that be possible?" I wondered. "How would Don react to my wish to see Merlin?"

The Paradox of Safety and Freedom

The days in Key West flew by and we had many amazing experiences with the dolphins and each other. It became apparent to me that being with dolphins opens people's hearts and bodies to more energy, and most participants felt inspired to be more alive.

Due to our daily routines, we tend to shrink in our expansion and get stuck in ruts. Shame, fear and false ideals all contribute to us replaying the same old track. If we want to grow, we need to open our energy flow to new patterns.

Sometimes healing happens simply by being with dolphins in the physical as well as in one's imagination. Due to the heightened energy that dolphins carry, we get an extra boost which provides us with a window to get ignited. If we go with that energy, we will grow. If we judge it and restrict our new flow in order to maintain the old habitual flow of Chi in our system, body, heart and mind, we don't grow.

Usually when I invite a dolphin into my mind to show me via feeling and imagery what I need to change in myself, I get the same answer: open your lower chakras to more flow, more joy and more light. And when I do that I am indeed more vibrant and feel more loving. Other participants got the messages – that they needed to open their hearts or voices, speak their truths more or let their hearts sing.

Leaving that magical world of light on the water, of turquoise dimensions, of telepathy and love was hard. Don and I flew back to our island north of Seattle. We came home to the most beautiful weather.

Sun, blues skies, eagles flying above our heads and fresh mountain air greeted us. The amount of oxygen in the Pacific Northwest is surreal.

One Sunday afternoon in August, Don and I took a walk along the cliff at the edge of the island's forest. We were high above the water overlooking the stony beaches, listening to the seagulls calling. We watched the eagles play as we stood in silence and were awed at the beauty of nature all around us.

I mentioned that I felt like traveling alone and that I was feeling drawn to Bali. We had been supporting a Balinese young man in his education and I felt like going there. This was my less courageous self talking, the self that also wanted to stop over in Australia on the way to see Merlin. But I didn't say that. Not yet.

As if Don had been reading my mind he said that I could just do a world-tour and end it Germany. I could stop in Australia to visit with Merlin, go to Bali and then onward to Germany for the seminars! I jumped at the idea and before Don knew it I had called our travel agent to inquire about ticket prices.

A few days later I got an email from a woman in Australia. Since I had been speaking at Prophet's Conferences in the company of prestigious speakers, people from around the world emailed me. She introduced herself as a coordinator for seminars and asked me if I would consider coming to Australia to teach a seminar near Nelson Bay. Since Nelson Bay was known for dolphins, at the conclusion of the seminar she wanted to offer an excursion on a sailboat called "Imagine" to watch them.

I felt upset. I was asked to work at the very moment I had concluded that I wanted to see Merlin. NO, I was not in the mood to work! Luckily I went to sleep asking my inner voices, guardians and advisors to help me find the right answer. I awoke in the morning with a larger perspective. I had seen that the larger purpose in my life was not just to have fun personally but also to teach. It was my gift this lifetime.

Being invited to teach, although it seemed to steal my time away from what I thought I really wanted, was in perfect alignment with my deeper desire to serve here on Earth. I had to laugh at myself. It was really funny that I didn't instantly see the amazing cosmic connection. One way or the other I was going to Australia. I agreed to teach the seminar in October 1999 and I ordered the airline ticket.

Don saw the cosmic perfection and we realized that the greater story was playing itself out. The trip to Australia, that seemed destined to happen now, was the continuation of the story we had embarked on earlier that spring in Mexico. We had opened our doors to love, to a larger field of love. Would we be strong enough to handle it? We decided to go with the flow of life.

Don and I wanted to be together no matter what, and we were willing to include others, rather than separate and have serial monogamous relationships.

Many people function much better at serial monogamy, and to try anything else causes them untold heartaches. But over the many years of teaching I have spoken with so many couples and individuals who confided in me that they would love to know the secret of how to love more than one person. They told me that if I break the code of loving more than one person at a time, to let them know. Secretly almost everyone wants freedom as well as safety. It is encoded in us. Unfortunately both traits are equally strong.

Most everyone has, during sometime in their life, been faced with love that was outside the norm. Attractions abound in nearly everyone's life, be they sexual, emotional, or from the depth of one's soul, despite thinking we shouldn't have them.

Most of the difficulties that result stem from lack of truth, or a lack of truly surrendering to the current partner or standing up for the deeper truths we feel. Many people suffer guilt from secretively having affairs of all kinds, and it is those secrets that build the walls within their marriages.

Closeness of the heart, even intimacy of soul with another person is usually enough to scare anyone. Lies and deceit in marriages and partnerships result because we cannot help but want to fulfill all the paradoxical longings in ourselves. Those that choose one side or the other of the paradox – the need to be safe or the need to be free – often do so at the expense of their aliveness.

I don't think that there is a recipe for everyone. Everyone's needs are different. I do know that in order to have long term relationships it is best to be really honest with one's self, with others, and to share, perhaps slowly, our deeper truths. We are really so very similar. In the beginning of any relationship, during the first years of courtship, our hormones are not even interested in being with another person. But as the years pass our love deepens, our security grows with our mates, and as this deeper love emerges, we also begin feeling our biological and spiritual availability for others once again.

In the book by Helen Fisher "Why We Love: The Nature and Chemistry of Romantic Love," she writes about nature's way to ensure reproduction, raise our offspring and the many different hormonal cocktails that our brain cooks up for us. We can be simultaneously attached to our mate, get infatuated with another person, have soul unions with yet another that rivals any marriage and have sexual desires for yet another.

It would be foolish to think that nature can be outwitted by the mind and willpower. Every person has a different mix and tendency for this brain cocktail. Here is a quote from page 78 in her book: "Feelings of male-female attachment are produced primarily by the hormones oxytocin and vasopressin."

Some of us bond easily, deeply, and for a long time. Others lack the long term bonding hormone "oxytocin." Others know how to open their hearts wide to most everyone and are excellent in the first stages of love.

They are the Casanovas. There are those that commit easily, yet again others who abhor the loss of freedom. Some are more sexual as partners, others are more loving. Some have a good mix in their partnership.

Don and I are very lucky. We have it all. We met each other on the premise that our life's purpose was to return to the oneness of God. That was THE most important purpose of our lives, individually, before we ever met. Igniting our own maturity as soul and having worked psychologically with ourselves via tools and methods we had studied in the early eighties, we were also vibrant in our emotional bodies. If we got stuck, we worked on ourselves. Mentally and spiritually we were well matched. And when we met and let the light of our souls rest within each other, we also had chemical fireworks. Over the years we found out we had great life skills that worked hand in hand. We had the same values and dreams since both of us had the same foundation: Self-Realization and God-Realization. We can only have illumined soul-mate relationships if both partners are able to delve into the light of their souls individually, before they meet.

I didn't need to remind Don to think of his spiritual evolution. He had been my teacher. And I was his best student ever. We were both eager to awaken, independently of each other.

Yet after years of walking this path of enlightenment together and after so many years of successfully arranging all aspects of our lives in harmony, we too were bumping up against the natural stumbling blocks of life. Life doesn't seem to want us to be comfortable. It wants us to grow, to explore and to expand. Unfortunately, steadiness is not the most growth inducing environment. So we had to face challenges and change voluntarily if we didn't want to succumb to the mill of nature. And this we did.

Merlin had walked into our lives as a result of our conscious acceptance of my dream. I wanted to stay with Don as my husband but I was told by the inner voice that had commented in my dream just a year earlier that I could stay with Don if we were willing to include the lessons, learning and the ignitions that we would receive from others into our marriage.

Don and I both looked at what we had with each other and we really wanted to stay together. Our life and relationship was too amazing to give up. The next best thing to do was to allow nature to have its way and to hope that we had a strong bond.

Most people have good reason to fear the loss of their partner. Most relationships are not made in heaven and the fire of beginning love with another can be extremely hot and mind blowing. Many people lose interest in their mate if they think they've found a better match or are simply experiencing more fire, physically, emotionally, or even cosmically with another.

I really don't recommend that anyone try what we did. We had the ability to step back, become aware of the larger pattern and to let our inner truths speak. It had been hard to acknowledge that we had sexual attractions to others. I thought my attraction to Merlin also had deeper soul components, but for now sexual attraction could easily disguise itself as coming from a higher order. Don and I were honest enough with ourselves to know that we were also creatures of nature, not just soul-mates. I wished it had been otherwise. But nature has its way. And we were wise enough to acknowledge that.

The next Sunday, another sunny day in August, Don and I had gone to a street fair in a small town north of us called Anacortes. I was to receive my flight tickets to Australia in a few days. A booth that displayed ancient looking stone-art attracted my attention. Gazing at these masterful etchings in stone, I was drawn to a particular slate upon which an animal, maybe a crocodile or gecko, had been painted in Australian Aboriginal style.

The owner of the booth saw me standing in a trance-like state near his booth and called me over. As we talked, a very special light started to surround our conversation. I was absorbing the beauty of all his stone pieces when he suddenly said, "Here, please take this stone-plate as a gift. My inner voice told me that you should have it." It was exactly the slate that I had been eyeing from a distance. He told me that he felt I had a deep connection with it and he wanted to gift it to me.

I had been preparing to go to Australia in my mind and heart. This gift certainly fit into the center of my dreaming universe. Maybe we live in a dream! Maybe all parts of our dreams interact. The man in the booth listened to his inner voice and I had the confirmation I wanted.

On our way home I had tears running down my face as I watched the brilliantly red sun setting. The magic of the coincidences were touching my heart and I felt guided as I embarked on this adventure to Australia which still had me wondering. I thanked the ancient spirits of the dreamtime for welcoming me via the light of the sun and the gift of the rock, which was an old Aboriginal motif.

The next day I received my tickets to fly to Australia. I wondered how all the elements of this trip were synchronized from a higher dimension. It seemed that although my personal wishes were involved, there was also a cooperation that superseded chance.

Don and I had been very much in love lately. We had intentionally focused our soul's attention on each other which always produced closeness, feelings of in-loveness and miracles. Maybe our hearts were opening even more to each other since we had opened the flood gates and our subconscious didn't feel like we were trapped.

We really had a choice to be in love together. Perhaps we also wanted to make sure that I came back and so we went deeper into love and became even more attractive to each other before I left. But that much love made leaving even harder.

Don and I had planned to spend some time in Hawaii together before I was to leave for Australia. To our amazement a woman whom we had met earlier at a gathering on Whidbey Island in Washington, announced her visit to us. Now Don was going to spend time alone with her. It was clear that Don had no problems manifesting plenty of "balance" in his life for my extravagant learning lessons.

Although I didn't feel quite ready to leave Don, schedules had been agreed upon and off I flew to Australia to see Merlin and to teach a seminar near Nelson Bay.

As the plane took off, taking me further and further west, I questioned what I was doing. I was following my heart, my vision and my inner guidance, but how much of it was really a good idea? I didn't know. What would this do to Don and me?

I felt my love for Don pulling at my heart and tears filled my eyes as the airplane took off.

The Gift of Australia

I called Don one more time from Honolulu airport, very sad to be leaving him behind. "Tears escape me when we're apart" were lyrics by Jon Anderson that best described my feelings for Don. But the plans were laid.

Sitting by the window I gazed at the Hawaiian Islands getting smaller and smaller, and the angels of the sky soon took me into their wings. I took advantage of the higher stratospheres. It seems much easier to meditate up high and I expanded easily into the space of light and clouds as I placed myself in the hands of God.

After a long flight I finally landed in Sydney, Australia. It was early morning and I was a bit nervous at the exit. I wondered how Merlin and I would feel. It had been four months since we had been together and much had changed in his life. I never really thought we would meet again.

A million people milled around and I couldn't see Merlin anywhere. Finally I resorted to asking a person if I could use his cell phone and called Merlin, thanking modern technology as I heard his reassuring voice answer. He had been waiting in a different area.

As Merlin walked up to where I was waiting, he carried a large red heart cut out from colored paper. I was touched. We walked up to each other silently and in slow motion gazed at each other as we got closer. In that same subtle way we started to hold each other. He took me gently into his arms as if to feel all the subtle nuances of me, opening the space for us to really meet. I really loved his subtle way of saying "Hello" instead of the usual frantic joyful hugs, which tend to lock up my awareness. But Merlin looked more worn out than when he had left Hawaii.

I felt motherly as I held him. He looked weaker, more tired, and not as radiant as when we had last seen each other. Life had been challenging for him. I could feel his spirit sigh as we were finally back together again.

He walked me to his VW bus. Bright orange, it looked like a Hippie vehicle. "Here is my Tweety," he said smilingly. It was to be our home for the next couple of weeks. We drove north in his VW bus, which reminded me of a honey bee flying along the highway toward the Blue Mountains. We were to explore this part of Australia for the next two weeks.

We had barely started to talk about our lives when Don called on Merlin's cell phone to see if I had landed safely and to see if Merlin had found me. Merlin parked on the side of a busy street and left the van so I could have some privacy to talk with Don. My heart missed Don already and I wasn't sure I really wanted to be away from him for very long.

Meanwhile Merlin ran over to a field of greens that were growing in an empty lot and came back with a handful of dill and fennel for lunch as I finished talking with Don. Merlin walked up to me with a smile, knowing that he had magically manifested food for us. Suddenly I felt a spark of magic. Here was a man who manifested lunch for us from a parking lot in the midst of a city!

OK, this was different for me. Normally I would go shopping and make the food, since Don was not really into cooking. He tried but it was not his natural talent, unlike fixing computers just by standing next to them.

I liked this new impulse in my life and something opened in me as I let this different wind touch my heart.

We were heading north into the Blue Mountains. That much we knew since we were on our way to Nelson Bay where the seminar would be held. Everything had worked out magically, a sign that my personal will and the greater will were cooperating. Freewill and the larger design were in harmony. I had no real idea what the larger plan was for my life. I didn't really want to know, although I could see glimpses.

Taking a turn off the highway we discovered a small quaint town called Lyra. It was a romantic, charming sort of village of artists and restaurants. As we got out of our Tweety, we were greeted by an ocean of Japanese cherry blossom trees. Although it was October in Australia, they were entering Spring, being in the Southern Hemisphere. Merlin and I had been blessed by warm weather.

We spotted an artistic restaurant with the magical afternoon sun lighting up its wooden floors and we felt drawn to enter. We picked vegetarian foods from the salad bar, placed the gourmet foods artistically on our plates and sat at a table in the midst of the restaurant. Unfettered by conventions and not knowing anyone around us, we felt as if we had our own cove.

Our eyes locked onto each other as we dove into our very own private world. Merlin and I started to feel the buzz arising from the deeper ability to connect in our souls. Intimacy comes from the ability to feel our souls touch. Merlin awoke to his natural talent of knowing how to woo me, how to gaze deeply into my eyes and he started to feed me pieces of food with his fingers.

Tantalizingly, he moved his fingers gently across my lips after each bite. Very slowly I responded and fed him a soft piece of papaya as if I intended to seduce him right there at the table. He then took a fresh red pepper into his mouth and started to feed it into mine. As our lips touched, we slipped into deeper and more ancient feeding impulses and started to slide the food back and forth between our mouths, intermingling kissing and breathing gently into each other.

I was getting high from this love play. Had I ever let anyone else do this to me? However, Merlin felt so clean to me, so similar in some basic instinctual way to my own vibration, that I easily could eat from his mouth.

As we touched and played with each other, we got drunk from our openness toward each other and we floated in a cocoon of in-loveness. We were absorbed in a world all our own, unaware that anyone else was watching. Our eyes glowed and I could feel our body chemistry igniting. He was making the most beautiful overtures to me, a sort of foreplay and the dance of our bodies opened me to his beingness in a most primal way. He knew how to enter me. Without any obvious moves, without any come-on, following the openness that we both felt and being willing to experiment in the moment, he won my heart over again.

As we stepped out of the restaurant we were high as kites. I ran across the street onto the green grass strip and pulled Merlin with me until we were standing in a massive ball of pink under the Japanese cherry trees. I held Merlin's hand as we stood in awe and wonder. A light wind came and blew a million petals upon us. We felt like lovers being rewarded by nature. What a miraculous day!

Night came and we drove a little further north and eventually pulled onto a small side road overlooking a great canyon. The view was fading slowly in the evening light and we made our dinner by candlelight in the small kitchen of the van. I felt like a gypsy and life away from my normal activities gave me a feeling of stealing a slice of heaven. Jubilantly I received this gift from the universe.

Had it been so easy to be in this moment of heaven only because a force larger than us was guiding and prodding us? Were we exactly where we were supposed to be? Had higher forces arranged this? Life had lined up perfectly to make this moment happen.

As we ate in silence I looked at Merlin across the dinner table and suddenly in the dim light of the candles I saw the face of Gopal Das, my inner guide, appear in the face of Merlin. This vision jolted me and I began to wonder if maybe Gopal Das was trying to have a moment with me here in this earthly realm via the body of another man once again. Gopal Das had played with me through the encounters of other men before, such as through Paul and Richard whom I had written about in my book, *Journey to the Center of Creation*.

Maybe Merlin was a surrogate for this interaction. Was my inner guide having a love affair with me here on Earth? Was he phase-shifting his essence into my physical world via the channel of another human? I was very puzzled. Maybe this was not a simple human encounter but rather my inner guide having a human encounter with me.

As we sat in deep silence together, we gazed into each other's eyes. I opened my energy field and the small van became a vast open space of stars. We rose in our awareness into subtler fields. I could see our earthly forms while we were also engaging our more celestial bodies.

We truly are not three-dimensional beings, even though we walk in bodies on the Earth. In truth we are stars made of light that are sheathed in varying cloths of ever finer vibrations, able to embody increasingly more beautiful spaces as we shift our attention from the denser to the finer realms.

In truth we are a point of consciousness that wears any number of dimensional coats, and even beyond this we are stars in the sublime worlds of God. The trick to ecstasy lies in moving into the higher and vaster states of identity and not become dominated by our five senses.

I gazed at Merlin and smiled since we were entering our home territory of being angels on Earth and we both knew it. We were entering increasingly complex states of simplicity and stillness. Within that light of stillness I could feel us touch each other, become one space together, still in eternity, feeling closer than one can imagine.

"Home, we are home," were the words that resonated in my mind. Our souls and hearts opened and we knew that we held the state of heaven open for each other. Gone was the look of tiredness from Merlin's face. Gone were all his worries, at least for now.

When I first met Merlin I knew where to "find" him inwardly. I rose in my awareness to a much higher space and found the seat of his soul. In Mexico on that bridge the night of our first kiss I could see that he had been lonely in this palatial inner dimension for a long time. There are not many souls able to enter such high states consciously with another and it can get lonely at times. Our next few days were filled with hikes surrounded by breathtaking mountains, rocks, waterfalls and by love.

The seminar was scheduled a few days after my arrival and we were heading north a little more each day until we reached Nelson Bay. We arrived there the day before the seminar and met with the captains of the sailboat "Imagine." The entire seminar group was set to go out on the sailboat on the Sunday night conclusion of the seminar to watch dolphins.

Marion was the woman who had offered her home to us for the weekend. I had to introduce Merlin to her as the man I was traveling with, with blessings from Don, and told her that I planned on spending the nights with Merlin. It truly was the most unorthodox way to show up as a seminar leader.

Marion was smitten by our unorthodox life. An artist herself, she understood right away. Although she had read my biography and my book and knew full well that I was married, she instinctively felt for Merlin and I. She took my hand and led me to her bedroom.

It was a masterfully decorated room in rich tones of burgundy velvet. It was her master-suite which she had decided to gift us for the weekend. Her life had been rich and full of love and she was as unorthodox as her gift to us. Being married and appearing to teach a seminar in the company of a lover didn't shock her. Indeed she felt like more of life should be that way!

Marion and I felt like sisters. She was a sculptor like my own sister, who was also named Marion. And Marion's sister was a published writer with a similar first name as mine. The similarities were remarkable.

After a potluck I was asked to sit on a huge puffy chair and people sat at my feet, asking questions. It was uncomfortable. In my heart of hearts I feel that we all need to see each another as equals. We are each a spark of God in form, partaking in the dance of creation and reflecting the many nuances of possibilities of Itself back to Itself. As such we are neither lower or higher than anyone else. Not to say that some of God's fractals were not starting out in Kindergarten on planet Earth and other sparks were about to graduate from the schoolhouse Earth. But that doesn't make anyone more or less valuable. I have superseded some of my teachers who once were way beyond my reach and yet other teachers are still waiting for me to wake up so they can start teaching me.

Of course I have preferences. We like being around beings that are in close resonance with us. Personally I prefer to be around people who vibrate with love, are awakening their souls, who don't get drunk or use drugs or foods to dull themselves. I like to be around people who are willing to grow and who want to shine and live in Heaven on Earth. But we are, in essence, the same at our cores. We are all made of the same starlight.

Night came and Merlin and I were finally able to retreat. I lit the candles in the bedroom while Merlin took a shower. Waiting for him to return I entered into a reverie. I knew tonight would be special. Synchronistic events seemed to lead us further and further into another kind of world. A feather quilt, a large queen size bed and candlelight were luring my mind and heart into opening up to Merlin even more.

The door opened and Merlin entered with a white towel wrapped around his long hair, resting like a turban upon his head. Another white

254

towel was wrapped around his waist. Walking into the room with a slow gate and a transfixed smile that lifted me into another world, he was like a dancer who was guided by celestial music from beyond.

Slowly, masterfully and in no rush, I felt myself rise into the timeless space of angels. As he lay down on the bed with me, he took me into his arms. I literally melted into him and all my will gave way to this eternally beautiful moment in time.

I wanted him, all of him. We had opened so many doors for and with each other. Life had been synchronizing our dance for so many months already. Whether we were just dancers on the strings of destiny or in our self-made heaven, I didn't care. We were in love and had entered the perfect moment of a trance-like dance with each other.

Merlin was so masterful in his gentleness. His kisses on my neck sent chills down my body and my nipples hardened under his arousing breath. Running his arms along my side, his hands never obviously touched any part of my body. Feeling the depth of his energy pulse into me, he was able to reach deeper into me than if he had tried to touch my erotic zones. I opened to him deeply. We moved ever so slowly, paying attention to our energies, to our merging of hearts and tried not to be climactic pursuers of a mountain top that we wanted to reach as soon as possible.

We lingered in the fields of flowering trees, in the melodic soul-filled sounds of the wind, floating rather than running, and feeling the energies inside of each other. The darkness and candlelight in the room reflected our deeply open mood as if stars were our bed and love was God's song to our dance.

I was not thinking of what the next move would be or how to prepare. It just felt right and Merlin held me from behind. Maybe was the most natural position for a man and a woman. When Merlin asked me to be very still I simply opened myself deeply. He started to enter me slowly and deeply, holding my body from behind with his arms wrapped around my heart. I received him fully in deep silence.

My body arched back and trembled and my temples touched his as if our minds could enter each other more in our perfect circle of energy. Merlin moved ever so slowly. It was as if we were in slow motion, breathing slowly, deeply and steadily. My heart was flying open in this momentous gift of his. He didn't rush. He didn't push. We felt only the intensity of our merging in a deep stillness. I felt like I could feel every fiber of his heart, energy and soul enter into mine. In that moment of deep interpenetration we loved each other. Our bodies opened to the depth of our desire to merge with each other and felt the vastness of the cosmos support us.

"I love you," he whispered into my ear. This memory would etch itself into my mind forever. I loved him in a way that words will never be able to describe. In that moment I could feel the vastness of our spirits merging through time and space, entering a field of energy that was coming from a dimension so vast it superseded our human ability to imagine. His soul and mine reached out to us from the vastness of eternity into this moment in time. We created a matrix together in another time-space and our love for each other was eternal.

Again I could see the vast ocean of who we were at a level of reality that supersedes and governs this earthly dimension. It was as if our future had reached back in time, calling our participation into being. I could feel who we were and who we were going to be. A vast play of love, awakening, enlightenment and living as sages, we were simultaneously living in a space that spanned and superseded time here as we knew it.

We slowly came to a point where we felt the fulfillment of our circulation of energy. He had not used a condom and had not come in the usual way. The only promise Don had asked of me was to use a condom, but I hadn't. But I also had not made love in the traditional sense. It was deeper than that.

Merlin was utterly grateful that I had allowed the feelings to be felt rather than get lost in the heat of our bodies. Our deep union was much more than our orgasms could have ever produced.

Later, as we lay in the semi-lit room slowly drifting off to sleep in each other's arms, I wondered if our future was speaking back to us or if we were stealing a moment from heaven, ahead of our time? Was our encounter to ensure that a certain future would unfold?

This room was a gift. The seminar was a synchronistic arrangement to make sure I would come to Australia. It seemed my life was in hands beyond my own. I felt like our future was working to get us together. Don had asked me not to get pregnant, and as yet I hadn't.

Commitment Phobia

The seminar was very fun to teach. Australians as a whole seemed more emotionally open, less success driven in their working life. Money didn't matter as much to them as living life, and the participants soaked up the information and exercises. Our culmination was a sailing-tour in Nelson Bay on the sailboat called "Imagine." Merlin and I stood at the helm like the main characters in the movie *Titanic*. Dolphins swam underneath of us in this very cold water. Since it was not permitted to swim with dolphins here, the boat had a net in which swimmers would be lowered, and with luck dolphins would swim around the humans in the net, as in a reverse zoo effect. We all just stayed on board watching these elegant beings swim underneath us.

The next day Merlin and I decided to go to a cove on Nelson Bay and just enjoy nature. With some luck, maybe dolphins would come around and swim with us.

We found an amazingly beautiful cove, with white sand and rock walls edging this piece of heaven. I could sense that Merlin needed time alone. The sensory overload created a subtle withdrawal in him. I decided to stay in a cove by myself, protected on all sides by large rock walls, basking in the warm sun. In my aloneness I pulled out my American-Indian Flute. Closing my eyes I started to play songs for the dolphins, imagining that somewhere out there they could hear me. Merlin sat further away alone in his space.

Suddenly a fisherman walked by and said: "You called them in!" as he pointed to a small group of dolphins swimming nearby. I couldn't believe it. There really were dolphins swimming along the edge of the beach in close reach of us. The fisherman told me that the dolphins didn't usually come that close to the beach and he felt they had come for the music.

I was touched. But the water was too cold for me to try to swim to them so I decided to just watch them. Merlin however ran into the freezing water and tried to swim to them. But the water was too cold for him too and he returned quickly. Shivering, he came to sit near me and after some silence he confessed that his heart was starting to freak out. He was feeling an intense pain in his heart and he felt like withdrawing. I didn't know at the time that he was plagued by a deep pattern in his life, the name of which I was to find out later: commitment phobia. When a man or a woman finds out that someone really wants them, after they have enjoyed their time pursuing the new attraction, they want to run to maintain their freedom.

Casanovas are good at the beginning stage of getting together, at flirting, at the opening scenes, at inviting intimacy. Usually they can engender intimacy very easily because they don't have the usual inhibitions most people have. These types are able to drop the typical layers of emotional protection, which most people let down only very slowly, and open their souls widely very quickly. Their amazing intimacy attracts others immensely. But when the time comes for deepening, being accountable, being wanted, being needed, being depended upon, they want to run.

Merlin was caught in his own inability to commit. Not that I wanted a commitment, not really, but I did want him to remain open to me, to stay here, now that I had opened my heart. So we worked through the pain with imagery work. It was a very, very slow session.

That night we were invited to have dinner on our sailboat captain's smaller boat. Lights were strung along all the boats among the various boardwalks, and they lit up the night sky. Merlin and I meandered arm in arm on the piers, searching for our captain's boat. Music filled the air from nearby and we stood still in a moment of magic and held each other in a very romantic embrace. Suddenly it sounded like wedding music and I could hear the bells ringing for us. In that very moment I felt a shift in Merlin. He disappeared from Earth right then and there. That depth of emotion, that kind of future was too much for him. He too had heard the same deeper meaning of the synchronistic music. As we entered the boat, I knew it was the end of our love. He had opened too far and didn't want to continue. We would not get any further.

The conversation that evening miraculously turned to making choices, to choosing to live and rise higher into one's soul's truth. Could Merlin hear what was being said? I could tell that he had made a 180 degree turn.

In desperation I tried to massage his feet, tried to get him connected to the earthly world. Maybe he didn't want that. Maybe he wanted to live as an angel, barely here, not quite touching down and only enticing the hearts and souls of women. But he didn't want them to bind him down here. Maybe the women were supposed to follow him up into Heaven.

I later learned that many people who are commitment phobic are very sensitive beings. Many have lived past lives as monks and they are not too good at relationships. They had lived in the safety of community, spiritual institutions in the past. So finding their purpose, having personal needs, and supporting themselves let alone a partner was too challenging. They also seem to lack a natural psychological boundary around themselves. They want to please, never hurt another and in the end, they give too much of themselves. The only way to regain their sense of self is to leave, to run. They are often also bonded deeply to their mothers, not ever having fully matured into manhood, but often somehow staying the "forever young" men, more boys than men.

In some ways they don't want to leave their mothers. Some of them don't have the usual strong sex drive that other men do, and they are able to relish the subtler joys of sensuality and attraction, not really wanting to fully take charge of their lives, or of sex.

Often, they were heavily criticized by their fathers and failed to develop their deeper sense of self love. As boys, they often remain close to their mothers, to protect her from the negativity or lack of love of the husband. Some of them had a mother who lived off the juicy love that her boy could offer, the innocent intimacy, which sucked the life-force out of that boy, misusing the closeness that a mother can offer. These boys also never grow up. Intimacy was experienced as a suffocation of their own needs. Of course not all mothers are like that.

I'd had an unconscious fear that if I had been a mother with a boy, I might be too close to him. I don't know where I got that idea, but I had that feeling. Maybe I was experiencing the boy now outside of myself, and was trying to fix the problem from the outside.

The remaining time Merlin and I had in Australia was filled with moments of intense closeness, followed by Merlin's intense fears and withdrawals, turning our time into a total emotional rollercoaster. In such states he could not see my spirit and I wanted to run.

What I didn't know was that withdrawals from a commitment phobic person work much like a vortex that suck more love out of one to compensate for the lack of love they feel. I didn't know that in a way it was very dangerous to open to a commitment phobic person. It felt like I was getting addicted to a force that seemed stronger than I was.

Commitment phobic types tend to feel less personal love, but are able to feel a more general, universal love. Their partner will often generate double the amount of love in their own heart in a desperate attempt to make up for the lack of love being returned to them.

It is said that a person getting involved with a commitment phobic, deep down in themselves is also not able, or willing, to commit. Though I was very committed to Don, I was not able to exclusively commit to Merlin since I was married already. In that sense this statement was true. I could only be connected with a person that didn't really want me, not fully.

I later learned many factors about commitment phobia from books. No matter how much I could see that Merlin couldn't open his heart completely, somehow I couldn't leave. My heart stayed attached to him, no matter what I tried. The experiences I had shared with him had been so very beautiful, that I didn't want my hope to die. I slowly realized hope could be detrimental. I wasn't very masterful at cutting ties, but that was because I really didn't believe in an end. Life goes on and on for eternity, which is a long, long time. Our love ties accompany us over many eons.

Deep within myself I felt that we return life after life to keep growing in our love with each other. I was willing to work with Merlin until we shared a deep respect and a free and unconditional love for each other, long after the embers of our hot love had died down.

According to Robert Monroe, founder of the Monroe Institute, we merge with our soul mate at a higher octave of existence into total oneness after a certain stage of evolution, to become part of a greater matrix. Once united, we seek another pair that has also united and which now serves as our new soul-mate matrix. Further on in evolution we find yet another unit made up of the same complexity and we keep going on in this unification process until we make a huge ball of light. We eventually become a union of souls so vast that it encompasses all into Oneness.

From that view I wanted to keep the love in my heart burning for all the close souls in my life, unless of course they were destructive to my being. If they were destructive, I let them hang out to dry, so to speak. Sometimes this drying period could last a year or longer, but most often the insights gained by both parties made it possible eventually to love each other again, with more depth, understanding and with more peace.

Merlin and I traveled together for the next week through Australia, followed by a trip to Bali. One morning in Bali, one of the Inn-keepers came to our little bungalow to serve us breakfast. Don and I had stayed in that very same bungalow years ago and he had recognized me from back then. Over breakfast he told us that his very own grandmother had had two husbands. I guess it was his way of making my obvious lifestyle an open and acceptable fact.

But the withdrawals on Merlin's side continued to plague us. I was not the kind of personality that handled those subtle abandonments very well. It was my Achilles heel, having had the imprint of my father dying when I was two years old. I abhorred abandonment. I did wonder many times, whether I needed two major loves in my life, because I had concluded as a very young girl, that it was obviously dangerous to be dependent on only one man. The one husband could die, or disappear. My mother must have felt distraught when she was left with two young children in a foreign country. This surely had left a deep impression on my heart as well. The message I might have learned was: "Don't wind up alone!"

Our time was at once magical as well as tormenting and painful, much like a roller coaster, and I got sick. My time to fly back home had arrived and I just wanted to be back in the arms of Don, my Love, my true Love. Don was the man who loved me beyond his own fears of loss, who said YES to me, YES to life and who loved me more than I did myself.

I flew home to Hawaii, weak on my legs and with a tattered heart. Don greeted me with a flower lei at the airport, but I was too hurt to appreciate it. Pain was clouding my heart and Don tried to cheer me up. I lay in bed for a week trying to heal my body and my heart. Merlin didn't email or call me even once to see how I was for one whole month. I didn't know that he had continued to travel around in Bali with a woman whom he had met shortly after I left. I became very depressed and my life seemed to have lost meaning. Why had I opened myself to love, and why had I been refused entry?

Was I able to let go of Merlin now that I had experienced the worst of it all? Karma wasn't that easy to shake off. Was there was a greater plan?

The Greater Purpose

The many months and years that followed were marked by my ups and downs of trying to let go of Merlin. Every time I told Don that I had really let go of Merlin, he laughed at me. Don had seen me change my mind all too often and he knew that I truly loved Merlin's soul, despite the fact that he couldn't open his heart.

The suction of this parallel life pulled at me often. Many times I felt that I was supposed to live a different life, one in which I was to have a child with Merlin and maybe even marry him. A supremely good and world-renowned psychic took one look at me while I was attending her seminar and told me that I was with the wrong man and was supposed to have a child with another.

But I did not want to let go of Don, nor he of me.

Were we too stubborn? We had to wonder. Our love was vast and made in heaven. Were we playing God with our destiny and refusing to do the obvious? In a dream in the autumn of 1998 I was told to leave Don and yet I tried to negotiate for a different destiny in which I wouldn't have to. In the big picture, leaving Don for one lifetime didn't seem to matter much. But from my personal perspective in this lifetime it mattered greatly, especially to my heart. I wanted to stay with Don.

To find out if we were just selfish and not listening to higher guidance, Don and I did some soul searching. What was the right course of action? In our preview of a future in which I would be with Merlin, we could see only a very painful life. Yet staying with Don I felt I was swimming upstream against an undertow of cosmic design, which kept pulling on my soul.

The following winter Merlin moved to Hawaii to be near me. Merlin and I never made love during those months, which would have been too difficult for me to handle, since Don was so close. But it gave us a chance to learn from one another.

One day, wondering what the right path was, Don and I went into deep meditation. From the highest place we could reach in our awareness we both saw the same answer: I should offer to live with Merlin for a period of time. There was something to be learned and it appeared wiser for us to finally surrender to that path.

Don and I agreed heavy-heartedly that we would give this experiment one to two years time, after which I would return to Don. We just couldn't bear the thought of fully letting go of our union.

One afternoon in the jungle on the Big Island of Hawaii, near Waa-Waa, while Merlin and I had taken an excursion to find native plants for our garden, I made the proposal to Merlin. I still recall how Merlin nearly fainted upon hearing it. He turned pale white. He was so shocked that he didn't know what to do. Eventually he declined our offer. He wasn't ready to commit.

Oddly, I wasn't shocked but rather delighted, because now I felt I was truly free. It had taken courage for Don and me to face our worst fear, to surrender to letting go of each other and be willing to allow a greater plan to take over. Instead, we were rewarded with a gift of freedom and our love-life was given back to us.

However, despite all my insights into the impossibility of our connection, and even with the decline of my latest offer, both Merlin and I were plagued with a recurring feeling that we had taken the wrong path for the next few years. Merlin couldn't say yes because his emotional pattern wouldn't let him and I didn't really want to let go of Don. But there was a calling from our souls that didn't let us go either.

Over and over Merlin and I searched out seers and therapists to help us. Again and again Merlin was told that I was his destiny. When I tried to go into my deep subconscious I found the same answer. He and I were necessary to each other's enlightenment.

During one seminar in Hawaii I had another profound insight. Don and I were holding a teacher training seminar for the *Living From Vision* course in which seven participants came from Singapore. They were teachers in training, taking turns at presenting the LFV course. I got to sit in on their practice session as a student. Several of them have since proven to be outstanding teachers in Singapore, reaching the corporate world and at-risk teens.

During one of their sessions I had very profound insights regarding my dynamics with Merlin.

Having closed my eyes, I had chosen to preview a life where I left Merlin behind and just dedicated myself to my own enlightenment.

Knowingly, I entered through a triangular shape into the next dimension as part of my own ascension. As I traversed the tunnel and entered into light, I was greeted by a small group of masters on the other side. They instantly let me know that I had failed in my life's purpose. Further back, behind this group of my life advisors, I saw Merlin. He shone in his most glorious colors and his true nature was revealed: he was an ascended master with a large following.

The advisors greeted me and told me in no uncertain terms that I had been sent to help Merlin at a time when he was down. My selfish choice to leave him behind in order to follow my own ascension was not rewarded at the end of my life. Rather than gaining greater enlightenment, it had diminished the scope of my work on the other side.

Needless to say I quickly back-paddled from this imaginary future life. I didn't want enlightenment at such a high price. By choosing to follow my own evolution I had indeed missed my own advancement.

Instead I returned to my choice point back in time and imagined myself available to help Merlin. Is this what a Bodhisattva feels? Merlin appeared splattered on the ground like a dark spot to my mind's eye, and he certainly needed help at that point in his life.

I was ready to help, and my vision unfolded into the most beautiful solution. Merlin and I were starting to teach together as we roamed the Earth, planting seeds of awakening. When it came time to exit this lifetime and enter the life beyond physical form, we were both greeted by a large group of people on the other side, all of whom had been ignited by our contribution to their lives. We reached our promised solution together.

The higher choice was about assisting Merlin to stay connected with the light, instead of being married or having children with him.

The true solution was about helping each other become masters and spreading the light together unto many others. Maybe we, or I, had personalized our attraction too much and forgotten the bigger picture. But we had both seen the vision and had been told by others that we needed to produce an offspring together.

I was glad that I had the chance to preview this second choice in my imagery exploration. Naturally this insight was a turning point in my attempts to run away from Merlin. From then on I committed to Merlin in a deeper way, more as a saintly friend, still in love, still suffering as a woman in my heart but now seeing a bigger picture.

Don't we all have times in our many lives when we need support? And wouldn't it be wonderful if a friend stuck it out with us? That is what I was willing to do.

In the many years that followed there were more trips Merlin and I took together. We took another trip to Australia to Ayers Rock, also called Uluru, sacred to all Australian Aborigines. It had been the wettest year to date and we were trying to go on a camel trek and a jeep safari, and sleep outdoors on sand dunes. Upon our arrival we were told that things might change due to inclement weather and mud everywhere. Merlin and I looked at each other with a knowing look. When we got into the jeep we went to work. We both knew about shifting reality. We had talked to the clouds before and now the time for good weather was really needed. By the end of the long drive from Alice Springs to our destination near Uluru rock, we were told that a miracle had happened. The weather had turned. One of our jeep companions had sensed something was different. He smiled as we were under vast blue skies and said, "When angels travel!" as he looked at Merlin and I, nodding up to the sky.

Months of rain turned into the clearest three weeks they had had all year. We were able to hike in summery clothes and sleep on the sand under clear skies and have the kind of vacation we had hoped for. Merlin and I knew how to make shifts in the time-space matrix together.

For the next three weeks we went on camel and jeep treks through the red rocks of the interior of Australia. Magic accompanied us wherever we went. The night before Merlin's birthday we slept in a dried out sandy riverbed. Falling asleep next to Merlin I had a vision of an old Aborigine woman greeting me. As I lay under the previous night skies, visions of dotted paintings had filled my mind but this was the only vision in which a real person appeared. An old woman greeted me and said, "Tomorrow I will take you to the *Valley of the Rainbows!*" I loved my vision and went to sleep. The next morning our guide announced that we were going to the *Valley of the Rainbow*. He used those identical words.

"Did I actually have an encounter in the inner dimensions that was real?" I wondered. We really did go to the Valley of the Rainbow, a flat area that filled with water in rainy seasons and made it look like a huge lake in the middle of the desert. The colors, the sand, rocks, sunsets and the stars were magical. Don didn't like to rough it like this, preferring more romantic, luxurious travel. This however was exactly Merlin's style of traveling. Perhaps my mother had been right when she told me to have different friends for all the different parts of myself.

A few years later Merlin accompanied me on a trip to Egypt. I had taken a German seminar group there. It was at a time when people looked down upon Americans because they had started waging war with the Middle East. Don didn't want to go. We were a group of only Germans but if Don had come along as an American, the government would have sent a convoy of military personnel with our group to watch over him. Don sent Merlin with me instead of coming himself. And Merlin did watch over me.

We were totally unromantic on that trip. We had passed that point by then.

Merlin and I had met in Mexico on Equinox 1999 at the Pyramid of Kukulkn, Chichen Itza on the Yucatan Peninsula during the Prophet's Conference where I was speaking. It seemed that as time went on we found ourselves at all the major energy spots on planet Earth: we have been on five continents and eight countries and numerous sacred sites together.

Never in my life have I had so many past life visions as with Merlin. My dreams were in full Technicolor. In one of my past life dreams where Merlin and I sang as opera-singers, it was so clear and powerful that I was awakened by the immensity we felt in the union of our voices.

In another vision, Merlin had been tortured for wanting me as his wife. I was lower in rank to him and was killed. He survived the torture and was forced to marry a woman of his standing. Loveless and broken-hearted he had to witness my death. Now he freaked out whenever he got close to deep personal love and commitment. Commitment had left a sour feeling in his heart. But no matter how many past lives I worked through, it didn't change our predicament.

During one six month period, while Merlin and I were desperately trying to separate our bonds, I received calls from several frantic husbands. They had all heard of his and my connection. Meanwhile their own wives had fallen for Merlin and they didn't know what to do about it so they turned to me for advice. I told them to hold onto their relationship and not get too worried about Merlin as a Casanova. Merlin didn't really want those women even if they were willing to give up house and children to be with him. Merlin was innocent in his heart. He was just very willing to be open and felt more like the Little Prince.

I was giving counsel to other men when in my heart I was still attached to Merlin myself. I knew all too well how strong his attraction was to women. His old lovers were writing me too, hoping to hear a few morsels of news about him.

Merlin meanwhile got more and more confused. He would look deeply into women's eyes and didn't know what he was doing wrong. From his perspective he just opened his soul to them, rising in his spirit to meet them. In his healing sessions, miracles happened. Bones healed, injected insulin was no longer needed and glasses became unnecessary.

But as far as the love that women felt, it was one-sided. Merlin loved them in a universal way but in the mind, heart and body of those women, his universal love started a different kind of fire. When they came crawling into his bed, he didn't want them. In his mind he was an innocent angel that was just willing to help those impoverished women have some light and love. He wanted to give them an experience of divine presence. What he didn't know was that mortal women didn't know how sweet the succor of divine presence can feel and how it made them feel attached to him.

Whether he was acting as a modern Krishna or a modern Casanova, one thing was for sure: his magnetism was very strong to many women but he didn't want them as earthly lovers. He had a deep wish now to find his true and right love!

Just shortly before we met, he sent a prayer to the universe that he wanted to learn how to love. Then we met. Was I really just a Dakini, a Heaven-dancer that carried the souls of my beloveds to Heaven? When my job was done did they then go on with their lives?

Was I lucky to have a husband who had accepted the deeper nature of his wife! I had read books about Buddhist women who had functioned as Dakinis and Yoginis and also lived in marital arrangements while they did their work at the same time.

I didn't really want to accept such a fate. But maybe it was true. I have met other women who have felt the same. Maybe our concepts are too narrow in this society. We may need to make space for our more mythical lives, which we may live side by side with our earthly, normal lives.

Wherever Merlin had lived previously, he left his things behind in storage, planning to return some day. Women were still waiting for him years later. But now it was my turn and I had his things stored in my house.

Toward the early winter of 2003 I finally told Merlin that he had to pick up his belongings or else I would throw his things out the door. I needed a clear cut ending. We had been caught between being masters for and with each other and being lovers, even if we were not sexual together anymore. It was not easy to be "just friends."

I had emotional strings with Merlin that were hard to let go of. No matter how much we tried to let go of each other, we had a difficult time. We wanted to keep our hearts open but it made the letting- go process very difficult. We talked for hours on the phone every week about ethical issues and all the subtle nuances of life. He was the only one, other than Don, that could endure such long conversations, diving into the smallest of details.

After many years I realized that rising into heaven together kept our human bonds alive. That is when I decided to stop doing that. Because every time we did, we would be drawn to remember who we really were and what we really felt in our hearts.

Sad as it seemed, Merlin wanted to learn to be human. Instead of going up, he wanted to come down. I had to respect that. Maybe that was indeed what he needed most for his evolution. It was just not the same direction I was going.

In the end we accepted that if he could not say YES in his heart, no matter how much I wanted to help him, I had to understand and accept that as a NO and act accordingly. It was a hard choice for both of us.

Eventually I knew I had to let go. But how was I to keep my commitment to his soul?

Re-Dreaming Reality

Since I had found the will to really let go of Merlin I had given him a dead-line of January 1st, 2003 to either come to Hawaii and pick his things up, or else have them thrown out. Yet I was not sure how to keep my promise to help his soul's evolution to mastery. I was willing to fulfill whatever that promise was, but I didn't how to express it, if Merlin kept pulling away.

Don and I had been spending our winters in Hawaii and it was a few days before New Years. As usual I had awoken from the loud chirping of the many birds that took sunrise as a cause to sing to their hearts content. Pulled by the light, I went to sit on the wooden bench on our balcony. This was my personal sacred space for my daily meditations and reading. Many times I had looked down from this high perch into our garden, and gazed at the trees in wonder and awe.

The water-droplets on the leaves were reflecting the sunshine as the sun rose above the forest's crown today. The sound of the birds and the sunlight gave me the feeling of truly being in another world.

In silence I sat in meditation and stretched into the vast space of God-consciousness. I rose to an exceedingly high space, a very special one. I was not able to reach that high every day. If I let some days slip and stopped meditating, I found myself needing to clean my emotional house and I did not get as high as previous days. Yet whenever I managed to meditate nearly every day for one to two hours, I was rewarded with amazingly high states and visions. In my quest for an answer I remembered that, in order to manifest what I wanted, I needed to live in the feeling / image of my future fulfilled.

Today I was so clear that I was willing to manifest my soul's commitment to Merlin, but at a higher level. I was ready for a miracle. Yet I also knew that if I was to meet Merlin in a more evolved form, I needed to let go of my expectation as to how that could manifest.

There were many ways this miracle could show up: Merlin could call and tell me that he had just woken up from years of sleep and was willing to be fully awake. Or maybe his soul had several bodies on this Earth and each human expression of his might be a fractal of his larger over-soul? Maybe one of his forms was a super-evolved fractal that I hadn't met so far. If so, I was willing to shift into that universe now and meet him again, to have another chance at our interaction at a higher octave. But I had to let go of thinking in linear terms.

Until now I had gotten stuck on thinking it had to be Merlin that was fulfilling my dreams. Yet Merlin could only go so far with me despite our heart's deep connection. I could feel our soul's longing to fulfill a larger purpose but we just couldn't fulfill this wish in this human story as we had experienced it so far. I was very willing to commit to the fulfillment of our soul's call, yet I could no longer go on with a being that was constantly pulling away. So how could I go on?

In my meditation I sent a message to the universe from the depth of my heart: "IF indeed there is a commitment to the soul of Merlin, I am very willing to keep it, but please send me a version of him where it is possible to keep my commitment. Please send me the essence of Merlin in a more advanced form, so that I can fulfill that commitment." I was clear in my request, and I believed it could be possible.

In a flash of illumination I entered the place of experiencing my wish fully manifested. In a moment of brilliance I was embraced by a soul that shone brightly together with me, as my wish fulfilled. If I could not change destiny fully, at least I wanted it easier.

Many personal choices in our lives can be changed, but there are forces and fields beyond our personal grasp that still affect our lives. The force fields "above us" so to speak, influence us. These fields, dimensions that are higher than our personal reach are the ones that we experience as destiny. The force fields "below us," which are well within our field of influence, are the playgrounds of our freewill. As we evolve, we advance from that which we call destiny and transform destiny into freewill.

Jesus was a miracle worker who had access to greater fields, largely because he believed so strongly in the power of God. Actually he had identified himself with God, quoted as saying: "The Father (God) and I are one." This gave him dominion over large areas of creation.

How we handle any given lessons depends on how mature we are, which shapes the outcome. Nothing is set in stone. If we manage to rise high enough in our states of awareness, if we truly understand the lessons, we rise beyond the level we call our destiny. We graduate a step closer to the Source. There will always be layers beyond our reach, which we call destiny, as well as layers that are below us, which are the fields we can influence.

Today in my meditation I had risen high enough to ask for a lighter version of my karma as I was asking to shift my destiny up a notch. I knew today was very potent, just a few days from New Year. Merlin didn't come to Hawaii to pick up his things and I was set to throw them out.

On the forth of January, just past the New Year deadline that I had given Merlin to gather his belongings, Don and I wanted to take a hike in the Volcano National Park on the Big Island of Hawaii. It was to be our New Year's walk, high up on the mountain ridge.

It was a sunny day, but up so high on the mountain it was cold, so we got dressed like Eskimos. We had chosen to walk the Iniki Trail, a crater-rim walk that would guide us along the edge of the volcano, down into the once active cauldron. The birds were singing, ancient ferns unfurled their stems and Ohia trees shaded our path along the edge of the crater.

It was a very narrow path and Don walked behind me. I was in a state of reverie when suddenly a radiant angel walked around the bend toward us. From a distance I could not tell if it was a man or a woman. His long blond hair made him look like he could be either. He walked in still, deep meditation, his hands in a position of blessing, his eyes turned inward. My breath stopped when he passed me and I gasped. Instantly I was transported into Heaven. I knew that he was a superluminal being and that we knew each other. As he passed I turned to look at him again and wanted to run back and speak to him. An angel had just walked by me.

Don laughed and said that he had never, ever heard my breath being taken away like this. But though the moment was short, I was transported into a heightened state of awareness, now able to see the world around me in an even more glowing radiance. Both Don and I felt like the heavens had opened and something very special had happened. The rest of the day I spent hoping the blond angel would cross our path again, and his every nuance was etched into my memory.

The next day was a Sunday and as we usually did, Don and I went to a dolphin beach, only minutes away from our home. A colorful mix of hippies, Rastafarians, tourists and dolphin lovers had joined in on this Sunday event. A drumming circle was in full bloom, sending rhythmic songs into the air. Dancers were waving in the soft breeze and friends met heart to heart everywhere.

We love to connect with our tribal pod on Hawaii. Everyone was very open, loving, and shared their hearts honestly. A couple that was sitting just a little further away from our spot on the beach had been watching me for a while. I had noticed them speaking German. When the man called me over to speak with them, I came over willingly, hoping I could be of help.

But I was not prepared for their sudden offer. He asked me rather quickly if I was open to join them in a sexual threesome! They had seen me naked, since we were at a clothing-optional beach and both had liked the look of my body and how I moved. I thank them, but bowed out politely.

Quickly, I begged Don to leave the beach. I did not want to be on display, a walking piece of meat on the beach. We were here to share our hearts, and being naked was part of being natural. Though flattering as this invitation was, I wanted to leave quickly.

No sooner did we reach the other end of the beach, just steps away from the path up the cliff, did we see our good looking friend Star. A few months earlier Don had warned me not to be too open to this particular male that looked like the most handsome mix of angel and pirate alive. Long dark hair, muscular body, deeply engaged in the spiritual worlds and eyes so soft and warm that any woman would have melted, Don sensed too much testosterone. I honor his perspectives and stayed within a good distance from this beautiful soul. I had no desire for him as a man. That is not how I operate, but Don still had to have his say, and I honored it.

Star was standing tall next to the blond angel we had seen on our volcano hike the previous day! Could it be true? I tugged on Don's shoulder, no longer in a hurry to leave and steered straight over to them. Both were engaged in spiritual conversation. I found out they were best friends and were happy to see us. Star introduced us to Amoraea.

While everyone was talking, I opened my telepathic mind. Reaching up higher, I tried to sense if my angel indeed could sense me in the higher spaces. As we stood next to each other, talking in the group, I could tell how Amoraea was keeping his multi-dimensional channels open with me. This much was clear: I liked him instantly and felt like we had known each other forever. Did it help that he was very similar looking to Merlin?

Later, when we had a moment to ourselves, he introduced himself and told me that he was into the White Lotus Tantra, the Tantra that was beyond the body, starting at the crown chakra, only engaging the highest form of union.

I could see that he was not the testosterone-rich man like his best friend by the name of Star, and Don gave me totally green lights to commune with this angel. We arranged for him to visit us a few days later. I loved living on Hawaii! Surprises never end.

The day for Amoraea's visit had arrived. And a new twist of fate beckoned me to reconsider the solidity of our Earthly life.

A few hours before Amoraea came to visit, Merlin had called and told me that he had been withholding information from me the day before.

During a conversation on the phone just a day earlier I had asked him if he was not telling me something. I just had that feeling. He had denied it and I told him, going on intuition alone, that lies are like nails in the coffin of a friendship. I guess that scared him so much that he wanted to come clean and tell me his truths: He had actually been getting closer to another female. He feared I would disconnect from him, if he told me that there was another woman. Since he had not really ever wanted me to leave, although he never wanted me completely either, he didn't want to tell me. Hearing that he was getting closer to another woman was the magic potion that gave my emotional body the fuel to let go of him even more.

I closed my eyes and let my prayer for a transformation of Merlin be heard by the heavens.

Four hours after that fated phone conversation and after my prayer to have Merlin's soul manifest in a higher vibrational form, Amoraea arrived at our house.

Since our garden was very unusual, designed along Permaculture principles, and since a tour of our grounds would give me a few moments of privacy with Amoraea, I offered to show him around our garden. There were the many fruit trees and nitrogen fixing plants that helped bring needed nutrients to the surface, and that had helped transform this barren lava-land into a tropical jungle within just a few years.

Merlin had done miracles in countless hours of working in the garden, when he was house-sitting some time ago. Bottle brush flowers in reds and pinks hung like a carpet overhead as we walked through the garden. Some trees had ripe papayas for us to pick and Don had just hung a rack of bananas to ripen near the stairway. As we walked from our hydroponic greenhouse back to the main house, Amoraea slowly turned to me and said, "I feel like I have lived here already."

I smiled, held my breath and almost said, "You have indeed! Just in another body!" But I didn't say anything. Could it be that my prayer had been heard? Or was I just projecting?

We went upstairs to greet Don and decided to have a meal together. The moment he brought his back-pack and unpacked his little bags of herbs, salts and his very own wooden spoon, I was certain. Merlin had always carried with him the identical arsenal of back-pack, spices and his wooden spoon. Both men were not only look-a-likes but had the same manners. Not only did he seem to remember to have lived at our place but he also wooed my soul in the same manner.

We cooked well together, dancing in the kitchen around each other and I felt like I was back in time. How could I manifest such similar beings into my life?

While waiting for some of the food to cook, I played my harp and Amoraea sat on the Bali-couch, in rapture. Hardly ever did anyone pay attention that deeply, listening with their entire soul to my music, except for Don. He was letting his entire heart and mind be taken into rapture. His sensitivity and the honor he bestowed my music was capturing my heart. This opened the doors for me to enter divine and subtle worlds, as only few people ever have.

Usually we engage with others in normal social behaviors. Only in the silence of our sacred space or in rare moments of deep surrender do we let our most precious pearl enter this earthly dimension. Rarely do we reveal ourselves in such vulnerability in the company of others. It appears easier to let that part of us come out when we fall in Love, before we again build the walls of self-protection.

We also get ignited at the presence of grand musical poetry or inspiring acts we may witness. But here was Amoraea, letting himself enter a state of bliss right in front of me. After playing my harp I put on music by Patrick Bernard and we started to move to this divine music in silent reverie. We didn't quite dance together, but there was a sphere in our movements that built a bubble of heaven around us. At a crucial moment when the music seemed to carry the most silence, rising into a sudden revelation, we both looked at each other in perfect harmonic rhythm and deeply glanced into each other's souls, and our souls locked on.

Amoraea had not known me before, but I knew already how much I would mean to him in time to come. He didn't know it yet. And it became clear to me during our first day together that my prayer had been heard.

It was awkward and I felt like I was like being caught in-between time.

I was literally walking in two worlds, one in which I continued a saga of Merlin and yet starting a fresh friendship with a human that didn't have any clue what he had walked into.

Dinner was ready and we called Don upstairs to join us. Don and I gave space to each other to have encounters of our souls with others. We were not looking for other mates, since had we been so very blessed with each other. That was clear to anyone who saw us. But we realized that our souls needed other encounters as well in order to grow. To live in Heaven on Earth we had to get used to the notion that deep encounters with others was, though maybe not the norm yet, very deeply enlivening and necessary to our core and our soul's growth.

Imagine a group of angels standing together and one of them saying: "Don't look at this angel. He/she is mine?" We would laugh at such a thought.

Don and I told each other of every nuance we felt and experienced with others. There were no secrets. And together we decided who was working for us and who wasn't. Some people just jibed better with the chemistry of both of us. Others didn't.

Don and I were most important to each other. Secrets didn't exist and we knew that the trust we had needed was nurtured by honesty. Earlier on, in our time together, Don had tried to hide some things from me. It was hard for him in the beginning to tell all. He thought he could hide his sexual attractions, his attempts at stealing some sexy moments. But I could see and read what was going on too well, and though I didn't know if I was right at first, I was either told by others, or the thoughts of others were so loud that I could hear them telling me the stories, which then came to light.

Don's karma didn't allow for secrets. He was too far along the path of evolution. Lies only work when we still believe in a universe with walls. But once we claim to live in a flexible universe in which we are conscious co-creators, lies fly in our face. The finer we vibrate, the faster they come flying back. I personally just couldn't stand to keep any secrets, small as they were, so I had to talk.

We certainly went through a growth-curve of learning that absolute honesty was the basis for deep intimacy. If our partner doesn't like whatever we are feeling or doing, then we need to give them the option of leaving, or change our behavior voluntarily.

For many years we experimented with what happens when we suppress our many different human drives. Either biologically driven feelings, whether or not we actually lived them or not, or our soul driven needs of entering the space of Allness with many others, regardless of sex, age, or looks, these needs all really wanted to be heard, addressed and lived whenever possible. But honest sharing was the number one baseline upon which we were able to build our love.

Most people want to have their mate entirely to themselves, but they themselves couldn't live up to never looking at anyone else. Our friendships are deep gifts to each other. When we find a master, an angel, we do well to keep their company.

Amoraea was such a master. But I could tell by the way we interacted that though he was obviously not a man of the body, he was a man of energy. He and I had a tie that was more that just masterful friends. I marvel at how I can be "just friends" with some men and yet I had no illusions of just being friends with Amoraea. But how would we work out the equation that Merlin and I had not been able to?

Night came and we asked Amoraea to stay downstairs in our guest room, which was my sacred meditation room. He was certainly the angel I would want to bless my room. We briefly went downstairs to the room before saying "Good Night." The room was just a simple screened-in room open to the outdoors. The many trees, flowering bushes, vines and the sounds of the night surrounded us magically.

We sat down on the floor, on my fur as I lit some candles and incense and we started to look into each other's eyes. Amoraea reached out to hold my hands. After a short while sitting like this, he pulled a little bottle of sparkling stardust out. Gently he placed this glitter on his right index finger and asked me to close my eyes. In a deeply reverent state he moved his hands and I suddenly felt his light touch land on my forehead, right were my third eye is. He anointed me. I sighed, deeply receptive to his touch, his energy now flowing into a most sensitive part of me. He was masterful at this. He knew who he was, what he could do and I was opening to him.

Gently, I opened my eyes and we gazed at each other. As much as I may have wanted to see him just as a friend, he was the continuation of Merlin indeed. Being much less sexual and more refined, he was a master of seeing the inner dimensions. "He is a real match for me," I thought.

As we sat in a silent meditation I was pulled into the most spectacular visions I had ever seen. It was as if I had entered a Technicolor studio, entering vast spheres of crystal worlds as exalted vibrations embraced me. We were rising within these palatial worlds, on an upward movement on a column of light. Spectacular visions of light-grids that surrounded the earth and stretched further into the cosmos filled my mind. Not only was I seeing these states, but as happens with true ascension, I was instantaneously pulled into hyper-dimensional space. Intertwined in the vision was the experience of BEING such a space. One becomes at once the entire form of light, where every movement has meaning and one becomes the entire wisdom enfolded within its space on such journeys within.

Just like grand music has the ability to take us on a journey and evoke in us entire states of grandeur, so can light take hold of us and we become a being whose body is simultaneously many dimensions at once. It has a magnitude of consciousness that impresses itself on our feeling-body and mind that is beyond any words.

Becoming the flame of God is a feeling that can be felt. But it is not just a feeling, it is a becoming that words can't express. It inspires awe in us, but somewhere we all know such states in ourselves. Somewhere in the far recesses of our soul we have such a memory. And sometimes by just having a person in front of us who himself goes into such states, or hearing a person tell us a few words about this state, will trigger the remembering that is deep within all of us. Such states are inherent in our core. We know such things exist or can exist. But they are elusive and it is hard to bring them to total recall even within minutes of being in them.

As we were ignited from our meeting, I opened my core to Amoraea and we met in a most sublime way. It felt like he was a flame of light that enfolded my flame of consciousness. It was spiritually erotic but in a most sublime way. Not calling on sexuality in its most physical form, but igniting the dance of our cores nevertheless had the same inherent pattern of desire for union, and a vision of the spiral dance came to me. We became a most radiant version of a sparkling DNA spiral together, ascending to God.

I knew my task was to rise up in the center column of light and not get lost in the beauty of the spheres. I kept ascending, scaling up the ladder of frequencies, until we reached the apex, the zero-point, the alpha and omega point of the central shaft in the DNA-looking spiral. I pulled and pulled and allowed our stars of awareness that I could barely differentiate any longer to fully overlap and merge into one singular event. The instant we landed within each other as one singularity, we popped into a silent, all pervasive brightness and stillness, a state that feels like it is All-that-is.

It was a bit challenging to maintain and stabilize our state here. It appears to me that this state of Allness is a state that is much like the center of a black hole. As the black hole becomes the white hole, the Big Bang ensues, desiring to birth again into form just at the very moment life had reached the Zero-point.

We certainly had a spiritual chemistry of the like I had hardly ever met. No wonder the Buddhists called the path of true Tantra the fast path to enlightenment. Amoraea had indeed introduced himself as a being of the path of the White Lotus Tantra. And he was!

Speechless, I eventually opened my eyes, waiting for him to open his. I was offering him the pearl of my soul. It seemed to be a bit soon and maybe that was too quick. But I was here and willing, building upon a past experience with a similar matrix that had refused to take the journey home. What baffled me the most was that when we went to the highest point of connection, he felt the same as Merlin had in his innermost core essence, in his soul. Maybe indeed Merlin and Amoraea were of the same soul-matrix?

After coming back to our senses, we told each other in a few words about what we had experienced. Both of us had a very similar vision.

Both of us were baffled. We gave each other a soft, gentle and very non-sexual hug, said "Good Night" and I went upstairs.

It was a bit quick to change from going into such high spaces in meditation to trying to be with Don. But he could see where I had been and smiled at me and we both met in our star of soul-light. I feel asleep quickly in Don's arms, just to be awakened in the middle of the night by an intense inner light surge.

Hyperdimensional Contact

In a half-sleep I felt myself being lifted into a surging light-storm.

A buzzing energy entered my entire body and Amoraea's energy was arcing into me from what appeared to be a hyper-dimensional space.

It's hard to say where he was, but since I was in bed, it seemed to me that he was floating in a hyperspace above me. This was not the sort of astral apparitions I had seen before. In the past I had had encounters at night, where I would meet people walking into my bedroom, whom I either was to meet in the future, or who projected their energy to me. Those apparitions had a more astral-human touch to them and they looked more physically real. Amoraea now, was also very real, but since our contact was at a higher frequency he wasn't humanly recognizable.

I felt like a supercharged current of energy was blitzing into my body and heart and as if this bolt of lightning was entering the core of my soul. It was extremely energizing and the last time I had felt such intensity was with dolphins one night while Don and I were camping on Kauai, in an amphitheater near the beach. In a dream a dolphin had touched my right toe with his nose which sent an electric current up my spine and out my crown chakra. This electrifying encounter with Amoraea had a similar quality.

A few years later I was to have that kind of experience while I was dreaming of the Dalai Lama, who at the time was teaching at the Kalachakra teachings in Amravati in 2006. A friend of mine reporting on that event had possibly set up this link. In my dream His Holiness the Dalai Lama kissed my crown chakra and I experienced an explosion at the top of my head. The charge I felt was enormous – like getting an initiation. Oddly enough it happened twice in the same night. The second administration came from His Holiness the Karmapa. The same kiss, the same explosion. That was in January 2006.

Back in January 2003 when Amoraea's surge entered me, the electrification of my chakras felt like an initiation type of energy as well. We merged in a heightened state of extraordinary reality in my dream-body.

It is so hard to describe higher dimensional experiences where we no longer experience things linearly. We start to experience simultaneous states, knowing space, able to feel and interact with time-space from a much larger perspective, able to know and feel ourselves in such a complex form, that it cannot be captured in words. As we enter more refined states we also experience more bliss and an all pervasive presence. This universe is made up of so many layers of dimensions, as well as the Zero-point or center of Isness.

Sharing my energy with Amoraea was more real than any human connection could produce in the three dimensional world. Even in my meditation experience I had never had such intensity. It was due to the fact that in my dream-body I had let go of all boundaries, and more of the information was allowed to enter my conscious mind, which otherwise would be censored by my five-sense oriented cognitive mind. It has been postulated that our brain has 90% more capacity than what we currently use. Well, until we include our multi-dimensional activities as part of "reality" we may not spend much time engaging that part of our mind.

If we start to include realities that are beyond our five senses, such as telepathy and existence and interaction in higher dimensions, which includes the ability to direct and redirect space-time, we will start to exercise the neurological pathways that need to be practiced in order to be noticed by our conscious mind. And the more we do so, the more we are able to live in a grander universe.

I had opened myself to Amoraea before going to sleep during our meditation and I was now experiencing the mix of our spiritual and psychic energies merging. It was extraordinary! Going in and out of sleepy awareness and meeting in a heightened dimension of an intense field of light continued for half an hour or longer. But our merging was not sexual, and he was sound asleep, downstairs, while I slept in bed next to Don.

Amoraea was a very luminous being; that much I could tell. He was dedicated to Love, to God and his spiritual practices. Our meeting was not based on sexual attraction; instead it was light-filled and focused on igniting each others' higher state of consciousness. As we connected, we exchanged our library files, ignited each other to higher spaces and it truly felt like we were being initiated in our cosmic bodies, which I believe was the real reason why we met. In a larger picture, what we gift each other with is enlightenment, which is the basis of all our future relationships.

At the same time as Amoraea and I had a very spiritual connection, we had a special heart to heart connection, which made it different than just meeting as spirits.

The effect our heart connection had on my heart and body was amazingly exhilarating. Not only did I explode in states above my crown chakra, I could also feel the pulsation in my heart reaching heights similar to a physical orgasm. Electric charges arced between us, which I was to experience more of in our future.

The next morning he was equally astounded as he had been aware of our meeting as well and felt that we had an amazing synergy. In the early morning sun we did some yoga together. Don and I did yoga daily and it was amazing to me that such soft movements were able to provide my body with such strength.

After finishing doing yoga, we all made breakfast together. Sitting at the table, the three of us held hands together and raised our energy levels to meet in union. As I held both Don and Amoraea's hands, I imagined that we all rose up in frequency and merged into a single star. We squeezed our hands at the end, to let each other know we were done. That is a prayer and blessing ritual we do with all our friends whenever we got together to share a meal. This was the real food for our souls. As we gazed at each other for a few silent moments before starting to eat we lingered in the reverent vibration and breathed a sigh of joy! "How great, to be in the company of masters!" Amoraea whispered. My wish for a Shangri-La pod was manifesting!

Amoraea announced that he was interested in house-sitting for us while we were gone on our tours, if we needed his help. We did indeed always need someone to house-sit for us, but Don was not sure that this New Age angel would have the muscles to deal with garden work required, or if he was very reliable. "We have just met him," Don reminded me.

But I batted my eyes and Don eventually agreed. He trusted my instincts. As we would find out later, we were richly rewarded.

Not only did all three of us share similar energies, lifestyles and ways of experiencing inner dimensions, Amoraea was also a musician! The match could not have been better. If the universe had been serious about sending me a lighter version of Merlin, it had succeeded.

Different from my experience with Merlin, Amoraea and I didn't have the rich interplay of sexual hormones. It made it easier on all of us and it didn't cause any uproar or hurt feelings in Don either. Don was very willing to help Amoraea in whatever ways he could and felt like he was mentoring his own past incarnation.

After staying one day with us, Amoraea left to see other friends on the island and we were planning on seeing each other again soon, before we had to leave on our seminar tour. But as soon as he had left I couldn't feel him anymore. It was as if the immense moments of energy, meditation, visions and developing closeness had vanished in an instant. I took note of it. It was as if I could no longer feel the bond with him at a distance. Almost as if the memories were dependant on me entering such high states to be able to recall the effect and I could not do that when I was in more normal states. This is what is called *state dependant memory*.

We did not share the kind of glue that pure sexual attraction offers and the usual daydreaming that is connected with romantic attraction never captured my mind. Though we had shared intense moments of closeness, we didn't get attached to each other.

A week later Don and I were planning to meet Amoraea and his friends at a Tibetan gathering, at Wood Valley, a Buddhist retreat on the Big Island of Hawaii, where some high Lamas from the Tibetan community were to create a Sand-Mandala. We arrived before the free lunch and were able to watch the making of a sand-mandala.

I stood in awe and silence next to a monk, as tears filled my throat. Every time I encountered a Tibetan I was moved to feel deep, deep sorrow and sadness. I felt deeply and irrationally connected to the monks. No longer did I want to be one of them, but I felt as one with them.

Suddenly I was drawn back into a room in a house which served as a temple, and turned out to be a library. I walked straight to a glass-bookcase, opened it, pulled out a book and read about the power of the path of Tibetan Buddhist Tantra. Buddhist Tantra spread out from Northern India, chiefly to Tibet, where it became known as the Vajrayana school of Buddhism.

The Kalachakra Tantra as taught by H. H., the Dalai Lama is sometimes said to be the non-dual Tantra. It appeared very late in the development of tantric Buddhism - in the mid-11th century.

The book described exactly the spiritual practices that Don and I had developed for ourselves and which I also had shared with Amoraea. In my own words I will summarize it in the following way: It described the ascension of two souls entering the state of union in spirit as being the fastest road to enlightenment.

I felt validation for all that I was doing, releasing doubts about myself. In a way I felt like I was doing what I remembered how to do from another life. We always take our past life lessons with us, not the money or the houses, but the wisdom. It feels important to me to practice deeper and deeper states of consciousness, since those are the only jewels that we take with us after death. Even artistic skills, though we usually take them with us too, are not always as prevalent in the next life as spiritual and emotional virtues. We are not here on Earth only to master artistic skills and take them from life to life, but are here mostly to discover our being as a co-creative energy in the entire spectrum of consciousness.

Although music came easily to me this life, it was a pale reflection of what I had done in some past lives. Perhaps in this life I was not destined to shine in that field, but in another. Maybe there were other fractals of my "self" living on Earth who lived that particular potential more masterfully while I expressed a different potential.

Amoraea never made it to Wood Valley and to the meeting of the monks that afternoon but we stayed in touch via the phone. He was soon planning to leave for Maui to visit friends there. One day we came up with the fanciful idea that I could fly to Maui so we could spend some time together. I had not seen Aimee for a while, who had been such a wonderful pod member at our house during the week of our seminar, way back when Merlin had come to stay on the Big Island of Hawaii.

After seeing her on Maui, I could spend a few days with Amoraea I reasoned. Don agreed, because it gave him a chance to visit with another dear woman friend of his, whom he had wanted to spend some time with as well.

Flight-tickets were cheap and I went to visit Aimee on Maui first.

We loved to share long "woman to woman talk while we sat in the garden in the sun, or made food together. We looked at each other deeply and for long moments, holding each other's hands. But whenever I would go very high, she would giggle and she felt like she was high enough, wanting to break the silence with her giggle. I honored that, never letting her know that she stopped us over and over again in our ascension. We all have levels of energy that we feel at home at, and our intimacy tolerance varies from person to person. Each person has a natural sense for how open they want to and can be. It is not good to push each other's limits too far, even if one could. There is no need to race to the top, since life is eternal, we can savor each and every step.

One moment as we sipped some tea, she told me how her husband of one year was making love to different women, withholding the information, or ignoring Aimee's requests for honoring the sacredness of their relationship. In a way he was telling her by his actions that she could not have him, even though they were married. Although she agreed in theory to his freedom, she was very hurt. She had become attached to him and her emotional pain was real. He had never surrendered to her, which was hard for her to take.

Had I not heard that story often enough!

I wondered why a man or woman bothered to stay in a relationship when they had a fear of surrender. I also realized that this same fear was facing us on our spiritual journey. We will have to face the fear to surrender completely to God, as we enter very high spiritual states. We need to let go our "self" and merge into the great One to get beyond the experience of separation. Nice as duality is, going beyond is what we are driven to do from deep within our core. But it is also the very thing we fear.

Without letting go of our identity and merging into oneness, we will sit on the outsides of the gates of Heaven, retaining a 'self' but never get to taste the succor of God.

Surrendering our heart and soul into the union of the two souls into God, opens the floodgates of heavenly love. It takes this divine triangle to make Love work. In surrendering to the trinity of two souls finding their pinnacle in the apex called God, we can open our hearts and soul and transcend our human limits. We are guided by a force larger than ourselves and in essence, as we ignite this new space of "us," we become much larger than the sum of the two combined.

Additionally we learn to transcend our self-centered nature. In deep love we give relentlessly of our selves. We can fully entrust ourselves into a union in which both parties will give their utmost best. We don't need to look back, cover our backs or wonder if our partner has taken on a new dyad already! When both partners give themselves fully to each other, serving together as the larger One, amazing creative potential is released and we experience divine love. But when one or both sit on the fence then one or the other starts measuring, making sure neither gives nor takes too much. Other telltale signs appear: One or the other starts feeling squeezed in, needing "space" more and more often and one has the feeling of needing to watch one's back.

Surrendering deeply to and with another person requires impeccable virtues on both sides. Both need to honor high principles of honesty, working for truth and not the ego, letting the higher truth win, instead of the greatest fear, or the loudest cry.

If one of the two partners is less developed, he or she will always give the feeling of pulling the higher one down, since falling is much easier than rising. Or the one that is less finely developed will always feel chided, or need to be reminded of higher standards more often. This wears both partners out. Both need to have reached similar levels of awareness, or at the least be very compatible in strengths, values, and virtues.

Honesty, selflessness, letting truth win instead of the ego, are all needed hallmarks of a relationship that allows for surrender. Each of the partners may have developed strength in different areas, but the general equilibrium needs to exist, before both partners can surrender their ego's guard.

Another reason for not wanting to surrender is the deeply imbedded drive for freedom, usually more dominant in men than in women. I believe it is based on biological traits. It ensures the spreading of the seed. But it is also a sign of our times as well as a general human dilemma.

At best we want to have our cake and eat it too. We want total surrender and oneness, and we want the freedom. Yet when we indeed surrender totally, we are set free because our mate knows we are truly with them.

Don and I had surrendered to God in our oneness together and because of it we were willing to give space to each other as well. We knew all too well that we cannot hold onto anything: not love, not enlightenment, not anything. I had to learn slowly but surely that I needed to allow change and the natural ebb and flow of intensity and when we worked with the natural rhythms of our human as well as celestial self, we had a greater chance to stay on a more stable course.

Don and I had learned to accept the facts, that life is the way it is. We also realized that we didn't want to make taboo that which was very human. We simply required of ourselves and each other that we were totally honest. In that light we let all our needs be seen, mutually approved, supported, and allowed into the light of consciousness. It was a hard learning curve. I wanted to cringe when I was telling Don about my spiritual intimacies with others. This was not done in normal society! My brain didn't like the feeling of baring my subconscious thoughts. But with time we got used to letting information that was delegated to the right side of the brain and our old mammalian brain, where most of our taboos are stored, enter our full awareness.

Societies the world over, in all of human recorded history have not managed to suppress, change, or eliminate the human needs, which at times contradict the societal norms. Such a challenge is normal, since we do need to suppress some needs in order to function together. In a partnership, or family, we do the same. We don't just do whatever we want, whenever we want. But to abandon the deeper needs or traits of our psyche altogether doesn't work either, as we all know.

I was on my way to visit with Amoraea, but as non-sexual as we were, we had a deep soul attraction. This could be felt as a more dangerous intrusion to a marriage than sex with another person.

But I didn't feel that I was at all lacking in my commitment to Don in either my sharing with Merlin or with Amoraea. Actually I felt like I had been so committed, that I tried to find a way to stay with Don. I missed Don already. Hardly being gone from home, I talked with him two times a day minimally. I knew that I had found my most amazing angel on Earth in Don. When Aimee listened in on Don and me speaking on the phone, she sighed. That is what she wanted.

I appreciated that Don allowed me to have deep and meaningful connections with others and that he didn't close his heart to me because of it. He had tried to keep me from connecting with others early on in our relationship, when we both were young. I was twenty-one when I met Don in 1983. It was now 20 years later, which had been a long time indeed and we had learned a lot together. To think that one person alone could stimulate all our areas of growth was a bit of a fairytale. And really we want to live in a community of like-minded beings, which for Don and I meant connecting as a muli-dimensional being with others.

In essence I feel that in connecting with others, whether in deep love or plain friendship, we ignite different vibrational states in each other. We stimulate different states of wisdom channels, becoming virtual keys to each other's cosmic library.

The other person's vast stores of experience, abilities and inherent dimensional designs are different from ours in some ways. By inter-braiding our consciousness, we cross-fertilize each other. In human terms we can stimulate each other. We might start on some exercise program, or do art together, explore a new author, or pass ideas back and forth. In multi-dimensional terms we are similarly stimulated by each other. Spiritual habits, inner movements of awareness and light patterns all can be absorbed into our auras, due to our shared energy. This can create a new stage of evolution in both people. We get ignited and inspired by our encounters.

On the other hand, when partners just take the space to connect intimately with others, without accord, it can have the effect of ripping the cocoon of the partnership.

Aimee was in tears from the pain she felt due to her partner's indiscretions. Her partner hadn't ask her permission to meet with other women; he just took what he wanted. In a way he was acting as if he was a separate individual that pretended to be in union. In a family, or in a relationship, we are actually creating a cocoon. The threads of light start flowing back and forth, intermingling and augmenting an energy cocoon. If we open ourselves to one another to share in this cocoon of light, we can build the energy; we can build trust and love-energy. The resulting energy of this cocoon becomes more than the sum of the two. If one doesn't want to be that tied down, it is better to be honest and not invoke a relationship that is more than just companionship.

How then can we enter deeper connections with others? In picking the people I connected with deeply, I had come to accept that Don had complete say over me. I have seen time and again that Don and I had to be in harmony about whom we connected to. We had the kind of freedom that we enjoyed, because we made all decisions together. Our union comes first. If there is a person that doesn't harmonize with both of us, we don't continue on that path.

What and who I carry in my energy field, in my mind and heart, is automatically also vibrating in Don's energy field, since we live in one cocoon. Of course our friend's thoughts and the energy they share with us bleed over into the cocoon of our marriage or main relationship. All additional friends need to feel a deep honor for the primary partnership or else it will bother the marriage to allow such a bond.

If Amoraea hadn't deeply honored Don as well and deeply honored our marriage union of our souls, then he would not have been allowed to share that deeply with me. But he did honor us and we didn't have that issue.

There have been women in Don's life who felt like they wanted my place, who tried to do things in secret, behind my back and without my consent, and that is when I got very jealous. However there were also women who wrote "Thank You" notes to me and sent gifts home with Don for me because they were so grateful to have been able to visit with him and share his masterful consciousness and be uplifted or healed by their encounter. Those were the women I liked. All our friends had to go through our mutual approval test.

Aimee's husband was by nature still not willing to surrender that deeply. I couldn't offer any consolation to her other than to say: "Why stay?" But she was too deeply attached to consider any other options for now. After a lot of heartache she did let go some time later.

Deep love is very willing to suffer and to give service. The beauty of love is the selflessness which we develop. In fly-by-night encounters we don't become selfless. We never really know the feeling of really loving another, or have a chance to learn to love someone for who they are, not for who we want them to be.

To be loved for who we are is an extraordinary experience. We are held in the cradle of a security that surpasses all other gifts of life. From this base, from this cradle we rise to face the world and encounter challenges with greater ease. When we are loved deeply, we start to glow and resources are released that are stunted when we are unsure of our love.

Don was the answer to my prayer. And I knew we had worked on a maturity that few people could sustain. I felt the grace of the universe touch us.

The day came when I left Aimee's house and was to meet Amoraea again. Since both of us were close to Pai'a, we decided to meet in the parking lot by Pai'a's health food store. How would he be with me alone, I wondered?

Magic on Maui

I stood in the parking lot of Pa'ia's Natural Food Store, waiting for Amoraea. Sunshine flooded through my closed eyes as I called upon all my guardian angels to arrange the most perfect alignment for our meeting. I wanted to surrender to whatever was in alignment with the highest. I didn't want to push for anything that was not of the highest design for all of us.

Like the wind Amoraea appeared in front of me as I opened my eyes at the perfect moment. Glowing like an angel, his long blond hair reflected the sunlight and gave him a golden halo. Speechless, I stood in front of him. We hugged deeply in reverent silence. God! How well I knew this way of communing! I knew it from my "other life" with Merlin.

With either Merlin or Amoraea, I seemed to be blessed with Don's permission and blessings. I had wanted to meet other men before, but nothing had worked out. Maybe Merlin and Amoraea shared the same over-soul and we had a destiny that forged paths through the thick of relationship taboos.

We had planned to explore the neighboring island Lanai for a great adventure of swimming with dolphins. We set out to drive north to Lahaina so we could catch a boat ride to Lanai. Yet as we drove north we were faced with a massive bank of gray clouds. We stopped at the side of the road to reconsider our path. The sky all around us was black and heavy rain seemed to be covering Lanai. We needed a new reality. Using our intuition to find better time-space coordinates, we quietly closed our eyes and tried to feel where we might find some sunshine.

How exactly does one do this? It takes practice to know how to enter a bigger space and encompass more time-space than the three-dimensional world which we inhabit with our physical body. As we practice shifting dimensions with our consciousness we learn to use our feeling body, or our imagination, as a tool for our brain to navigate in these dimensions. Images and feelings translate the subtler input that our consciousness receives from those finer dimensions. Feeling-images become more meaningful signals for our human mind to understand. Schools in the West do not usually train us in navigating the subtler dimensions.

Through the imagination and our inner feeling body, we can ride the elevator of our awareness to any dimension and commune with any reality at any given point. This allows us to interact with Creation, allowing us to become an active co-creative dreamer in a dreaming universe, or if you prefer, an awakened soul that consciously dances in the surf of time-space, adoring the beauty of the creator. Ultimately we want to use our ability to move our awareness in order to arrive at the zero point, and enter unity consciousness.

Amoraea and I needed to have earthly changes in the here and now. I rose to the level of the heavy clouds that were all around us. Suddenly something within my body or my imagery gave me the feeling that I really made contact with the consciousness of the clouds. This ability can be applied to anything whatsoever in life. To develop accurateness, it had taken time and practice, and learning from feedback. The internal symbolism we receive from our inter-dimensional communications, represented in the form of images or feelings, truly represent an interaction on another level of reality. We receive signals which our minds turns into imagery and feelings that help translate the inner experiences of the inner-dimensional terrain into symbols that we can understand.

It is very necessary to have feedback from the 3-D world so we don't get lost in stories of inner fantasies. We need the valuable feedback of our three-dimensional reality to develop accuracy. Later, when we have a good track record, we can be bolder and enter dominions that are harder to verify and still know that we are accurate. But feedback remains our best teacher at every stage of evolution.

As we connected with the weather pattern over Maui in our minds, Amoraea and I both got a message in the form of an image: To go back to where we came from to catch some sun!

We promptly got back into the car and turned around. Amoraea recalled a sacred spot he wanted to show me, which was just a little north of Pa'ia. We drove to a retreat-center, down a private road called: "SHANGRI- LA." I was moved to tears when I saw the sign. The word stirred my memory of another time, of another land, hidden deep within my memory of a thousand years ago. In Tibet it was said that there was a place called Shambala, known in the West as Shangri-La. It was said to be a place where beings of the highest order lived in surreal surroundings, in Heaven on Earth.

We walked silently past the retreat center. Like deer we slowly ventured deeper into the jungle, climbing down rocks, holding onto vines and feeling the magic of nature pulse through us. The sound of water rushing over rocks grew louder as we continued climbing down toward a hidden waterfall. We finally landed in a cove where a waterfall greeted us to our right and a vast vista opened to our left, overlooking a deep canyon.

The solid blue sky above us let golden sunlight stream down upon us. It was the only hole of blue sky we could see, but that was all we needed there in Shangri-La! Later we found out that Pa'ia had been deluged with a torrential downpour while we were sitting in bliss in the sun. However, the blue sky stayed with us all afternoon like a gift from the heavens. Hidden away, safe from the tourists' view, we took off our clothing to bathe in the sun. We sat on a rock on top of the waterfall, which gushed down 200 feet into a great canyon below us.

As I raised my energy I became even more aware of the breathtaking beauty that surrounded us. Everything took on a celestial glow. The majesty of the great flat rocks, the waterfall which cascaded down and fell far below us into the belly of the island, the sparkling light reflecting on the water, all gave me the feeling of being in Shangri-La, truly in Heaven on Earth!

After some time alone in silence we joined together in a picnic, feasting on avocados, tomatoes, rice bread, herbal salt, some sun dried olives and a date for desert. Food tastes so much better when eaten in silence and outside in nature.

As we came to the end of our picnic we started to gaze into each other's eyes. We became ever so still. Opening our core to one another, we slowly climbed in our subtle perception on ladders of light.

Etheric imagery enraptured me. Spires of light, columns of luminous color engulfed me, raised me, and beckoned me to greet Amoraea in his innermost temple. I opened the wings of my heart, allowing him to see the beauty of my soul. Together we rose on the currents of light ever higher, into less and less personal realms. Each dimension filled me with deep meaning – ecstasy.

My wings became the entire space of the cosmos and I took on the wisdom contained within this space. The space within my cosmic body then filled me with living information. Light became movement, an undulating dance of our light lines. Primordial galactic memories surfaced to carry us into a realm of promised futures. Galactic heights seemed to call us from somewhere deep inside. It ignited a memory so vast, we could hardly contain it. We became alive in worlds far beyond any ordinary concepts of reality, and tears streamed down my face from sheer joy.

Indescribable beauty surrounded us in visions which we seemed to mutually share. I felt like I had finally found a playmate again, other than Don, who could meet me in the vast multi-dimensional cosmos. Bliss, joy and love filled our hearts. Our mutual presence and focus with each other pulled us up ever higher. We functioned like a stairway to heaven for each other, to keep going beyond any form, into the most refined states of consciousness, beckoning us into total union with the mystical source.

I was certain that much of what I felt was shared by both of us. Indeed, as we later found out, both of us felt that our future was calling us. We were simultaneously sitting as bodies on a rock surrounded by waterfalls, as well as becoming vastly advanced structures of consciousness. As such, I saw and felt us functioning together as a unit, in vast cosmic spaces. It felt to us as if we were the alpha and omega of a gigantic future form, which we were a part of. If our future incarnations were to truly take us into ever more complex forms of consciousness, we got a taste of who we would become. We felt destiny talking to us.

I surrendered. If that was who we were to be in some dimension, some future time-zone, I was willing to become that, to be that. So was Amoraea.

But we didn't know if that was the potential still awaiting us, or if it was a primordial archetype that we were tapping into, due to our heightened awareness. How exchangeable are we? Are we archetypes encountering one another? Are we truly an individual soul that has its unique expression and consequences?

I was certain that Amoraea was an expression of the same multi-fractal creation as Merlin, which I had been able to tap into. However, when Merlin's human self had to bow out, I met Amoraea, who was much more able to sustain this high current of potential.

One thing was for sure; I was very high and blissful due to our inner merging. This was merging at its best. Plain sex pales in comparison.

Time and again I have found that as a result of spending time in these vast and increasingly finer states of consciousness, entering into moments of unity with the Allness, more synchronistic events happen in my daily life. I don't need to work so hard at manifesting in the three dimensional world when I spend a good amount of time in such refined spaces.

I do find that I have to be more attentive about the thoughts I think. The higher we are situated in the seat of our soul, the more intense the laser beam of our awareness becomes. The increased light shining through the images and feeling of our minds makes things manifest increasingly faster.

Naturally I have to guard against any misuse such as angry thoughts and revengeful feelings when I enter more often into these heightened states. When we work from a higher vantage place and have increased power within us, we also have more responsibility.

It is very important to have a tool which allows us to easily transform fears, anger, and blockages on our own, as we still have to deal with our human limitations. The Tracking Process, which I wrote about in my last book *Journey to the Center of Creation,* allows me to deal with fears, pains and anger very easily, and transform them into allies.

Sitting with Amoraea was like sitting with a master, a yogi, an angel. Everything glowed around me and I was taken by the beauty of my surroundings. Seeing beauty and feeling deep gratitude is a clear indication of being in a higher state. It is a great barometer of our true vibrational state. The world around us takes on a supernatural glow when we are inwardly expanded.

Amoraea and I sighed, held each other's hands and could hardly contain our awe at having found a cosmic consort in each other. The sun had started to sink and we got dressed. It was time to look for a B&B for the night. Since we were surrounded by dark clouds, other than the spot we were sitting in, we were not ready to camp in a tent. It truly was magical how nature, the clouds and all the elements seemed to cooperate with consciousness. It had been a miracle, a gift to have this afternoon in the sun and we were utterly grateful!

The Spyglass B&B was right on the ocean, north of Pai'a and we were lucky to get a great room. Amoraea knew the woman there and I felt a little awkward about asking for a room, sharing a bed with such a younger man. Amoraea was 14 years younger than I. We didn't think too much of it, since we were not looking for a hot night, but I was aware that we also left much to her imagination!

After we had cooked some dinner together, flawless in our harmony, we had the use of the hot tub and I offered to float Amoraea under the majesty of the stars. This form of floating is totally non-sexual, giving a safe space to the one who is being floated, as if in the arms of the great Mother.

As I held Amoraea in my arms, he entrusted himself as a baby would, and let his mind go. To him it felt as if he was being carried in the cosmic womb, totally able to let go, letting his mind, heart and soul soar into the cosmos. Indeed this form of floating is now known by the name of WATSU, Water Shiatsu.

For a long, long time, I held Amoraea. I floated him and let him feel the support that such selfless attention and support can give. I did have a moment when I felt a bit more sensual, I admit, but it just didn't feel right to break our trust. I was made aware later, when I asked for feedback, that it was the most profound experience for him being held so safely. The tone for our non-sexual connection had been set. Amoraea also verbally made sure I didn't get the wrong idea or hopes.

In my heart of hearts it hurt being told over and over again that he was not attracted to me. But I accepted that new version of my higher Karma.

The next morning at breakfast however, I felt Amoraea pulling away ever so subtly. Did I not know that feeling all too well from Merlin?

Very subtly I could tell that Amoraea was drawing the curtains shut ever so lightly, making sure that I was not getting too attached to him. It hurt!

While sitting at the table, finishing my breakfast, I started crying.

"Why would he want to open his soul so much and then withdraw from me again?" I asked myself.

I accepted the non-sexual part. That was not the issue for me. But if Amoraea didn't want to open his heart, at the very least, I wanted out right now. This reminded me too much of my struggles with Merlin. Trying to get a "yes" or a "no" from him for years hadn't born any fruit. Nothing ever changed, no matter how patient, careful, or forgiving I was. Merlin's indecision always broke the energy bond we had.

By now, I certainly knew the emotional signals of a person that would not commit. Had I really encountered the same soul matrix? It seemed so. If nothing else, I had encountered the same archetype. The issue appeared to be the same. I did not want to go through the same pain again!

He was very good at cosmic union, but he couldn't and wouldn't open his personal heart. I later found out that his father had been similar – emotionally cool. Maybe in another lifetime, deep within him he had made a vow not to attach himself to anything. Had he encountered so much pain in another life that he would not risk getting close again?

What seemed clear to me was that he had not taken "residence" down here on Earth. Amoraea and Merlin were both beings that lived a bit in a higher stratosphere, who never quite said YES to life, to living in this dimension.

This placed their home a little above ordinary reality and that was perfect for me, since I love to go to the levels they call "Home."

Yet not quite being anchored in the physical dimension, I felt that Amoraea's human heart didn't have the same bonding ability that most humans have. I perceived it as a lack of love.

I was not willing to offer the most precious innermost pearl of my soul to him for just a "quickie" when he might just drop me the next day! For that I required love. Love ensures that we care and take care of each other.

Amoraea looked at me in despair at the breakfast table, as I was ready to run. He asked me to stay and help him figure out how to love. He told me that he sensed that I knew something about matters of the heart that he still needed to learn. He was indeed very humble and wise. I was willing to help Amoraea open his personal heart. I agreed.

Heart Chakra Orgasm

The days and nights on Maui with Amoraea were filled with spiritual practices, meditations, yoga, eye gazing and hikes in nature. Our crown chakras were buzzing and I had many realizations.

Each day I vibrated higher, sustaining a high degree of awareness as often as I could. We both felt like we were in an intensive one-on-one seminar, being teacher and student to one another at the same time. Both of us were very compatible in experiencing the inner worlds and the inner experiences we shared were truly phenomenal.

The next step in my evolution was to take the solitary practice of heightened awareness states from previous lifetimes into a shared reality. I wanted to bring this awareness into active life, eye opened awakening. Bringing increased presence and higher vibrations into my body and human mind nurtured new neural pathways. Sharing intimacy in the higher dimensions by being jointly focused on God was my new growing edge. Amoraea and I used each other as incentives to open our doorways to heaven.

In the midst of being married I was experiencing the luxury of intimacy usually forbidden. But it was more as if I took lessons in evolution. There were many things I loved very much about Amoraea. He encouraged me to be more silent, which is a great feat for my Gemini mind and mouth. By acting like a saint and moving like a holy person from India, he created an environment that was outside of my norm. His body movements and his silent gazes encouraged me to act and behave differently from what I was used to. I was encouraged to step outside of my comfort zone behavior. Through him I was now exposed to a new vocabulary of thoughts, behaviors, movements and interactions.

Normally our behavior is a copy from our general socio-cultural background. In essence we copy the behavior of those closest to us. We imitate our family members and those in our larger environment, such as those in our country. We copy the smallest of details; how we smile to express joy, how we greet each other, how we dress and which colors we wear that identify our social status. We learn how and when to be silent, when to talk, how much to open and reveal to one another, how to move our bodies relative to each other. Amoraea dared to be different and I loved being around his very different way of being. It opened new doors of feelings in me.

Amoraea walked around the woods caressing the many trees and standing in silent adoration beneath them. On the walk to the seven pools in Hana, on the eastern side of Maui, he showed me one of his favorite Banyan trees. This tree was a pilgrimage spot for him. We stood inside the Banyan tree with its many roots and entered long moments of silence. I stretched my feeling to sense the air between the roots. Taking this silent time to truly feel nature opened both of us to a much subtler and richer world. I could breathe easier in that kind of silence.

Don and I go into deep silence when we are walking in nature as well, but we keep the star of our soul's union ignited, even though we may be walking 150 feet apart. This is the place of our union at a higher dimension. Even when we want to have space alone in order to commune with nature, we still keep the union-spot of our souls connected at a very high space.

Even while I was sharing time with Amoraea, I still kept the flame of my union with Don alight.

Amoraea didn't keep that space of union with me naturally. When he walked alone, he walked alone. But he had told me that he wanted to learn about union. I could see that the subtle light-lines were not running back and forth from his heart to mine, and it was painful. We were so close, yet so far apart.

Even later at a Mexican restaurant he kept closing the doors in a subtle way. He touched my hands and moved his fingers in a fine dance with me, but didn't really penetrate my energy. To him it was normal and at that point in time he didn't notice the lack of connection that I did.

We experimented: I moved my fingers over his hand in a nice, but superficial way. I was not really connecting my heart through my touch.

Next I moved my fingers over his hand in a deeply connected way, pulsing energy into his hands and heart. Outwardly it looked the same and in fact he said he didn't notice the difference. We were still in very different worlds, and because I could feel a lot more than he could be aware of, I felt alone. He didn't really want to bond deeply and his desire to remain separate and free was apparent.

It hurt to feel his detachment, his separation. Although he wanted to share himself deeply, his energy didn't really open to me in a connected way. One moment he was able to open wide, the next moment he was detached. As we walked in nature there were a number of times when he was off in his lonely world and I cried silently.

How different it was for me. I felt no need to keep my freedom. I had it by giving it up. Although I asked Don for permission about everything in my life now, which could have been constricting, I felt absolutely free. Within the synergy of Don and me, we were able to create a life that was bigger than we could create individually. Being alone to do as I please any moment didn't appear to me as a greater freedom.

Lyrics from a song once said: "Freedom is just another word for nothing left to lose." How true! When we have something dear that we can lose, we are open for pain. I had chosen to be open to the potential of loss and pain. To be in love and to be willing to bond always harbors the risk of getting hurt eventually. But avoiding that kind of pain and living in a passionless world of detachment just so that I may not experience pain at some point seems to me to be missing the essence of life. We will eventually rise to form ever more complex and universal structures. Yes, bonding implies loss but it also implies aliveness and expansion.

This lifetime I had chosen to interact within the very human realm of being emotionally bonded, loving and feeling attached. However Don and I were practicing feeling the connection in a larger multidimensional framework. We felt our identity in the form of a space of union that was beyond the normal human form of feeling connected. We were practicing feeling the union at a higher level, which is different than being a monk. Within this life I practice my focus on the eternal force, on the God force.

Being alive in duality, while at the same time being aligned with the Oneness, the center of creation, gives us a true and deep satisfaction.

The answer to the riddle of life that has plagued mankind forever lies in becoming the paradox. We are the one and the one is us. God needs us to reflect back onto Itself, to see the one in the many. We are it and it is us.

We are the form which reflects its light of awareness back into the Oneness from whence we come. We are the happiest when we are being fully alive in the world of form, while being impeccably in touch with the Oneness. This is my sense for our true salvation.

Amoraea and I spent our days holding high states of consciousness, sitting in meditation, communing with each other while eye-gazing, adoring nature, sharing our mesmerizing inner experiences. We were nectar for each other's souls.

W e spent nights in the same bed. Since we had been so attentive to our meditations, I did not slow my vibration even when going to sleep. We were both on our best behavior with each other. We never became lazy in our awareness and although this constant attentiveness wore us out somewhat, we also loved the intensity of light that we generated together.

We spent the third night in a very rustic and romantic B&B tree-house. The bedroom was built high into a tree and we felt like Tarzan and Jane. After a simple dinner, which we cooked over a camp stove, we lay down at sunset and cuddled in bed. Amoraea and I we were not sexual, that seemed to be an unspoken command. But the silken movements of his body took my breath away. His gaze was fixed on mine as he slowly arched his arm over my back. In my mind I traced the body movements, but mostly I felt the waves of his mind create ripples as he pulled his hands slowly from my heart chakra onto my hips.

It was like a choreographed dance and we shared incredibly beautiful movements like dancers that know each other very well. Like cats from the same tribe, we moved similarly and artistically together, creating a form of sensuality which was not hot and heavy as one might expect, but instead so subtle that the smallest movement reached our souls. Amoraea called it the art of creating "torque." One creates this torque by being not the body, but the cocoon of energy which is able to ignite at any point of union within a larger field of merging. I truly no longer identified with being a body, but relished this moment of finding a play partner who was able to meet me as a wave of energy, and melting point of union in God.

Eventually we fell asleep in each other's arms. Even though we were sleeping, I also stayed alert in a semi-conscious state throughout the night. It was not particularly restful, but I loved to feel Amoraea's arms wrapped around me as we tried to sleep. Again and again I felt him touch me on my heart and we continued feeling the energy run between us in slumbery moments of awakened sleep. In this semi-sleep state the current of energy kept running through our bodies from his hand over my heart and back into him. In my drifting, sleepy mind I started to notice that Amoraea was pulsing me with energy from a deep part within himself, and I soon drifted off fully into sleep.

Suddenly I was awakened by an intense electric charge that surged through his hands into my heart. Amoraea had touched the backside of my heart chakra again and this time it ignited such a charge between us that I arched my body in full ecstasy into his arms. An orgasmic heart surge was pulsing through me! He held me strongly in his arms as he too was fully engaged in the arcing of our energies. My whole being surrendered into his arms, his soul, and into God. We were one circuit of energy. We stayed in this silent state of union for a long time.

The next morning I described what I had experienced and wanted to know if he too had had this immense experience. He smiled, telling me that, yes, he had. He had tapped into an ancient wisdom during nightly trainings from inner beings. But it is an art which we can all learn, when we are able to listen to the silent teachings from within.

I loved it.

During those few days we grew closer in some ways. It was challenging to feel our immense soul closeness, and yet to also feel the tendency in him to remain inwardly separate.

The day for me to go back home to the Big Island had arrived and we made plans for Amoraea to come and house-sit our house within a few weeks time.

As wonderful as my time with Amoraea had been, I could hardly wait to see Don. All the detachment energy had worn me out, and although I had experienced great heights spiritually, my heart felt shredded. To be so very close and yet to remain so aloof was confusing to it.

Don knew how I felt since we had talked every day on the phone. He greeted me with a purple orchid lei at the airport as if I was the long lost love of his life! On a grassy spot by the Hilo Bay we lay on a blanket near the ocean, and Don held me in his arms forever. His love cocooned me as he poured balm over my heart and smoothed my ruffled feathers. As much as I had learned new things, I also felt like I had been shaken up. I was grateful to have the kind of deeply attached love that Don and I share.

Attachment in this day and age has gotten such a bad name. More and more people show signs of commitment phobia. In our western culture we have become increasingly individualized and able to survive without a family. As a result we are also starting to show signs of attachment difficulties. Don soothed my feathers and we were in love. I loved being back with Don again!

Several weeks later, Amoraea arrived again at our house on the Big Island and stayed with us for a week before starting his house-sitting job.

Don needed to teach him how to fill the solar panel batteries with distilled water, as well as how to feed the fish that in turn nurtured our hydroponics green house. Trees needed to be pruned and it took time to learn how to do everything that needed to be done to keep a self sufficient home running.

Our synergy together as a threesome was surprising to all of us. Since we were all musicians, we started recording music together. Amoraea wanted to record his next album. Since Don had been his own sound engineer since he was in his teens, he was willing to teach Amoraea. We laid down tracks of Amoraea's Didgeridoo and crystal bowls, added my various silver and wooden flutes and harp, and then layered Don's guitars, cello and synthesizer onto these sound tracks. We started to feel a greater purpose of our union develop in our multi-layered sharing.

Our recordings turned into several CDs with joint tracks, which were then published by the Monroe Institute and elsewhere. We definitely had a successful, co-creative energy together that nurtured and helped each other.

Don and I had to leave for Seattle, and Amoraea started to live at our house in Hawaii, house-sitting as it is called, tending the garden.

We needed to spend time with our secretary back in Washington at our main home, before flying to Germany and then onward to Egypt for a German-speaking seminar. I was looking forward to the great pyramids and the silence of the desert. The time alone in our "'real" home on our island in the Pacific Northwest, was like balm to our souls.

Egypt, Pyramids and the Desert

Crisp Spring weather greeted us as we arrived in the Pacific Northwest. Something in the cool air stirred a change in us. The balmy tropical air we had enjoyed all winter long, had slowed us down and had lulled us into a soft tropical slumber. Here in the Pacific Northwest however, the air was rich in oxygen, unlike in the tropical islands.

In the fresh cool Spring air we completed a zillion tasks each day. After a few weeks in our cocoon it was time to leave for the seminar in Egypt.

It was April 2003. The political situation in Egypt was such that Don didn't want to be the only American traveling in an Islamic state with our otherwise German group. This was prudent. We found out, that had Don come along on that seminar trip, the Egyptian military would have sent a security convoy along with the whole group to keep watch over this American passenger to ensure his safety. Since we didn't want to hinder the group, Don asked Merlin to accompany me in his place through the desert. And so it happened that magically again I had to travel to another amazing power site on Earth with Merlin.

Don and I flew to Germany and I went on to accompany the group to Egypt, along with Merlin. Don went onward to Vienna to help a woman friend deal with her cancer surgery.

Although I loved my life near the water, the desert was another kind of home for me. As a child I was mysteriously attracted to the Tuareks, the mysterious nomads living in the north African desert. It was like going back home for me.

Cairo airport was filled with strange sights, and luckily we were greeted by guides in the baggage claim area, who then took us to meet Rosemaria, a Swiss woman who was going to be our guide through the desert. She had married an Egyptian tour guide and together they now arranged adventure trips into the silence of the deserts of Egypt.

We were going to travel by camel and by jeep. Rosemaria was leading the physical part of our two week adventure in the desert, while I was going to offer meditations.

Our first stop was at the three monumental pyramids of Giza. We didn't know if we could enter the King's Chamber because with low oxygen levels in the King's Chamber only a limited number of people are admitted each day. Many of us in our group had had visions or a feeling of having lived in Egypt before. And all of us wished to be lucky enough to enter the pyramid that day. Magically we got tickets and soon found ourselves reverently walking up the steep catwalk that took us deeper and higher into the pyramid to the much talked about King's Chamber. It was April 26th 2003.

One by one we filed into the room where the King's sarcophagus stood in silent testimony of a ritual that no one understood for certain. Only a few other visitors were with us as we gathered in a circle around the supposed tomb.

The shaft that extended from this room upward and outward was said to lead the soul of the King toward Orion's belt, as it would have been positioned back in time. Some research has shown that this chamber was aligned with the Belt of Orion, if the pyramid was rotated to the map of an ancient sky.

Here a few excerpts from the website http://interoz.com/EGYPT/cheops.htm:

The southern shaft from the King's Chamber points directly to where Orion's Belt would have been in the ancient sky. The southern shaft of the Queen's Chamber points to Sirius. The northern shaft of the King's Chamber points to the circumpolar stars. These stars never disappear in the sky. It is thought that these shafts were to help the spirit of the dead pharaoh find the important stars.

It was the pharaoh's transcendental launching pad and it propelled his soul into the sky. There he marshaled the forces of cosmic order and stabilized the universe, just as he had organized society and governed Egypt.

I wondered if this was only for the time of his death or possibly even for his and other's journeys during their lifetime to enter higher states of consciousness.

The Egyptians were obsessed with the journey of the soul into the afterlife. Reminiscent of Tibetans, they felt that we need to prepare in our earthly life for the journey of our soul that awaits us all.

Inevitably when training our mind to see beyond the walls of the three dimensional boundaries our experience of the physical life becomes magical and the life of our Soul becomes more important and more real. Ancient civilizations knew of the capabilities of entering the higher dimensions, and only in our modern times have we shunned such realms with such great fervor. Even in the Christian modern schools of thought the adherence to and interpretation of scripture surpasses the importance of mystical experiences that we can personally gain and verify.

Standing in a circle we stood in silence together, chanting a soft Om to begin our group meditation. In my mind this room had always been a training room for ascension of the soul and not a tomb for a dead King, as is popularly believed. Several of us felt like we had been trained in ancient Egypt as seers, as kings, as prophets. Some of us recalled a connection of Star People to the Egyptians. During several ReCreation seminars I have led, where we dive into past and parallel lives, several participants saw how their embalmed body was a genetic gateway used for eventual revival of the DNA by the ETs. The embalmed body was often buried near the pyramid, but not in it, serving as a homing station for the extraterrestrial energy. I also saw legions of Roman soldiers entering this room later in time and wondered about the historical correctness of my vision.

Large Orbs, soap-bubble like light balls, showed up in the digital photographs that we took during our meditation in the King's Chamber. These Orbs are now thought to be a manifestation of a high presence of prana, energy, or life force. Standing together silently in a circle around the sarcophagus we tried to tune into the secret realms hidden in this majestic keeper of time.

Each of us had a different experience during our meditation in the King's Chamber. I had expected to be surrounded only by silence and was surprised at the vividness of the imagery that unfolded before me. In my mind I traveled the shaft to what we might call Outer Space. In truth it is the deeper Inner Space as well. We were blessed with a visit into the King's Chamber.

Now we were ready for the depth of the desert. Over the next few days we drove south in Jeeps to our first destination at Umm El Dabadib, close to the Libyan border. The sparse shade of 2000 year old Acacia trees greeted us and gave us shelter from the scorching desert sun. This refuge was at a crossroads of Roman ruins, which had served as an outpost at this once lucrative trading route of wines. With the help of water ducts, wine had been produced here thousands of years ago.

We were invited to explore the ruins. In mild shock I stood in front of a tower built of mud bricks.

It was the same kind of tower that I had seen in a vision years ago, regarding a past life with Merlin. In that vision I had searched for an understanding of our love that was so torn when a brilliantly vivid vision unfolded before my closed eyes.

I was wearing sandals, a long dress and had been captured and placed in the bottom of a tall tower. Slowly, water was let into the cell and I eventually drowned. Merlin had been placed a little higher in the same tower, in a room that had a window, and had been made to witness my death, while also being tortured. He was allowed to survive however, since he was of nobility and was forced to marry another woman of a higher standing. His illicit relationship with me was not tolerated in the social order, and when we didn't cooperate willingly we were forced to let go of each other. Both of us were within earshot of each other and I could hear him scream before I drowned, while he had to witness my drowning.

That experience had left deep wounds in both our memories. My wounds were less intense, since I had willingly surrendered to death. Merlin however was left with the pain of loss of his love which he carried in his heart from then on.

In Umm El Dabadib I now stood in front of the same tower and I wondered if this was indeed the actual place where the event that I had recalled in Technicolor, had actually taken place. I knew it had happened in northern Africa, in a desert-like environment. Here was a desert and the riddle of how water was let into such a tower was now solved by the presence of water ducts. The event could have actually happened here.

Our age-old struggle continued to play out in the present as well. On one hand we wanted to feel our higher connection of soul love, but somehow Merlin would not let it come to fruition. By now I could predict with precision how Merlin would make sure he didn't open his heart. During brief moments he let me peer into his soul and we were both taken by the immensity of our merging. Our souls were deeply in love and we felt like we were spanning the entire cosmos.

However I had to learn to close the curtain of my inner sight and open it only briefly in very specific moments. If I opened my inner sight to Merlin too much, my heart just leaped, my hopes rose to the heavens and I couldn't tolerate the distance we kept. But we hadn't been able to break through the wall of his fears and I didn't expect it to happen anymore.

So we kept the curtains drawn until such a day when his human self will be able to walk in unison with his celestial self. As much as I heard his soul cry out for me not to abandon him, his human self was telling me to let go of him.

I hesitantly accepted the clues that I received from Merlin's emotional body, which told me that he didn't want to bond. I bowed to his personality even if our souls wanted something else, and even though I heard him cry out for me to stay open to him. But a love connection is a two way street that builds magically over time. I could not sustain my openness and be abandoned by him whenever he felt like it.

Souls form bonds over time. High Tibetan Lamas know this as they seek to sustain the same relations in their continuous reincarnations. We all re-encounter each other again and again. Recognizing each other proves to be a test of being anchored in our eternal soul. But it takes both parties. And Merlin was scared by the loss of self that love would bring. Surrender to a greater whole is scary.

Our Swiss guide, Rosemaria, was excellent. She took us through the vast openness of the desert, into old canyons which provided us with a sound chamber made of rock for our group chantings. One day she took us hiking onto high plateaus to see with our own eyes the majesty of the river-like meandering sand dunes, which had been traveling from China through Africa on the wings of the wind.

Just like water, sand travels in crescents of waves of dunes, which form a large river. This ancient desert offered our minds a vast geological perspective of history. In hundreds of millions of years, oceans, tropical landscapes, and now the desert have covered this landscape. We traveled back in time in our minds and we traced the images left upon the land. I could feel the oceans that once had covered this land, see our primate ancestors, and watch time pass by as if in time-lapse photography in front of my mind's eye.

Since we were in the desert, there was no privacy as such. Open space engulfed us at night, where we had a choice of finding a sand-dune, a semi- crescent hill of sand, for an illusory sense of privacy. Here we could sleep alone, in the wind-shade of the crescent, or share the crescent dune with others. The nightly hike back into the vast darkness was adventurous. I was glad Don had sent Merlin along as my guarding companion. The sand-dune kept us safe from the wind at night, at least to some degree, and the crescent gave us a feeling of having a large, vast bedroom to ourselves, until someone walked by. We didn't cuddle at all during this trip. Merlin and I wanted to make sure we didn't use the seminar space for our own personal fun. Rumors abounded but we kept painfully separate.

It was different for some of our participants. It soon became obvious that Richard, a young man, and Regina, a young woman participant, both of whom had partners at home, started to flirt. Soon the flirt developed into a full affair and we all knew it.

"What was I to do?" I wondered. It brought up the questions of integrity, of honesty and Richard promised me that back home he would tell all.

The virtues we demonstrate in our real life reveal the true evolution of our soul. Virtues are not some abstract rules we abide by. They can only spring forth from the depth of our soul. The more awake we are in our consciousness, the more we naturally want to 'clean up our act.'

We realize that our actions have repercussions and we choose to do good things voluntarily. Killing, stealing, lying, all become things of the past. Later on even the ego's attempts of whitewashing our truths fall back and secrets become a thing of the past for more evolved beings.

Kindness, compassion, the desire to accept and allow, to understand, to be loving, respectful and caring, to share, and to be truthful, are all virtues that arise from our heart into the world of action.

The manifestation of thoughts, wishes, and the boomerang effect of our actions happen ever more rapidly as we accelerate in our vibrational rate. The purer we become in our energy field, the faster the effects.

After a while we cannot afford to lie, cheat, or be unkind. The loss of vibration such behavior brings with it is so painful to us that we would rather deal with the pain of truthfulness than the loss of our vibration.

I couldn't make Richard and Regina do anything differently, as their own vibrational rate dictated how they handled their life. However, later during a seminar in the fall of the same year, Richard had to come face to face with his attempts to cover up part of his life.

Somehow, miraculously, he and his girl-friend, as well as the lover from the desert chose to attend the same seminar with us. Richard still had not told his girl-friend anything, and I told him that I was not going to cover for him.

Many of us who had traveled with them in the desert of Egypt partook in this seminar. It just so happened that the two women volunteered to play in a role play about a betrayed wife. They signed up without knowing in advance what was coming. As they played the play of a betrayal with a different man in lieu of Richard, the rest of us sat raptured at the edge of our seats. All of us who knew how true this role play was, listened to every word they shared. Using the methods of the seminar this role play and real life play had a happy ending. I realized how much one single lie pulls all of us into a spin, and how relieved we were, when the truth was shining again.

Regina was an exemplary angel. In her Higher Self, and with the methods of Tracking, she was able to handle the betrayal and turn their relationship around.

"Dolphin Strategy" in Business

Egypt was by now many months in the past and July was around the corner We were going to swim with dolphins again.

A seminar participant by the name of Gerold and his wife Elke, whom we had met a year earlier had wanted us to lead a Dolphin

Swim Program for handicapped children this coming summer. Gerold and his most beautiful wife Elke were visionary business people. With her long blond hair and blue eyes, she looked like a Plaeidian. Elke also resembled a female version of my inner guide Gopal Das.

After they had read my book, they attended our seminar at the Jonathan Seminar House near the Chiemsee Lake in Germany. During the seminar we struck up a soul-filled connection that opened doors to future adventures. Gerold is the owner of a very dolphin-like run company in Germany. His company employs nearly 200 people and deals with customers who have bodily handicaps of varying degrees.

The company itself operates with higher principles and ethics and has developed business strategies for a healthier work environment. The employees were carefully hired to fit into the team spirit and are involved in innovatively running the business.

We had given a presentation to the CEOs of the company some time before. As a result, with the support of the employees the company had collectively chosen to sponsor twelve handicapped children under the guardianship of ten adults plus Don and myself as guides to swim with wild dolphins in Key West.

When Don and I gave the presentation to the CEOs I noticed that something was different about this company. Eventually I took time to interview Gerold about what attracted him to dolphins and how he runs his company. Here is what he told me:

Normally one would find employers simply hiring employees to work, to get the job done. But in the end the employees provide a service, which in the truest sense of the word implies serving, which can ultimately only be done best with the heart. Therefore, to be authentic, this kind of energy has to be demonstrated, set as an energetic example by the company itself. If serving from the heart is to be exemplified by the employees, it must also come from its CEOs and be exemplified in all its departments. Ultimately a caring and cared for employee will treat a customer with more care.

The CEOs of this sizable innovative German company believe that this is the key to success. Customers feel that if they are treated well, they will come back for more, and refer more clients to a company that cares.

For Gerold, the well-being of the employees is not just a slogan, it is a lived reality. As such his employees are given the option to receive physiotherapy treatments free of charge, including energy touch treatments during working hours. Clean, filtered water, fruits, fitness rooms and time to relax are all part of the daily service to the employee. To create a better work environment, the company also integrated Feng-Shui advice into the layout of the office rooms, moving away from the usually sterile office environment. They included more color, allowing the feeling of "flow" in offices.

The energy flow, as seen in Feng-Shui, dictates the position of the desks, chairs, plants, and shelves. Not sales, best utility, or the cheapest price guide the principles for the layout of the office furniture and room designs, but rather how the energy of the employees is best served.

Motivated by the ability to govern one's own time at work, the usual punch-clock to keep track of working hours has been replaced. Instead the company extends its trust to the employees, giving them freedom to choose their time of work, so that the employee can demonstrate that they are capable of self-directed discipline, earning the trust of the employers. Gerold and the other two CEOs feel that a free person is more likely to be self-responsible and therefore more motivated.

Since the team depends on each other's contributions, each individual's act affects the well being of everyone. Starting with requiring self generated dependable timing, to completing cooperatively created projects, the team spirit and the ability to function as a unit is stimulated.

Working proactively as a group belongs to the higher functions of human evolution, which is what Gerold's company wants to support.

To support the feeling of caring and working from the heart, the salespeople are asked to find out what the real needs of the clients are in order to sell only that which is truly needed by the client. The employee is motivated to truly understand the client and listen to his needs in order to address the client in a way that fulfills his or her true needs not only to make a sale, but to understand the client and serve him as well. With this approach, sales become service and not a performance under pressure or a number to be pushed.

"The principles are being lived and exemplified by the CEOs, and not dogmatically ordered," Gerold emphasized.

What really proves that this style of running a company pays off is that his company is annually evaluated by the German version of UL laboratories, the TÜV as well as other agencies, and each year they receive outstanding medals for the company's superior performance.

Gerold and his CEOs wanted to be part of an experiment where they supported the freedom of the dolphins and explored their alternative healing ability. There are plenty of centers where captive dolphins are exploited for what they can "give" to humans. That is neither how Gerold's company runs, nor did he want to support such exploitation.

He also wanted to involve both the teachers and the handicapped children with the dolphin encounter, to allow changes in the children, as well as the adults.

Gerold believes in a win-win attitude for everyone: old customers, new ones, children, and dolphins. If and when all parties involved are well cared for, everyone benefits. Such cannot be said for dolphins kept in captivity who are coerced into "giving" their service.

As a part of making a profit, Gerold's company wanted to give something back to the community by supporting the dolphin therapy in the wild with handicapped children. Of course it would be an experiment, since we did not know what the results would be. We had known of one case where a child was able to walk up a flight of stairs after just two days of swimming with or near wild dolphins in the deep waters of Hawaii. The results had been published in a local newspaper. The physiotherapist had measured the angle and range of motion before and after the dolphin encounter. To create a healing effect swimming with wild dolphins was going to be an experiment. We had never done it before.

The message Gerold's company wanted to give to the world was clear:

"We will only support encounters with free living dolphins!"

We can, and do, vote with our money. The same message was given by Ric O'Barry in his world-lecture-tour on captive dolphins years later. His slogan was: "Boycott visiting captive dolphin or whale shows!" After his work as the trainer of the famous TV dolphin "Flipper," he had a change of heart and dedicated his life to fighting for dolphins' freedom.

If we don't visit dolphinariums, don't support any captive dolphin situations and refuse to give our dollars to such companies, they will soon feel the lack of support for such shows and stop them altogether. Ric O'Barry's book "How to Free a Dolphin" tells about his attempt to free dolphins.

Gerold and Elke's wish was that the children interact only with dolphins in the wild, without the customary zoo-like and demeaning encounter dolphinariums usually offer.

Curious to see if the handicapped children would show signs of improvement, as has been touted by many of the captive dolphin-swim programs, Don and I accepted to guide the children.

Since Gerold and Elke needed to learn how to navigate in the water with wild dolphins, they joined us for the wild-dolphin-encounter seminar the week prior to the arrival of the children. They wanted to learn the general ethics involved in swimming with dolphins in the wild before helping the following week with the handicapped children.

A group of German-speaking participants had arrived for a one week adventure of swimming with wild dolphins. The first day we went to the public beach at Fort Zachary. The white sand and the green trees were in brilliant contrast to the blue sky dotted with white clouds. We were all very excited to meet the dolphins so we practiced snorkeling and swimming, and I explained our dolphin-swim ethics.

No touching of wild dolphins was allowed and I gave the example of how you would not touch a stranger at a farmer's market either. I explained how we would slide into the water gently, without making huge splashes since dolphins are very sound sensitive. We practiced holding our breath, and looking at each other's eyes as we dove under the water. I explained about not swimming head on toward a dolphin but to veer to the side and invite and allow the dolphins to swim toward us.

We laughed and had fun in the water. The warm sun and the bright colors lifted everyone's mood and we started to connect with each other. After we got out of the water we were hungry and sat under the shade of pine trees in the white sand to eat our sandwiches. As usual, I guided our group in guided imagery exercises and we started to see the world through different eyes.

Soon it was getting late and upon returning home we showered and got ready for our evening walk to our favorite restaurant "Blue Heaven." Lights strung through the trees created a magical atmosphere as we ate in the garden setting of this restaurant. Filled with Creole food, we strolled back home to our B&B, passing artistic houses and their gardens of old town Key West, adoring the lit up trunks of the trees, which looked like a creation of art in the evening light.

The next morning our B&B hosts served us great American breakfasts with eggs, toast, oats, pancakes, fresh fruit, teas and juices. Our B&B truly was a tropical paradise.

Half the group went out on the boat with Don, while the other half stayed with me to train our imagery minds. We sat together in the shade of the garden and in a gentle guided imagery meditation we pre-envisioned how we wanted to feel as we swam with dolphins.

We made sure we imagined the end-result of how we wanted to feel. Independent of actually achieving the result, we have the power to feel the joy and satisfaction within our minds and hearts. This empowers us from the inside out and makes us independent of external events. When we have reached such a state of mastery, the universe is able to fulfill our desires.

Odd as it seems, we need to feel the potential future in advance before we can receive its manifestation. Such are the rules in this dreaming universe.

Naturally each of us had a different image, goal or wish as to how we wanted to encounter "our" dolphins. What matters to the universe is that we feel and imagine the end result in advance. Of course over the years I have come to realize that we do indeed get what we envision but that may include the manifestations of our subconscious expectations, either good or bad.

It is the negative, often unconscious programs that we need to alter, because they get in the way of manifesting what we truly want. However, we get many opportunities to clean our slates and update our dreaming minds through learning life's lessons in order to become increasingly more brilliant beings.

Each day that we went out to swim with dolphins we were rewarded with the cooperation of the dolphins. The hardest thing was to learn to trust that they would and could hear us telepathically. We needed to find the right channel for projecting our feelings and thoughts so that they could cooperate with our visions. When one of our group members rushed after a dolphin, they were only disappointed when the dolphin swam just a little faster ahead of them. Rushing after a dolphin was like saying to the universe "Hey, I believe I am not going to get it, and so I have to chase what I want." But instead, all it takes is feeling the end result already within us. Sooner or later it will happen. It is always in harmony with our deeper, often unconscious, expectations. What we feel to be true will manifest.

Actually, as with all things in life, there is no way in the world we can chase a free dolphin into giving us what we want. Nor can we make a mate give us what we want. But what we can do is to "already be" in the state we want to be and feel the dolphins around us, or our mate. When we do, the magic happens.

Whenever Don returned with half of the group from the boat, I took the other half to meet the dolphins. It was then that Don spent the other half of the day experiencing radionics and inner exercises with his group. The imagery that worked best to manifest results was from our course, Living From Vision®. The miracles that can come from daily imaging and pre-creating one's life are astounding.

One afternoon on the boat, I sat in the shade on deck of the catamaran boat, bathing in the light of the turquoise water and watching the dolphins. When they came close to the boat, we stood in rapture, bent over the railing, trying to gaze into their eyes. We squealed for joy when they returned our gaze.

Just to watch dolphins from the boat and being within two feet of them was amazing. When the captain felt that the dolphins were not feeding or resting, he told us to get our snorkel gear ready. Alternating, we took turns getting into the water, usually in groups of three and sometimes six to swim with the dolphins. He asked us to stay in our group and not to swim toward them.

Since they were usually 50 yards away, which was the suggested guideline, we would just wait and let the dolphins find us. Some good swimmers would at times dive down to see if they could hear the dolphins' sonar locating us. Gerold and Elke were amazing swimmers and soon learned the art of letting the dolphins come to them.

Our captain also got his turn in the water with his beloved dolphins. The dolphins were super friendly that day and swam around us in circles. The captain was a very good swimmer. With a deep breath he dove down. Swimming backward in a circle he started showing a dolphin his belly as a sign of intimacy and trust. As he pulled slightly backward, the dolphin followed his invitation. The dolphin found this game interesting and swam in circles around him. It was obvious that the dolphin was engaging with him because it was fun. Certainly being able to dive, hold one's breath and be mobile under water is enticing for the dolphins. However, as we would see the following week with the children, these skills were really not necessary either.

One other afternoon, while Don was out on the boat with half of the group, I sat with the others in meditation in the shade by the pool. I enjoyed these sacred hours nearly as much as swimming with dolphins. The meditations gave us a chance to get in touch with our silent, inner center and we could feel ourselves as energy beings.

With soft music floating in the air we drifted into a guided meditation. In the silence of our own minds, we pondered everything that was beautiful in our lives. I started out by gazing physically at everything around me and noticed how beautiful everything was. Then I closed my eyes and I wandered into larger and larger spaces in my mind, spanning the beauty of my universe.

For fifteen minutes we basked in this silent reverie. Thinking of everything that is beautiful raises my vibration every time. At first just the obviously beautiful things came to my mind, but as I sat in this balmy silence I realized that everything in my life started to look beautiful. Everything was perfect. Even the small propeller airplanes that made a loud noise flying overhead didn't disturb my sense of paradise. The more I spread my mind into all areas of my life and saw the beauty, the happier I became.

I guided the group through a variety of thoughts that worked like mantras, giving our chatty minds a focal point. Each thought, such as focusing on beauty, gratitude, love or awe at life, was leading our minds into greater levels of expansion.

Finally we reached the level of contact with the source of life, with God. Sitting next to Elke, I felt our energies arcing into greater levels of consciousness, reaching unprecedented heights together.

In my vision I rose into a field of pure electric charge. I saw how the totality of the field of energy that existed at this level was in no way partial to how the charge was expressed in the manifested world below it. Much like lightning was a field of charge in the sky, able to strike here and there, that field of energy was also pure potential. It didn't seem to matter through which vehicle the charge expressed itself as long as this charge was expressed.

The field of Isness, the field of charge, is alive. Period. The forms that express this charge of Isness don't have greater or lesser importance or value relative to each other. We are all expressions of this Isness and as such we are all the same. If we want to we can choose to be the most beautiful expressions of this charge or we can choose to express more contracted forms of energy flow. The choice is ours.

We can choose to be a huge energy field or a small one, it doesn't matter.

We can choose to be any part, at any time. It doesn't seem to even matter what we choose, if it is good or bad. We will bear the results and be full of joy or anger. It is up to us. The universe simply supplies the energy.

In this field of pure potential, I felt Elke's soul and mine arc our energy together. We were both fully present in that dimension. I could feel her there, in that heightened place I had entered.

At this level of existence karma is mutable. IF we are able to occupy a higher state of potential within our minds, we can be the recipient of this particular energy. Although Karma is thought to be immutable, it actually is mutable IF we can move ourselves truly into the place of a higher potential.

I realized how the holographic imagery was a key to shifting Karma. Once we transform the old energy into a fulfilled form of a future potential, we can experience the expression of the new energy. IF we can jump into a new time-space configuration, we can experience miracles. The only trick is really moving into such a new state. I had indeed experienced plenty of miracles this way as I have previously written about, and realized that this was also the key to changing my own destiny.

Afterwards we talked about our experiences, and Elke shared a very similar one. We realized that we had indeed arced our higher minds together and reached heights that took us beyond the ordinary. Together we had truly felt each other in the matrix of light. We became aware that we were both part of this vast field of charge. We had both risen to a state in consciousness in which we were no longer form, where we felt ourselves touch the same space of aliveness.

I looked into her brilliant blue eyes as she told us of her experience and we both knew that we had touched heaven together. With a glimmer in our eyes, we winked at each other. This sense of sharing was deeply fulfilling and built a foundation for our friendship for a lifetime to come.

As the week came to a close, we were ready for the children to arrive in Key West. Some of them had previously never left home and had never swum in open waters so this trip would be an adventure of a lifetime.

Three teachers from the handicapped school that had been selected for this Dolphin Swim Program picked a group of twelve children. A total crew of nine adults, plus Gerold, Elke, Don and I were to be guardians for the children. Together we were a large group of twenty-four people. The children had been prepared to meet dolphins in the wild through many different school activities. In sports classes they learned how to snorkel. In art class they had painted dolphins in the ocean, and in geography they had learned about the dolphins' habitat.

The children had different handicaps. Some of them were emotionally underdeveloped, while others had physical handicaps. Some handicaps were mental, some were circumstantial or combinations of other factors, but all the children were able to swim!

We had rented two boats and were going to take two trips per day with each boat so that there were only six passengers at any one time. Since we didn't want to overload the dolphins with too many people at once, small boats were our preferred choice. Even so, each day all twenty four of us got to go out to where the dolphins lived.

The two boats went to two different areas in the languid waters surrounding Key West. One boat went to an area that is about five square miles where the dolphins live in shallow waters during the day to play, rest, and nurse. When they were hungry they fished in the deeper channel that goes out to sea. The other boat went to another area the dolphins frequented, the Atlantic side of Key West, between some small islands.

Half the day we went out in the boats to find the dolphins. Each adult had one child to supervise. We felt that one adult for each child was the most secure setting to work in.

But for the children, the safety of their home was gone, the rules at school didn't apply, and there were no regular patterns to follow. Home, school and familiar environments are very important to people living with handicaps. Here however, everything was new and different. We knew that this could increase insecurities. Just how would the children respond to this wild world of open waters, six feet deep that was so foreign to them?

Dolphin Assisted Therapy in the Wild

Just like the week before, we started the first day of the seminar with the children and adults by practicing snorkeling together in the warm ocean water at the Fort Zachary Taylor beach. We talked about the dos and don'ts of swimming with dolphins, played a name game where each child got to choose a name of an animal they liked. The children had prepared a gift for each of the adults. A T-shirt with our name and a jumping dolphin on it was presented to us with glee.

They had dreamed of the dolphins for a long time and the teachers had done a wonderful job preparing them. Before going to sleep the first night, we sat on the balcony of the quaint, Key West style B&B with its wooden steps. The palms and many tropical flowers surrounded us, swaying in the balmy evening air. Everyone's senses were filled with new impressions and visions of the past day.

Twenty four of us, children and adults, piled onto the steps halfway down to the street. We were singing Swiss German songs that the children knew. Singing harmonized the group and gave us a commonly shared activity. It reminded me of my childhood, when I lived with my grandparents, my mother, sister, uncle and aunt in one house. We didn't have a TV in the mid- sixties. Many nights we would sit, eat fruit, crack nuts, or knit while we sang songs. What a great experience it was for all of us. The mood between us was harmonized, our hearts opened and we felt each other deeply. Later when my grandparents got a TV, this experience fell away to my regret. I wonder how it would affect families nowadays, if they would sing every evening together.

As we hugged each child "goodnight," we told them to dream of the dolphins and to imagine how they wanted to experience them underwater. Dolphins are beings that have evolved a greater brain. They have a very refined social awareness, and apparently other magical mental abilities such as telepathy and the ability to cause inexplicable healings. Some dolphin researchers have been astute enough to notice these abilities. But to the general scientific community, dolphins have not been recognized properly due to our human arrogance. This is similar to the view about women, who have been thought of as being less intelligent than men until just recently.

But what gave these children, who lacked much of the normal cognitive functions of the mind, such trust in these creatures? Intuitively they felt love for dolphins. What makes many people dream of dolphins, miss them and want to connect with them? Many say it was the movie Flipper and surely that movie helped raise our desire for contact with dolphins. But maybe there is a much greater picture is at work.

Dolphins, in my opinion, are already living at a heightened level of awareness, being very telepathic. They seem to be able to read our minds and feel our feelings, and even know where we experience pain. A certain number of humans feel the call from the dolphins because they connect with them at a higher octave. Most humans do this without knowing how and why they desire dolphins. I believe it is because those that feel the call of the dolphins are on the same path of evolution.

Those of us who are drawn to dolphins are usually interested in the higher aspects of life, knowingly or unknowingly. Dolphins instill love in our hearts, raise our spirits, and many people report some kind of healing or a change of mind that moves them closer to living in alignment with their souls after encountering dolphins.

Maybe we were ready to hear their call in order to make such a jump, since dolphins served as a model for having made such a huge evolutionary jump themselves. Although the jury is still out about their brain power, they do have amazing mind power. Perhaps they are calling us to the seas to inspire us and to imprint us with information. Who knows what kind of an imprint we receive in their midst?

And just maybe they also need us, because our human evolution is currently threatening their very survival. If we, who have thumbs and can do things they can't, get excited about dolphins in the wild, we are also more willing to help ensure their survival.

Currently the Navy is using Low Frequency Active Sonar, which has been heavily associated with the stranding of whales and dolphins when they were in some proximity to the underwater sound exercises.

The intense sound explosions of the LFAS seem to damage the navigational system of the cetaceans, burst their hearing and cause internal bleeding. We, as a group of informed humans, need to take action and support the groups that effectively put a halt to dangerous practices, which may otherwise drive a species to extinction.

Dolphins, as a species, seem to be actively calling for our human help. Never in time has the desire for contact with dolphins been as high as in the last two decades. Dolphins and whales have evolved to live in constant states of extraordinary consciousness and at such levels they are touching our hearts and minds, long distance. When I am in high spirits and meditate well, I often start dreaming of dolphins. I believe humans start dreaming of them whenever their souls are reaching into higher realms and dolphins are the symbolic messengers from our higher minds, which let us know that a rise in consciousness is happening within us.

We are at the stage in our evolution, where humans and dolphins can hear each other in the subtle realms. We would do well to support our human-dolphin exchange, which can be an exchange at a distance, through telepathy, or physically. To be true friends, we need to make sure the dolphins and whales have a chance to survive.

I was excited to witness how the children might change as a result of unstructured encounters. We could not guarantee contact, as in a captive situation, but in the wild we could experience true, functioning relationships and observe unadulterated dolphin behavior. We didn't feed the dolphins any fish as they do in captivity when they perform a trick, because we wanted that all encounters are fully desired by the dolphins themselves.

Dolphins seemed to have already had a healing effect on the children and adults this week. One morning, while half the group was out on the boat, the other half of us sat again on the very large balcony of the B&B. White, artfully curved railings surrounded us, balmy warm wind touched our skin, and the palm trees just feet away swayed in the wind as we gathered for our morning meditation on the Victorian style balcony.

I had the children close their eyes and guided them to find their place of peace and their most beautiful future self. When I asked everyone how their best future-self looked, one girl that had not talked before started to open up by saying: Blue! Her teacher that was sitting with us felt perplexed.

While walking next to the girl one day and trying to engage her in conversation, I was told by one of the teachers that all she ever did was just nod "yes" or "no," and I should not bother asking her any questions or expect any answers from her. This girl, so I had been told, never answered any questions at school in Switzerland. But I just included her anyway in the circle since I just didn't have the memory of her failed communications. And I was expecting changes.

Indeed, each day as she sat in our circle she increased her capacity to communicate. She even started to hug everyone, which she had not done before. At school she never wanted to do that. But as we were hugging all the children in the morning and before going to sleep, she now picked up this behavior and her light started to shine.

One boy was autistic and never greeted anyone by name. As he was standing with three boys and Don in a circle one day, he named each one. We didn't know what to think. Some of the accompanying adults tried to pass it off as accidental.

The children also envisioned how the dolphins would interact with them. Later, as the children came back from swimming with the dolphins, several of them told me that the dolphins had behaved just the way they had imagined. Adults from our regular seminars usually tell me the same story. As such I expected to hear that from the children as well. But it was amazing to me that these children could recognize the connection between imagery and reality.

When we were not doing imagery work, collages, or other such activities, we went out on the boat. Each day we rotated who went out on which boat and who was responsible for which child. I got to take care of several of the girls during this week. Each of them had a beauty about them. Isabelle was beautiful but never dared do anything alone. She would not even go into another room by herself at home. What a change she went through after the week was over! To our amazement the children, who at school would fight and be rebellious, were totally peaceful in the presence of dolphins and this new world. One teacher commented halfway through the week how cooperative the children were.

One day we trekked with three adults and three children to the Waterfront Market where we picked up our sandwiches and waited for the others to return from the boat. Soon the catamaran was gliding into its docking space. The children that came off the boat where thrilled and told the girls in my group what they had experienced. We were eager to get to the see the dolphins ourselves.

Since the boat was a catamaran, the deck of the boat was very low to the surface of the water and dolphins could be seen easily. As soon as dolphins were near the boat, the children would jump for joy and run to watch them swim in the bow wave by the front of the boat. The dolphins seemed as curious to look at us as we were to watch them. Maybe because of the high pitch of children screaming for joy, they took notice of us.

The dolphins turned on their sides to look at us as they swam beside the boat. Our hearts were captured by their intelligent eyes. The children were so excited! Our captain loved to see such enthusiasm. It was a treat for him as well to witness the dolphins interact with us.

When the dolphins seemed to invite us into the water, our captain motioned for us to get the snorkel gear ready. He also worked within the guidelines of the marine fishery department, which has suggested safe distances for humans and dolphins. We couldn't always keep the fifty yards distance because the dolphins swam right up to the boat, and sometimes swam in the wake or by the side of the boat to look at us too. But he did make sure he didn't chase them with the boat, and when he let us in the water he didn't drop us off on top of the dolphins, but kept the distance of the suggested guidelines.

He told us to get ready to get into the water and waited until we were far enough away from the dolphins to turn the motors off. This safe distance allowed the dolphins to either choose to come to us, as we hoped, or to swim away. Slowly and gently we slid into the water. Since dolphins are very sound sensitive and may get skittish if we were to jump into the water with a loud splash, we practiced sensitivity and respect with the children.

It seemed that as soon as the children were in the water, the dolphins swam straight over to us. We even were able to capture such meetings on video. That day in the water I held the hand of the girl that hadn't talked before. She was not the least bit scared and paddled fast with her little legs because she wanted to be close to the dolphins. I didn't have to pull her, and actually had to swim to keep up with her. I kept an eye above water to look for the directions of the fins so that we were not just spending all our energy swimming blindly in the water. Somehow this girl had set in her mind that she was going to swim with dolphins. I heard sonar sounds from dolphins scanning us but couldn't see any dolphins ahead of us.

Suddenly the girl squeezed my hands with excitement. From behind us a group of dolphins had been swimming up to us, scanning us with their sonar and as they dove beneath us they were starting to come into view below us. Together, she and I watched in awe as they slowly swam underneath of us.

One of the dolphins seemed to look at us. The little girl was paddling and paddling and gone were all her fears. Universally, humans seem to get fully absorbed in the presence of dolphins and forget others, the boat, the distance, the depth and vastness of the water. All that counts is the present moment. As if they have a hypnotic attraction upon our soul, we feel blessed when they are near us. The little girl squeezed my hand in pure joy. Her dream had come true!

Was her new behavior – hugging children and adults, and starting to verbalize – due to the encounters with the dolphins? Or was it due to the imagery work, or the expectations of strangers like us, who didn't know we weren't supposed to expect anything less of her? We will never know which component of this week worked the most magic on the children but my feeling is that it was a combination of the adventuresome dolphin contacts, their sonar and the power of the imagery work.

Another day, I went out on the other boat which we had rented. It was much more like a normal little boat. We had a female captain and she was moored in a marina that was a little outside of town. Don and Gerold took turns every day, driving our little group of six in a minivan to the second boat.

As we climbed on board we were greeted by the captain's motherly energy. She took us to a different place than the captain of the catamaran. On our way out, the children were holding onto the towels which they had wrapped around the railing, pretending that they were holding the reins of a horse. In their minds they were riding the wild waves into a new adventure.

As we arrived at our destination, another spot where many dolphins convened, the water was deeper and we found a different group of them. I knew some of the dolphins from the shallow bank by name since we had come to swim with them for nearly ten years. But I didn't know all of them. Some of the dolphins rotate between different groups. I knew that Grandy, the old female that had mothered many of dolphins, had been seen here, as well as in the sand bank area.

As we slowed to watch some of the fins break the surface, gray clouds gathered in the sky, threatening to rain. I wondered if we would get to swim with dolphins at all today.

Not making the situation any easier, one of the accompanying adults was a man whom I found difficult to be with. He had been selected to participate due to his marine biology background and represented the typically left-brained, dominant male that had a very macho attitude in my eyes. He refused to participate in any of the imagery work because he didn't see any value in it. At times he challenged my work and didn't think any therapeutic effects could be gained from this week with the dolphins.

All the changes that we were observing in the children were simply coincidental in his mind. It was interesting for me to note that no matter how hard he tried to swim near dolphins, he didn't encounter any underwater the entire week.

Time and time again I have witnessed that dolphins shower us with love and their presence when we are selfless, giving, thinking of others, and yet they seemed to shun those that show none of those signs of communal conscience.

Sprinkles started drizzling upon us, then quickly turned into rain and the gray clouds cast a big shadow on the joy of our day. But since dolphins kept swimming around the boat, the captain thought we could experiment with swimming in the ocean while it rained to see if they wanted to interact with us.

Gregor, a lightly handicapped boy, was on my right side and together we swam into the dark, warm water. As soon as we had entered the water, heavy rain started pelting down on us. As I looked up from the water's depth and glanced into the horizon, I was hypnotized. The water drops that were pounding the surface of the warm water and bouncing created a million splashes. The temperature differential caused a small haze to rise up from the surface of the ocean and combined with the vision of the dancing raindrops, I was transfixed.

This effect mesmerized both Gregor and I, and we felt as if we were in an adventure movie. This beauty impressed itself on my mind forever. In the midst of an adverse situation we were gifted with some of the greatest beauty I have ever seen.

Our adventure filled me with many impressions. We had dared the rainy oceans and were rewarded with dolphin encounters. We made it back safely that afternoon and gathered again in the evening light after dinner to sing some evening songs.

Teaching the daily imagery exercises, I had a strong realization. I saw a correlation between the *ability* to use the imagination and becoming successful. This applied both to the handicapped children and everyone else. The children from this group, as well as the handicapped children the following year, all displayed different degrees of ability to concentrate and to imagine non-existent, abstract things. In general they were markedly less able to use their imagination than children without handicaps.

I noticed that the less they were able to work with abstract imagery, the more handicapped they were. I concluded that a handicapped person is not so closely in touch with their astral body, which expresses itself in the inability to utilize the imagination. I wondered then, if one could counterbalance any impedance by strengthening their power to use imagery. This seems certainly true for other people.

Over the years of teaching seminars I noticed that the greater the coherence in a person's imagery, the greater their health, joy, wealth and success. Most successful people in life have the ability to imagine their future in advance, in a successful way. The clearer an image is in a person's mind, the more successful they are. Conversely, those that have more difficulty using imagery also find their lives to be more difficult. People usually come to our seminars to improve these skills in order to enrich their lives and teach others.

The ability to pre-create the future in one's mind creates success. We know that from the many training programs now available for sports and business people. The secret is out. Imagery works.

I am using the word "imagination" but it is exchangeable for using any of the other inner ways of perceiving, either feeling or just knowing.

I could see a clear correlation between how "able" a person is with how well they can imagine things. The more restricted the inner imagery life is, the less successful a person is likely to be.

Not surprisingly, inventors, geniuses and artists have been extremely gifted in this department. Einstein, Tesla, as well as many others used imagery as a way to think and create.

Many successful people use imagery to pre-create their success. They know the secret to the universe. We live in a giant dream. We manifest that which we can see and feel as true, first in our inner mind. That is the reason why the *Living from Vision* course is so powerful for people. In the course, one learns specific imagery tools to be used in daily life. We should all be taught this skill in school or even in Kindergarten, but life seems to want us to awaken to the magic in our own time. When we are ready, we find the right person, the right book or the right movie that inspires us. Or we may figure things out by observation.

No one can make us "get it," but once we catch on, the sky is the limit. However it is a secret that requires us to practice it every second of our lives. Moment by moment we have the choice to focus on what we want or what we don't want. When we manage to rip our riveted attention away from our drama, from an experience which is not fulfilling, and re-focus on what we really want to feel, we are suddenly rewarded with a turn-around in life.

Life will give us what we hold in our mind and energy field. The feeling of fulfillment is the greatest attraction force that pulls manifestation into being, even if we fake the feeling at the beginning. The universe, even our brain, cannot distinguish what is real now or what is imagined. So we can all dream anything that we want. Big or small, it is up to us. We can create the house we want, or the state of love we want. We can be as enlightened as we feel is right for us. We can be an angel, a star, or a galaxy.

During the week, the children were dreaming of their future selves. Most of their lives, they had limited their expectation of themselves. We wanted them to think outside of the box. We gave them the space to be grand. I believed in their dreams because I knew that thousands of humans had overcome obstacles and created majestic changes in their lives before them.

We were eager to see how the week was going to change the children.

More Healings with Dolphins

The next day I was taken into another realm of experience with the children and the dolphins. Again I joined the smaller boat that went out to the deeper waters. Our ride out to the dolphins' playground, which was different from where the catamaran took us, brought us along some small islands.

The sky had cleared and there was absolutely no wind at all. The vast expanse of the Atlantic waters was as clear as glass. In a very surreal ride, we passed over the low waters from which tiny islands emerged like elegant cranes, silent in their serene beauty.

Everything was mirrored in the water: the clouds, the island greenery, the light from the sky. It was as if we were gliding along on a glassy, mirror-like surface. Our boat was floating like a sailing star in utter beauty. Heaven on Earth was all I could feel. The water's color shifted from turquoise to deep blue, and then to a brilliant light. Occasionally we came close to a little island that spread its green hues like a green cloud hovering barely above the surface of the water.

Today was magical and the children were also in total silent awe at the beauty. This was better than TV. We were taken by the beauty of life. For half an hour we glided on top of the glassy silent water, until we stopped.

We waited to see if dolphin fins would break the surface. The captain was an advocate of sound interface experimentation and had installed speakers in the hull of the boat. She started to play some music via the loudspeakers under water. She also started to play some singing bowls on the surface of the water. Sure enough, dolphins emerged from the mysterious depths of the water. How they located us and why they came is a mystery. But they seemed to seek us out deliberately.

Our captain gave us the sign to put on flippers, masks and snorkels, and to glide as silently as possible into the water. Each adult took a child by the hand and off we went into the deeper water together. Today I accompanied a different girl. I still recall Jen, her little hands holding onto mine and fearlessly diving into the great unknown. The dolphins had done their magic in evoking courage in the children. Years ago the dolphins had coaxed me out of my fear of the water and now I was witnessing the same courage blossoming in these children.

Soon, Jen and I were swimming in the deep, blue waters. The bottom was invisible and far below us. Noisy chatter and clapping sounds surrounded us, yet we couldn't locate the dolphins. Then a huge group of smaller bottlenose dolphins were swimming just ahead of us. I figured they were juveniles due to their size. There were a lot of them, maybe ten or twelve. I had never seen a group of similar aged dolphins; they were maybe three to seven years old. Normally there were adults among them but I couldn't tell if there were any today.

These juvenile dolphins were so rambunctious and playful today. They swam in circles like a column around each other, playing catch, and roughhousing with each other. We saw them from a short distance but Jen wanted to be right in their midst and kept swimming straight over to them.

I didn't really want to be so close, but Jen didn't give up. She pulled me and paddled as fast as she could and I slowly gave in. Soon the column of dolphins was swimming in circles below us. They swam on top of each other and Jen loved peering down on them, being right in the middle of the vortex above them. Despite my many, many years of swimming with dolphins, even in close proximity, I had never seen them in such a feisty mood. Not only were they quickly turning around each other, they seemed to be engaged in some form of fighting. They used their jaws to rake each other, and used their teeth to scratch their sensitive skin, leaving scars for years to come. They clapped their jaws at each other producing loud noises. Dolphins usually punish each other with loud sounds, or use it to tell other dolphins to back off.

They were very rowdy with each other. I thought I was out on the school courtyard, where the children were roughing it up with each other. Was this a reflection of what my little girl had in her mind? How could I have missed such behavior before? True, in Hawaii I had seen some squabbles in a dolphin pod, but within minutes other larger dolphins would come in and disperse such squabbles. Here they were playing all out. The noises they made were loud and a testament of too much energy.

Once we were swimming on top of the juvenile dolphins, they seemed to stay with us and we didn't have to swim hard at all to be right in their midst. It was breathtaking and my little girl squeezed my hands from sheer excitement. This was her dream come true. And mine as well. Jen and I were able to witness this whole display of power and play for maybe twenty minutes. Gone were all concerns about the boat and how far away the others were. Safety didn't matter at all to us. Since the dolphins were near we didn't mind if no one else was around. All that mattered were the dolphins. All that mattered was the moment. We were riveted, excited, and at one with our dolphins.

As we swam with the dolphins I heard the familiar sonar with which they were scanning us. It has become my belief that it is the sonar that causes beneficial changes in our human system. Sonar applied in medicine has not only been used to scan the interior of the body, but also to break up kidney stones, and lately used by the military to stop internal bleeding from war wounds. In captivity it has been observed that dolphins find the sore spots in humans and then rest their noses on those areas. When they apply sonar to a specific area, it reduces or eliminates pain. It was also postulated by Dr. Michael Hyson, a Hawaiian based biologist, that the sonar of the dolphins can affect the structure of our DNA. If so, it would make dolphins "midwives" to the evolution of humanity.

I had certainly felt their amazing effect on Don and me in our lives.

If we were to take their abilities seriously, wouldn't we think that they need to be treated with all the same rights that we apply to humans, another highly sentient species on this planet? We, as a species, are ever evolving and maybe the cetaceans are igniting higher functions in those who are willing and receptive to be ignited by them.

Meanwhile, Jen and I were simply enthralled by swimming with these rowdy teens. Exposed to the dolphins' natural energy, our hearts were wide open. Somehow humans feel special when a dolphin comes near them, or even swims toward them. Jen felt like she was special. Later as we climbed aboard the boat, we took each others hands and jumped up and down for joy. Jen could hardly contain herself. I was so very happy for her and us! She had been taken into the midst of dolphins in a way that I had never seen before. It was a most amazing experience. Every child had a unique experience that day.

The days passed. We went out on the boat for half the day, and swam with dolphins whenever they were open to us. The universe arranges itself holographically perfectly around us, whether we are aware of it or not. Life is highly interactive, and when we live in heightened levels of consciousness we have more amperage, which makes the manifestation process more quickly visible.

How our minds interact with the weather became so brilliantly clear the following year when Gerald and Elke came to be with us again, with yet another group of handicapped teens. One of the afternoons had been very cloudy, and rain threatened to interrupt our dolphin adventure that day. But Anna, who was our captain that afternoon on the catamaran, dared the seas regardless, with gleeful teens in tow.

Since we didn't have any thunderstorms or lightening, we simply had to deal with the gray weather, light rain and the lack of sunshine. But as soon as we went out on the water, we were met by increasingly more rain. The gray sky alone can feel ominous enough and we didn't really feel like getting into the water. Our captain felt sorry for the kids, knowing how eager they were to meet the dolphins. I closed my eyes. Being with dolphins was about living in a magical universe. Our group just needed to have a small area of sunshine, some dolphins and calm enough water. I visualized how we would feel if we were swimming with dolphins this very day in the sun. Anna must have seen what I was doing, and she winked at me. Despite the rain and gray we kept going further and further out to sea.

Suddenly the sun broke through! The clouds parted and formed a large circular halo right above us. The sea became calm around us and light filled the water. Then dolphins appeared as if out of nowhere, just like the sunshine. It was as if we had magically entered into another world.

Realizing that this was perhaps the only chance for the children to be in the waters with the dolphins, Anna stopped the boat in this vortex of light and calm, and let us into the water. As if the dolphins had been waiting for this moment, they swam right over to us, around us, and under us.

Mysteriously, we shared a slice of heaven together. After some time we felt the clouds moving back in, and we all got back on board. Radio contact let us know that heavy rains were on the way and that we needed to make our way back to Key West soon. Navigating in the rain is not much fun. Cold rain can pelt against the skin, make us shiver and render all navigation markers invisible.

The children, adults and I huddled in the lower cabin of the boat, out of the rain. Sitting on the captain's seat, Anna braved the wind, the rain and the vanishing visibility. No other boat was to be seen anywhere. It was just us in the middle of gray water, gray skies and Key West had disappeared.

Gone was the island. Gone were all cues. Luckily we had GPS, the satellite guiding system. Gerold climbed up to the steering wheel to give Anna moral support. Together they stood in the cold and wet. We were a team together and we envisioned ourselves arriving safely in the harbor.

Below in the cabin of the boat, we were still awed at how nature had conspired to give the children a window in time and space so to speak. The very moment we had sunshine, dolphins had shown up and the children were able to swim with them in the water.

The whole universe is intelligent and once we can hold a vision in our energy field, it can interact with us. Do we live in our privately created movies? What we had experienced that day was a dream co-created by several of us, the weather and dolphins. All of us wanted to be together in the same happy universe.

I asked myself if I was the script writer. Were the children the script writers? Was it our captain who later told us how she too had been talking to the clouds? When we have a deep wish, collectively or alone, if it is a wish that makes the heavens and our hearts sing, we can experience it " if we can believe it. That was the message today for sure.

The time had come for our first group of twelve children to leave Key West. They had grown in our hearts, and we gave them each many big hugs before they left. A small conch shell served as a souvenir, and we waved good bye as the twelve children and ten adults drove off to Miami International Airport. A long flight home was ahead of them.

We had been thrilled with the changes we had observed in just this one week. But would the changes last at home? How long were the children positively changed by this one week with wild dolphins?

A meeting was scheduled in two months time, when Don and I would be back in Europe for the fall seminars in Germany and Switzerland. Of all places in the world, the children's home and school was located only twenty minutes by car from the location where we had been holding the seminars in Switzerland for years. Gerold and Elke organized a dinner for the parents and the children. Don had prepared a film of our many adventures with the dolphins and children in Key West, which he was going to show the parents and children. At the end of the presentation we gave each child a video of their dolphin adventures.

After our presentation, parents met with us and told us of the many changes their children had gone through. One girl was too fearful to do anything on her own. She had not been willing to go into her own room alone but was now making her own sandwiches and even rode a horse by herself, whereas before she had refused to do any of these things.

The girl that had never spoken but just nodded her head "yes" and "no," at the beginning of the week with us, and who, I was so emphatically told, would not be able to answer my questions, was now speaking. She was a different girl, and gave hugs.

One boy, who had not felt very proud of himself, was now sure he was special and had special plans for his life.

Another girl who had never thought of herself as being very pretty now wrote that she was a kind being, she liked herself and felt that she was pretty.

One foreign girl felt quite special from the kind of love she had received from us. We had indeed felt very close, and she really started believing that her mind had an effect on life, and told me that she was visualizing her future. She was the one that was able to make the most of her life in years to follow.

Not everyone had experienced dramatic changes, but one of the teachers told me that the children who had gone to swim with the dolphins had demonstrated greater self-confidence, were more harmonious, less stressed, and had become more at ease with themselves upon returning home. The teacher herself also felt that her own life had opened up and changed.

Love was all around us as we met again in Switzerland for our rendezvous dinner with the children. It was a very special evening and our hearts were wide open.

Manifesting Flowers

Soon we flew home, for just a few weeks of res in the cooler Northwest. Next on our itinerary was the Prophet's Conference in Palm Springs, California where I was about give a talk to about seven hundred people on the skills of manifestation and living from inner vision. At a previous Prophet's Conference, I had hear Edgar Mitchell, the astronaut, speak about his sudden epiphany when he saw Earth from space. I listened to him raptly as I had always dreamed of being an astronaut when I grew up. He had belonged to a think-tank group and their research brought about the same suspicion that I have had for years: "Consciousness is gravity."

When we realize that our thoughts create gravitational fields which are the formative power that manifests reality, we can truly make huge shifts in our ability to navigate reality, and fully enter the cosmic creation chamber.

As usual, I meditated before appearing on stage. In my meditation I pondered my limited beliefs about manifesting. By now I had gotten used to manifest some things within hours, or possibly even minutes. But to manifest instantly was still beyond my comfort. Since my talk was on the subject of manifestation in part, I tried to go beyond my current limits that I had reached so far and wanted to see if I could perform a real miracle on stage today. I wanted to manifest a flower in the palm of my hand in plain view of everyone.

"If yogis in India can do it, so can I," I reasoned. "If one human can do it, so can anyone, sooner or later. So why not sooner?" I concluded.

As I visualized the flower appearing in the palm of my hand, I could really feel and see myself being able to manifest a flower in my hand today. No doubt entered my mind as I visualized the flower in the palm of my hand, imagining myself on stage. I knew that today I could do it, because I got this feeling in the back of my spine, which I always get when I know something is true.

I had tried to manifest an orange for the last fifteen years in seminars. But I had always failed. Just like I expected, but that was because I really didn't want to manifest an orange and believed it impossible in a very subtle way.

Standing on stage later, I held the microphone in my right hand. Blinded by the stage lights shining down on me, I couldn't really see the hundreds of people in the audience. I told everyone in advance that I was about to manifest a flower in my hand. Incidentally this whole event was filmed by a film crew and later aired on TV.

In order to manifest my flower, I made a large swinging motion with my left arm like I had seen Sai Baba do, when manifesting holy ashes. I held the feeling of fully accomplishing my wish in my body and mind.

Lo and behold! Suddenly I held a huge pink Hawaiian torch-ginger flower in my left hand, complete with its long stem.

I looked at my left hand in shock and amazement for a split second.

"Wow! I must be getting good!" I said out loud, because I was caught off guard. But my left brain instantly got busy finding a reasonable explanation. 'How could this be?' my mind whirled. 'What had really happened?'

Right away I realized what had happened. As I had made my large, magic-like hand motions, I had accidentally swooped up a flower from the big flower arrangement behind me. My miracle had an explanation!

But whether or not I had a good explanation, I actually was holding a flower in my hand, in plain view of the whole crowd. I had instantly manifested the flower, just like I had imagined.

I had not been a trick, and I was quite shocked myself when I first saw the flower. It had worked to fully feel and expect such a miracle. My earnest meditation had worked, albeit in a way that was harmonious with my deeper beliefs and concerns.

We truly are in a school here on Earth, each of us is learning at our own speed and level, without competition. This understanding gives us more compassion toward ourselves and others.

Everyone of us plays our own part. It takes all of us to create the whole tapestry of life. That is what makes life beautiful. Some beings are dolphins, others are humans, some are clouds, and others are the stars.

Manifesting something is often understood to be in contradiction to being truly enlightened. As a result people feel guilty about consciously manifesting, or fulfilling their wishes. For many in the spiritual movement making enough money to fulfill their dreams is a taboo and as a result many New Agers find it hard to make a decent living, let alone make extra money. Either they feel undeserving when they try to manifest something, or judge it as unspiritual. Some people had given oaths of poverty in past lives, and still adhere to that believe in this live time. Some people are still working on the basics of understanding the physical laws of manifestation.

What we need to realize fundamentally is, that we already create non-stop. Usually it is our deep unconscious mind that does the manifesting. Our patterns, pains, believes and wishes manifest as a mixed salad of creations. Manifestation is an everlasting aspect of God. The in-breath and the out-breath of God is eternal. The cycle of birth and death is eternal.

The existence of Nothingness is simultaneous to the cycles of manifestation and decay. Nothingness *is* the basis of manifestation.

In Buddhism and some other Eastern teachings it is taught, that we are supposed to get beyond our desires and get *off* the wheel of reincarnation, in order to enter this Nothingness forever. Yet I see no proof that this state of 'Forever' is forever, or that there is an imagery or real place outside somewhere. Neither Enlightenment, nor any other state, seems to be permanent. Even if one were to try *no*t to be, it will not last. God *is* forever, and will not stop, even if we complain about suffering.

God is forever *both* the Nothingness *and* manifestation . God's in-breath and out-breath, and anything in between, is eternal and simultaneous, as the eternal Isness of Oneness. Manifestation in both aspects of becoming and decaying, exists simultaneously as the Oneness.

We are the part and the whole, the all-encompassing Oneness. THAT is the answer to deep bliss.

When we are able to hold the paradox of any creation within the palm of our hand, so to speak, we become the master to that particular dimension and we will be able to express our human potential to its maximum.

Journey into Oneness

After the conference we flew back home to the Northwest and oxygen rich air embraced us as again we walked up the stairs to our dome house on our little island. Key West and the Prophet's conference had been incredibly rich. Now I was looking forward to having some time to myself, without a schedule to follow. After breakfast, I sat on the balcony to meditate, as I needed time alone after this last marathon of being with people. Mountain peaks, glowing in pink and orange, were visible from the deck as I looked across the water. They reflected the early morning sun and reminded me of the glowing Alps that Heidi loved so much in the book from my childhood.

I closed my eyes, and let the sun caress my whole being. In my lap I held my long treasured book, *Enlightenment,* by MSI, which is a translation and interpretation of the well known Yoga Sutras by Patanjali. The Sutras were most likely written somewhere between 1,700 and 2,200 years ago, although they may have existed long before that time in unwritten form. Tradition has it that Patanjali is the *compiler*, but not author of the <u>Yoga Sutras</u>. This modern rendition by MSI, more than any other, stimulated me into ascension and I loved to read a passage before going into meditation.

I had opened to the Pada II Sutra 36, and it read: "Satya pratistayamkriya phala asrayatvam." It was translated as: "From reversing to stability of truthfulness, all actions quickly result in their fruits."

The interpretation of this text by the author MSI told us to no longer undermine our thoughts, speech, desires and actions by self-contradictory and self-destructive thoughts, speech, desires and actions. It said we will thereby receive full support from the Law of Nature, and all desires will quickly be fulfilled – if we live in truthfulness.

A paragraph later made the point more interesting to me. It continued by saying that masters of the *Observance of Truthfulness* can verbalize anything and it will instantly be fulfilled. One who lives in full inner and outer truth has risen to the level of cosmic universality. He or she resides as the Self that is All that is. All desires of the Self are holy and reach instantaneous fulfillment.

These Yoga Sutras also showed us that the ability of manifestation is totally connected to the vibratory state of the soul. Not only do our wishes determine the outcome, but the capacity of our soul, our vibrational state also determines the speed of manifestation. The higher the seat of our soul is, the easier it is to manifest our wishes. We naturally become clearer in our radiance and more potent as we move into greater states of awareness. Our identity changes as we increase the velocity of our soul. More pristine states of consciousness in which we fully align with the Oneness allow us to be at the core of the creation force.

After reading that passage in the *Enlightenment* book, I closed my eyes and rose up in my mind to higher spheres. I concentrated my attention on solely being in the center of the star above my head. It placed me into a vast space of stillness, becoming the center of consciousness until I finally entered into a singular point, which took all of me into IT. I lost all sense of individuality, but gained the sense of Allness. On my voyage to this space of Isness, I felt light fill me and I literally felt like I was *becoming the wisdom of space.*

Even though I would describe my journey as an upward movement, really what I was doing was simply increasing my vibratory state. As we located our attention ever higher, we simultaneously become ever more brilliant as we move our location of Isness into the center of the cosmos, or into the center of Allness.

Yet at the same time I was not separated from the body, as I truly didn't go anywhere. In essence there was no time-space travel involved in my ascension. In moving our soul's attention into the center of Allness, we simply locate our attention in the non-dual aspect of reality. It is beyond the highest vibration we can conceive of, which then becomes our primal residence. Within it we lose our association with our identity until we reengage the brain, which will tell us that the body is still alive and well, and ready to receive our main focus again.

Suddenly I felt Amoraea's presence join me in the upward spiral to God. I felt the urge to call him right then, to continue on my upward journey together with him on the phone. I dialed his number, hoping he would answer. As the phone rang, my breath stopped for a moment, awaiting Amoraea's voice.

"Hi Beauty," he answered the phone. Caller ID had given away my presence before he picked up the phone. His voice was full of pure pulsing light as he too had just started his morning with yoga and meditation.

I was thrilled to hear his loving voice. We briefly talked about my arrival back home and soon I felt our vibrations mingle and we became silent simultaneously. We had long practiced meeting in silence.

Opening into a space that was simply pure consciousness, we floated in a vast sea of light. Amoraea had arrived at the same dimensional focal point as I had, and we both sent a resonant sonar beam out to locate each other.

Instantly, we both started to rise higher, forming a pulsing luminous spiral together, moving ever higher, into finer dimensions. In my mind's eye, I saw a double helix spiral, much like the DNA coil, doubly wound, rising toward the heavens. A pillar of light beamed brilliantly upward in the middle of the spiral. Colors of pink and lavender, as well as golden and blue hues surrounded me, as I rose on this spiral towards the heavens. I was enraptured and my heart was wide open. The radiant DNA spiral was our joint lights creating an ever greater transporter beam into higher dimensions. We were each other's elevator into a grander universe.

Passing the land of living jewels we burst forth into the center of creation as one.

As we birthed our new consciousness into being, we entered into a mysterious space of omnipresence. It was as if our innermost jewels had opened into each other's lotuses and together we were truly entering the secret highway to unified consciousness.

Enlightenment filled us in stages upon stages as we share our light and consciousness. I understood that one part of the dance of life is the co-creation of increasingly complex states of consciousness. Often God is understood as the all-perfect, never changing existence. God is the consciousness that animates all life. It is the light that illumines all, but it is NOT forever stagnant. IT is the zero point, the ground upon which creation comes into being, but it is not only that. The zero point, the ground, and creation belong together. Consciousness and form are part and parcel of each other.

It has been believed that soul's only purpose is to witness God. It is also true that souls are the vehicles that partake in the ever new creation of manifesting the possible. We can be become *the gardeners in the cosmic garden creating ever new seeds of creation"* as borrowed from the bio-feedback game, *Wild Divine*.

Co-creation allows for new evolution and prevents a stagnant universe. If it were otherwise we would find totally predestined futures in which it wouldn't matter if we evolved or not. This would turn creation into a mere spectacle of predicable repetition.

All of the many facets of creation of course serve the One to recognize Itself in a million more facets, and see Itself from the eyes of a million more of these facets. God is forever exploring its own potential by giving free will to each of its manifested drops of consciousness, which in turn are creative units of awareness.

I understood that we do have free will and that we grow accordingly. We can grow slowly, or easily. That is up to us. But grow we will.

We felt that this eternity was all that mattered in that moment and bliss filled our hearts and souls. Eventually Amoraea and I were coming to completion. Our journey had reached my limits of endurance, as a refined state of consciousness requires a lot of focus, and I slowly returned the spiraling pathway downward to where he and I had started our journey.

We were stunned by our visions and complexity of feelings, and we just awed at our experience. As we spoke we sounded like cosmic poets, sounding like Rumi alive. Words could never come close to capturing our experience, but since we both had experienced the same thing, we both knew what each of us meant.

It felt so archaic to use words and our laughter expressed more readily how much our hearts soared. It was awesome to have a consort in heaven that could effortlessly feel all the subtle nuances of movements in our consciousness. It was as real, as taking a walk in the woods. We were rare gems for each other. We knew that for sure. Floating on cloud nine we ended our meeting on the phone.

Shortly after our phone call Amoraea wrote me a short email:

Dear Soul Flame,

Our last communion over the phone was ecstatic; I felt such an Oversoul contact with you. Now, as I write, I arc my light again with your diamond love, so pure and established in the Supreme Realms of Devotion to the One.

I am consoled and honored to have such a Love as you that will always meet me at the Highest Ranks of Mastery and Tantra in offering up our Soul's Light to the Collective, and fulfilling the journey of incarnating God's force and Consciousness into form-Identity.

We are lifted from above into the Celestial Currents of the Divine, ever higher if we choose to surrender to its Mystery.

Holding together strong presence here in Southern California, ceremonies are going well, and my soul remains enraptured in the folds of Love, heart centered in devotion and willingness to respond to the Calling to surrender ever deeper.

Today the sun shines bright and clear — I will go to Laguna Beach for the day to recharge my solar battery and swim in the Mother Ocean.

In Essence, Amoraea

Having such multi-dimensional friendships, loves and marriages is a huge blessing in our lives. Deep in all our hearts, we all seem to know of this potential, and we long to find our soul connections while here on Earth.

Understanding the Grander Design of Destiny and Free Will

I loved living in the immense light worlds with my friends. Connecting with other sensitive beings who share the ability to meet in higher dimensions gives me a sense of living on higher grounds and yet not being alone. We don't need to separate our spiritual time and sit hidden away from others in caves or on mountaintops to be in bliss. I believe many of us have come down from the mountain tops to live regular lives and to intertwine Heaven into our Earthly lives.

We can build and share this heavenly field together and walk like masters in Heaven on Earth with our eyes open. Our human potential is awaiting us, to become multi-dimensionally conscious beings by creating new neurological pathways in our human bio-system. Our inner heart knows that this is possible. We dream of our soul mates and our spiritual family. Down here on Earth we can walk tall, with our heads in the clouds, and our feet on the ground.

Imagine communicating with your beloved partner, your friends, family members, or your coworkers while being in your higher dimensional bodies. You can see each other not only as a 3-D body with a personality, but can feel each other's light, feel each other's thoughts, and look at each other like two angels in heaven.

Now and then we find people who touch us deeply, who walk tall, who live in higher consciousness, and with whom we can connect soul to soul deeply. But they usually live further away, sometimes across the planet. In order to feel like we have a lot of these kinds of friends we have to start thinking globally. But if one expands the sense of feeling connected across the planet, and allows one's mind to feel that the inner meetings are as real as any physical meeting would be, we can have a global village of beloved angelic friends.

Don and I are rarely home for very long. Instead we travel all over the world, teaching seminars. Since we don't have the luxury of having regular afternoon tea with our friends, we have developed connections with people who are multi-dimensionally awake wherever we go. I choose to think of all our spirit friends as being inwardly close, although they live physically far away. If we only take into account those people who live close by, we can feel quite alone in our heightened state of consciousness. Feeling the global village of likeminded souls requires that we tune into the silent code of telepathy and practice our connection with each other.

Daily training in refinement of our higher senses, such as in meditation, helps us to perceive subtler dimensions as fully real. We can feel the subtle shifts in ourselves as we touch each other at a higher level. It does not matter if we are of the same or opposite sex. The love of soul is deep no matter which body we find ourselves in.

One of my dearest girlfriends is an international traveling flautist. As we hardly ever get to see each other due to our intense travel-schedules, we make it a point to find each other in the highest dimensions daily and to shine the light together upon each other.

When she places her attention on my soul I feel and see her wave of incredible luminosity touch my soul's star. It pulls me into such heightened states that I feel like a master is touching my soul. Not only is it pleasurable in the moment, but we also amplify each other's capacity and potential in our daily lives. Luckily she feels the same in return and we keep pulling each other into higher states by contacting each other in those invisible realms of light.

In the beginning of our friendship we took the time to verify our experiences with each other. Although we could have dismissed the moments of luminous meetings of our souls as mere personal fantasies, we checked on our accuracy of inner perception by emailing each other the very second we felt each other inwardly. We did this for the first few years. Now I know her soul's signature, and her light takes my breath away.

Another girlfriend from Germany often met with me in higher dimensions when we visited on the phone. We made sure we had some silent times together after we finished talking about the issues of our daily lives. Her work reflects her soul's nature. She has restored paintings of angels and other holy imagery on cathedral ceilings of old churches, and also paints angels on people's bedroom walls.

After we have covered our human stories sufficiently we will often go into silence and meet each other as soul in the high light grid around the earth, spanning the world below us with our luminous wings. When we expand our wings we both feel like we are truly more in touch with each other than if we talked for another hour about worldly issues. In these moments of silence we become vaster fields of dimensions together and we intertwine at higher and finer levels, beyond the five senses. Sometimes, if we are blessed in these communions with our soul friends, we touch the face of God together. Those are my most memorable moments in my life.

Don is my constant daily co-creator of Heaven on Earth. We shine as much love and light together, and onto each other, as we can. With our resulting extra energy we create projects and hope to be good vessels for divine energy on Earth.

When I found Amoraea it was just four days after I had promised God that I was willing to live my commitment to the essence of Merlin's soul. Back in December 2002, I had asked God for a higher version of his soul. I imagined that the soul I knew of as Merlin could easily manifest in the form of someone who was able to fulfill a higher purpose than what Merlin and I had been able to achieve.

And that is when Amoraea walked into my life, exactly four days later. I really felt I had been blessed with the next higher vibrating version of the same soul pattern that I had met in Merlin. Something very deep, ancient and from a dimension far beyond my conscious mind had drawn me into Merlin's orbit. This same energy was embracing me now with Amoraea.

When Merlin and I had originally met in 1999, karma pulled hard on both our hearts despite our best intentions. Destiny pulled us strongly toward a future we both sensed.

In my dream in November 1998, I had begged the higher forces in the universe to allow me to stay married with Don, despite the fact that I was told that we were done. And indeed, Don and I were given the chance to stay in love together. However, we had been asked to allow other beings and other lessons into our lives in order to grow. I had agreed and my life had become a living reflection of that promise.

Don and I had to rearrange our lives in ways I never dreamed possible.

As I was about to leave Mexico and I was told in my mind that Merlin was to be my future husband, I was baffled. Later as he came to stay with us in Hawaii, things became more complex as my passion and heart became involved.

But as intrigued as I was by Merlin, I could see my future all too well, if I were to mate with him. Beyond the amazing allure of our souls, and our powerful future potential, I saw that I would suffer greatly due to Merlin's seeming inability to commit. He would be the first one to agree how hard it would be, being together with him. Although he felt very angelic and shared a light that lifted me above and beyond the ordinary, at times into states of the purest bliss, not being able to commit was his own problem he was determined to solve in this life.

Indeed, the experiences we shared in the following years were filled with a lot of emotional pain. Our only way through and out was to learn to love each other despite the apparent difficulties. Finally we learned to see through the veils of illusion and to enter into true unconditional love. We worked together intensely and always returned to an open heart, until eventually Merlin and I couldn't go any further as he felt he needed to become more human and I was on my way to becoming more celestial.

My lessons were transferred to Amoraea, who seemed to be a finer version of the same pattern. With both Merlin and Amoraea, I shared a sense of belovedness. Both were cosmic consorts. One was more powerfully emotional and sexual, and the other more visionary and celestial. Both of them could tap pure states of soul and God with me.

Merlin was becoming my best friend, and we shared deep, long conversations on the phone, hours at a time. But to his regret he had come to realize that he always hit a wall of fear in his heart when we opened even a little too much. Our inner meetings of soul were getting rarer. The intensity of opening our soul's love and light toward each other caused him to freeze and so we chose not to enter that realm too often. However, many years later, he missed the union of our souls in those pure realms and slowly but surely we reopened those doors, once I had been able to let go of him as my Beloved.

I realized that it is best to open our energy only as much as our counterpart is capable of. It is a hard realization, one that keeps challenging me, because I really want to see the greatest possibility in a new love. But the limits are real, and eventually the relationship becomes lopsided if both do not give equally, and if both are not at equal levels of evolution. One of the two will feel undernourished, while the other one will feel overly demanded of their capacity.

This holds true in any relationship, group, family or work situation. It is good to be matched in intensity, values, levels of evolution and levels of intensity.

Merlin kept saying to me that he wanted to bake smaller breads, borrowing a metaphor from his expertise in bread baking. He felt that I was a "shoe size" too large and he felt he was overdriving his electric circuitry when we opened our souls up to each other deeply. Sad as it was, we had to let go. It is a common occurrence in relationships to come to such a realization.

It really took us six years until we both were comfortable in realizing that this had happened. After six long years of capitulating to the apparent human emotional limits, we accepted that our capacity as souls was large, yet our human expression was limited and not able to fully embody our potential.

Perhaps it was my flaw to see the potential of someone and then ask them to live up to it. At our highest potential, his and my souls were co-creators in a grand design, but down here in our human lives, I had to accept the limitations. Slowly but surely I surrendered and resigned to this truth. I kept a lid on my soul, though I never closed my deeper parts off from him.

Merlin would forever tell me later, that he felt like he had taken the wrong turn, and he sought the silent moments on the phone with me, where once again we opened the doors to Heaven. This time around I reminded myself that we were just masters in the grand design, not Lovers, not Beloved.

We had opted not to have a child together and for many years we pondered the rightness of this choice. Deep in our subconscious we knew that we had taken a different turn off the path than had been designed for us. We had chosen a different path of destiny. Although the magnetic pull of destiny had been strong, we had the choice not to walk that path. Only time will tell if we made the right choices.

The one question of whether karma and destiny could really be changed was forever pulling me onward. It started to look like it could. Amoraea and I had a much lighter load to bear with each other. I still had to deal with the issue of non-commitment with him, but in a much lighter version. He was willing to say YES more often, and only ran every now and then.

But how exacting karma is, was going to reveal itself in a mysterious future. We were going to find out how this destiny had altered its form, as we chose to play our parts differently.

Destiny is an energy pattern larger than ourselves and is situated at a higher time-space matrix juncture than we are ordinarily able to reach. It is an energy pattern which is usually beyond our ability to control. And because it radiates from a higher time-space nodal point into our lives, and therefore is usually beyond our human reach, it gives us the feeling of being in the hands of destiny or fate.

Normally, step by step, we learn by making mistakes, adjusting our course until we find the doorway into a higher perspective. Once we are able to reach a higher vantage point and we are able to hold any given paradox in the palms of our hands, not as a paradox any longer, but as the two sides of the same coin, we are able to start influencing the realms of creation below us.

It may look like we all live on the same Earth, but some souls are further evolved than others. Each time we are able to move to a higher perspective, we are able to solve the riddle of what previously appeared to us as a paradox. Holding a paradox within oneself and containing both sides of the truth within one's heart, is one of the signposts of rising beyond the previous limitations into the next higher dimension.

Mechanical evolution requires that we walk step by step with pain as our teacher. When we hurt, we try another approach, until we expand to a greater perspective, greater love, greater forgiveness, and are able to rise to the next level of understanding. Pleasure and pain are our guides.

As such, we walk through life step by step and learn from experience.

But Don and I had risen to higher ground in order to see if we could alter our path of destiny. I was not sure if I could avoid the pain of separating from Don and still learn my lessons and reach mastery. But we wanted to try. Instead of the mechanical learning process of pain, we chose conscious evolution. We opted to work voluntarily with life in order to reach the new shores of love.

Don and I wanted to stay together and go through whatever we needed to go through. As I had been told in my dream in November 1998 before I met Merlin, Don and I could stay together if we were willing to allow other souls and their lessons into our lives. IF we could be grand enough in our hearts and love each other enough, we would be spared separation. Usually people learn their lessons in serial relationships. It is called serial monogamy. Don and I had been touched by the brilliance of our future with each other and wanted to stay together. We were willing to learn the lessons with other people that normally would have to be learned sequentially.

This we had now done, and by the grace of God I was now allowed to work out the lessons with Amoraea in a much finer and potentially more fulfilling way. He had so many patterns in common with Merlin at a deep level. But Amoraea had realized that he wanted to say YES to Love instead of NO. Amoraea's NO came only every few months, not every moment he felt deep love.

We *can* be given a lighter version of our lessons, if we refuse to be pulled into the mire of negative projections. If instead we create positive future memories and become aligned with the purest form of love that we can hold in our visions, we will be rewarded with the realization of those truer visions.

In the many years which Amoraea and I eventually shared, we were again and again faced with our willingness to focus on our future of brilliance or to be destroyed by the lack of trusting the higher love. Anytime I let myself sink into the mire of despair because it looked like I was about to lose the love of Amoraea, I created more lack. Of course, since he too shared the fear of opening his heart like Merlin had, he ran into similar walls. But instead I kept imagining and feeling my fulfilled future of this love.

Again and again Amoraea rose like a phoenix from the ashes to share with me in the next chapter of our saga of love divine. And when he graduated from being with me and went on to look for his true Soul-mate, we let go of each other and simply became true masters walking the path to Heaven together.

The final mystery to be solved was the vision I had of Mother Mary telling me to have a child with Merlin. It was just as magical as the transformation of Merlin into Amoraea.

Babies, Birth and Dolphins

The puzzling vision of Mother Mary and the baby still made me wonder how this potential fate could resolve. A question remained in me; are we able to change karma, fate or destiny? Many religions would say no. In the Vedic teachings, Karma has been described as both mutable and immutable.

I would say that our effect on the time space matrix depends on our soul's evolution, and our ability to focus.

A karmic time-space energy pattern seems to be located in various layers of the time-space matrix. Some patterns are more universal, less mutable while others are more temporary. If we can learn and grow, Karma will change. Depending on the development of our awareness levels, we may have the sensitivity to enter those realms to some degree and alter our future, or not.

Some fundamental soul patterns are deeply seated within us. These are usually referred to as Seed Karma. The universe however, seems willing to allow us to shift into any space-time zone that we are capable of switching to, as a result of learning. This learning however can be done effortlessly. Holographic Imaging can move us out of old patterns, as well as enhance our ability to enter the Akashic fields. IF we can do it, we are allowed to make the jump.

In my meditation in the spring of 1999, the directive to have a baby by Mother Mary came from a deeper level of time-space. I didn't know if I had to abide, if it was carved in stone, or if I still had a choice.

As I pondered my past, I started seeing the thread that conception, birth and dolphins had played in my life. Some part of my soul really wanted to contribute to conscious parenting.

My mother was the most fabulous mother I could have asked for. She had worked as a seminar teacher and trainer of seminar teachers and had been a very aware person back in the sixties. I thank the universe to have been blessed with my mother! Her extraordinary soul's maturity helped shape my life here on Earth. I miss her very much and always felt that I owe it to life to pass on these wonderful gifts to yet another soul. Although my father died when I was two years old, together my parents gifted me with a great creation myth for my life's path.

In the fall of 1960, on the eve of September 27th, I had been conceived consciously by my mother and father. Don and I still have the fur in our living room upon which my parents made love and created the opening for my soul to come into this world. My mother loved to tell my sister and me that we were consciously conceived. What a novelty that was, especially back in 1960!

My parents traveled from Afghanistan on a road trip through the Himalayan Mountains to India when my mother was three months pregnant with me. For the next three months they traveled around the country. Together they adored the Taj Mahal, the symbol of deep love, and absorbed the vast and mystical culture of India at a time when going to India wasn't yet "in."

I always felt that my mother had picked up my soul in India. Growing up as a child I remember always wanting to wear a sari, and paint a spot on my third eye. I tried to stretch my eyes sideways into the Indian slanted almond shape.

Since I had been raised for the first years of my life in the Far East, my mother made sure we heard the stories from the collection of *One Thousand and One Nights*. *Aladdin and the Wonder Lamp* was my favorite story. Images of beauty, grace, palaces and miracles filled my young mind. I longed to walk in grace like the princess did in the fairytale, looking at her palace that looked like the Taj Mahal with her beloved Aladdin.

How much of it was actually going to manifest into my life I had no idea at that age! We do need to be aware that the heroic tales and images that children fill their minds with are going to be the images that may well manifest in their later adult life.

Being consciously conceived, being wanted, and being bathed in the energy of the ancient land of India during the time of my gestation, I was ushered into life with a magical creation myth. Our gestation tale is a potent story which accompanies us throughout our lives. We can make the gestation period magical and offer this as a gift to our children.

At a time in my life when I had no desire to leave Don, Mother Mary had come to me in a vision giving me the future vision of having a baby with Merlin. Don had had a vasectomy, so I knew that we would not have children. But to be impregnated by a man, even if I was told inwardly that he was to be my future husband, and even if it was by the voice of God, was totally out of the norm. The vision of Mother Mary, however, had stirred my soul.

Over the next few years all three of us, Merlin, Don and I, wondered if we should follow that idea or not. Merlin's parents would indeed have been my grandparents of choice. Even though they were very traditional, caring people, they were vegetarian, healthy, practicing Yoga and open to all the crazy new ideas their son brought home to them. One day they told me they would be OK with the unorthodox situation we all presented to them.

I loved them both and spending time with them was fun for me. I recall their white linen table, laden with Sunday's coffee and cake when we all came to visit. The German good old life was still fully expressed in Merlin's family which I had missed ever since I had moved to America. They never blinked an eye at the very unusual situation, since we were both open and honest.

We eventually decided that it would be too much to ask of us and a newborn soul, to bring a baby into this kind of constellation. We decided not to fulfill Mother Mary's design. Although the vision of Mother Mary had been very clear and Merlin too had received the same message within the same time period, we felt it was humanly too daunting.

I wondered how this story of a child announced by Mother Mary was going to turn out differently since we hadn't played according to what seemed like a higher plan. The answer turned out to be as mysterious as my original vision had been.

Karma appears to need to be expressed, but different players can choose to play the role of expressing it:

Don and I had announced in my regular round of letters that we were going to Bonaire for a dolphin exploration vacation the coming

February. Once there, we were going to connect with Roberta Goodman, the dolphin researcher, to see if Bonaire would be a good place to have dolphin contact. We also wanted to see if there was a place for birthing babies in the water near dolphins.

I had held the vision in my heart of water births near dolphins ever since 1991, after reading my first book on dolphins. If I was ever to have a child, I wanted it to be born in the water, ushered into the world by dolphins as my midwives. I was mesmerized by that dream. And indeed, we found a bay on Bonaire that held warm and shallow water.

But the longer we discussed the ins and outs of this dream with Roberta, the more we realized the real problems with our dream. There were many hurdles facing a pregnant mom. Flying at nine months of pregnancy is not allowed. Pregnant women can only fly up to the eighth month. There were the hazards of bacteria and possible staff infections in tropical waters. Blood can flow and would need to be taken out of the bay.

Dolphins may just not show up at the right time, since they have their own rhythms and needs. If there were complications during the birth, a hospital needed to be nearby. A midwife would need to accompany the mother. The local laws did not allow for non-local midwifes. Bonding well with a local midwife could also be an issue. Most people cannot really afford to take off work for such a long time, especially the husbands.

If the water is deeper, it is usually colder and rougher, and women would need to swim and support themselves while giving birth. Complications faced us at every turn.

Don and I had been looking forward to some time alone, but since I had announced our upcoming vacation near dolphins on Bonaire in a public letter, several readers picked up on the cue and had made arrangements to come to the same island for the same time period.

This trip taught me never to announce my personal vacation destination again in a newsletter! Gone was our privacy.

But as all things can have a good side, we were also gifted with meeting Ingrid, an author, film maker, musician and dolphin proponent, who wholeheartedly supports the interspecies communication between mankind and cetaceans.

Upon hearing that I was to be on Bonaire, along with Roberta Goodman, she flew out to meet us in order to interview me for a television show. We struck up a great friendship right away. We had originally met her when she came to a Holographic Imaging Seminar that we taught in Germany. We had instantly liked each other and we shared a very easy telepathic link. Don and I both loved her right away and we vowed to stay in touch.

A few months later Don and I were leading a seminar with German participants in Florida when the captain of our boat called me to her side one afternoon. She was glowing with excitement and told me that she had had a marvelous dream the night before about me.

"Ilona," she told me, "I saw you with a golden baby in my dream. It was a boy, like a little Buddha and he was radiantly wise. I think you are to have that baby."

She commonly had premonitions and trusted her prophetic dreams. I smiled, knowing that Mother Mary was still waiting for me. Merlin was still in our lives and we not yet completely closed the door on the option of having a baby.

Again, a couple months later, during our seminar-tour during the fall in Germany, we took time to visit Ingrid in Bavaria. After spending the night in her and her daughter's home, Ingrid told us over tea at breakfast the next morning excitedly, "Ilona, I dreamt that you were going to have a baby, it was like a wise Buddha boy."

Don and I looked at each other and Don said jokingly, "Why don't you have the baby for us!"

We all laughed.

Ingrid's husband of over twelve years was a musician and due to technicalities they had to live in different regions of Germany, not seeing each other very often. Several months later, we were greatly surprised when she called to tell us that during her recent visit with him she had gotten pregnant.

The timing was perplexing. Had we not jokingly suggested to Ingrid to have the child in lieu of us? But could that even happen? Could she have a soul that might have been waiting for us?

Ingrid's pregnancy was an epic journey. As she was a film maker and author, she had a lively lifestyle. Her dream was to give birth near dolphins. Inspired and directed by her unborn child, she promoted the power of women listening to their inner voices. Her deepest desire was to empower women, who were usually bombarded by society to follow the standard protocol with regard to pregnancy and birthing. Instead, she helped them find their own inner wisdom, follow their inner voice, and listen to their child.

Much research has been done around the fact that an unborn child is indeed able to communicate with the mother and that she can ask for the cooperation of the child in utero. Telepathy before, during and after pregnancy was not new to many mothers and Ingrid saw the time of pregnancy as a fertile time for opening to inter-dimensional communication.

After she met the Russian couple Vladimir and Katja Bagrianski in Paris who gave birth to their children "in the wild" both in the Black Sea and in Corse, she had been inspired to be near dolphins for her birth. She had also read about the work of Dr. Igor Charkovsky and his birthing camps in the Black Sea.

Elena Tonetti had worked with Dr. Igor Charkovsky on water birth and had managed the Black Sea's birthing project for several years.

Elena had stayed with us in Hawaii and we had watched the amazing video on water birthing with her.

About twenty years ago, after developing and confirming the benefits of water birth, Igor Charkovsky began to birth human babies in the Black Sea, sometimes with dolphins present. Some of the reported occurrences include a mother and a baby playing with the dolphins within forty-five minutes of the birth.

Another story is the instance of a free dolphin escorting a newborn human baby to the surface for its first breath. According to Igor Smirnoff, their research director, water babies develop six months faster during their first two years, and the development of walking, talking etc. occur earlier.

While Elena stayed with us in Hawaii we brainstormed on the dolphin-human birthing possibility in Hawaii. But the waters there were too rough and unpredictable. The closest we could find were tide pools right by the ocean, which offered warm water but no dolphin contact during birth.

Ingrid's baby's due date was the 18th of June. But instead of being able to drive to Croatia where she had wanted to birth her child in the water, suddenly at four in the morning of the 10th of June Ingrid woke up and had her first contractions. She knew right away that the baby was on its way. Her husband quickly let warm water into the bathtub and within a short time her son Nick was born at home. She told me the baby boy looked Tibetan. Something in our hearts made Don and me feel that it could have been our child. Our joke had possibly turned into a real life alternative. But we still didn't know for sure.

In order to stay connected with them, we sent Ingrid and her husband a DVD of our trip to India and a seminar we had just recently held in Bali. As they watched the DVD a breathtaking event took place.

Ingrid called and told me on the phone excitedly, "As we were watching your adventures of India and Bali, Nick saw you both in the film, pointed to you on the TV screen and said: "Mommy, Daddy!" I was nearly in tears as she told me that.

Had Ingrid indeed taken on the little Buddha soul as her own, as we had jokingly suggested during that breakfast morning at her house? Had the soul that could have lived with us, now found a new home and parents who were able to give him the similar kinds of lessons which he needed? We all felt that was the case. His current parents are very similar in style, energy, and even professions as Don and I. His mother's energy was similar to mine. Even the issues she and her husband share had elements of what Merlin and I would have shared.

The mosaic of free will, destiny and fate came into view ever more clearly in my mind. I started to see how we can collectively share our fates and destinies, and how conscious evolution allows us to shape our futures.

Mother Mary had brought a potential future to me. But when we chose differently, life found a creative way to solve the puzzle. Ingrid had the child for us and she assured me that he was very cooperative as she traveled with him on her many lectures and film projects through Germany. This had been one of my main concerns, since my lifestyle rarely left me any time in one place, let alone much time at home. Don and I were living like global nomads and a I felt that the child would have suffered greatly. But Nick had found a place in a home of parents with a similar signature as ours. And he was going to learn similar lessons in their hands.

All was well.

Don and I kept evolving on our path of learning to navigate time and space. We learned how to rise beyond fate, which was our creative part in this entire story. We were practicing surfing the Akashic fields and rising beyond the mire of karmic fate.

Again and again we lifted our gaze above and beyond the horizon of 3D time-space to higher stratospheres, where we had a grander overview and the option to be co-creators in the grand design. We were free to live alternate futures.

As one ascends in one's soul's frequency, one is able to rise above various horizons of the timeline, and gains greater freedom. Experiences in time and space become increasingly a matter of choice. Fate can be harsh and often we don't know what is coming. But we can elevate ourselves to a higher octave as we evolve our soul and turn fate into choice, turning our sketched life's plan into a greater and more beautiful painting.

We normally see our personal lessons only in linear time. When we grow beyond the limited version of "self," we can include others into a greater sense of "self." We can transform our lessons into a multi-human design, a mandala of human bodies, minds and souls, all dancing to a higher tune, co-creatively learning and fulfilling our life lessons together.

As such, Amoraea was the continuation of my lesson with Merlin and the baby had found a parallel home. All of the experiences taught me how we actually form a mosaic of souls, and in this mosaic we are acting collectively, acting as a larger unit of "us."

Ingrid's story and the brainstorming with many dolphin assisted births enthusiasts have changed my perspective on creating dolphin-assisted water-birthing centers in the wild. I have come to the conclusion that it is best to swim with dolphins during the time of pregnancy and bring a beautiful creation and gestation story to the riches of the baby's birth.

The stories of our creation before and during our gestation, as well as all the experiences and consciousness that a mother goes through in her time before and after conception, contribute to the kind of soul she will attract and which kind of gifts the child will bring to the world.

How magnificently we can help others by blessing the unborn child. Receiving blessings, be they from humans, dolphins, or any other species is an amazing gift to the child.

How much the DNA and soul is affected by blessings and sonar is yet to be discovered, but we know that we can grow gigantic seeds and fruit just with the pure power of prayer!

One thing is for sure, quoting Henry David Thoreau:

"I learned this, at least by my experiment: that if you advance confidently in the direction of your dreams, and endeavor to live the life which you have imagined, you will meet with a success unexpected in common hours. You will put some things behind, will pass an invisible boundary.

"New, universal and more liberal laws will begin to establish themselves around and within you; or the old laws will be expanded, and interpreted in your favor in a more liberal sense, and you will live with the license of a higher order of beings.

"In proportion as you simplify your life, the laws of the universe will appear less complex, and solitude will not be solitude, nor poverty poverty, nor weakness weakness. If you have built castles in the air, your work need not be lost, that is what they should be. Now put foundations under them."

We change the kind of reality we live in by vibrating at increasingly finer levels in our body, mind and soul. New laws will apply to us when we walk with the laws of beings of a higher order."

Epilogue

In essence, we all emerge from the same pure state: From God, the only Source there is.

We carry that memory deep within us, experiencing ourselves as individualized Soul, as the I Am, as well as the All.

As such we desire to be seen by others as we truly are.

Deep within we wish we could be seen by each other as pure souls, as the seat of God we truly are. Once we get that hang of how to share our essence we usually want to share this with everyone and share our purest heart of hearts. Love is all that remains in this state. God is all that engulfs us. God, the zero point is the ground we walk on. Playing "just being human" appears like a game at that point, like we are trying to play being small, when in truth we are the vast Isness at our core.

Yet here on Earth, in our various levels and forms of manifestation, each one of us is unique. There is beauty in creation and limitation. The choice of what we want to embody, manifest, attain, and experience is ours alone. In the grand design of creation the palate is full of many colors and we are able to paint any kind of picture we want.

But behind the many different paintings we paint, we are all ultimately drawing upon the same canvas.

The canvas we paint upon is pure beingness and aliveness. When we awaken, and merge our minds with the canvas itself, we realize that we are, at our core, the colors *and* the canvas itself. When we are awake and operate in time-space, we are always able to simultaneously be the design, as well as the canvas and the painter.

From a distance we can see that the many different paintings we create, form a collective mosaic. We are co-creating a collage of aliveness. Each dot is connecting us with each other. This super-string of vibrations that we collectively manifest, is the symphony of God.

In our daily lives our souls vibrate with the greatest joy when we simultaneously touch the center of creation, the Oneness, while painting our particular painting and live our specific dance to a tune we design. We are best serving the All when we express our specific individualized aliveness.

People often ask Don and I often how we manage to be so in love. We do it by **merging** our souls in union as I have described. Because so many people are yearning to experience themselves as Soul-aware, and to be in touch with others in this more heavenly form of love, we decided to teach these steps toward reaching soul awareness, and returning to the One in our *Soul Seminars*.

This union of our souls is the basis of our life together, our love and purpose. It is what feeds Don and I, guides us, and enlivens us.

Being in touch with soul's light is the very purpose of our human life in general. Without it we live like dolls on the strings of fate, usually directed by karma or unconscious programs. Yet by being alive in our soul's light, we are free to ignite our potential and touch the sky!

During one of the ReCreation seminars we taught, I experienced an epiphany.

Don had created a collage that represented his inner life. This collage was a mandala of his soul that represented the innermost gestalt of his deeper consciousness.

His collage showed many luminous images which he had found in magazines, depicting the inner landscape of his mind, heart and soul.

There was the light of God at the top. Below that image Don had pasted an image of a star, representing our Soul Star. The soul star is Don and me together at our highest merging point, our union.

Below that he had pasted what was a most amazing image to me. It honored me to my depth. I stood in silence as tears rolled down my cheeks, while I listened to Don explain the meaning of this image in his collage to the group.

The image was of five luminous masters walking together. They walked linked together, arm in arm, down the marbled steps of a temple, descending from the light of God toward the viewer.

Don explained the meaning of this image to the group in the following way:

"This is Ilona and I, as our Soul Star." He paused as he looked over at me. His eyes were filled with a glistening light.

"Below the star, we are walking with the other masters, like Merlin and Amoraea, and Ilona's girlfriend, the flautist (whom Don had wanted to marry when he was nineteen, and whom I love as my own soul now), as well as other friends. We all are walking together as masters, holding the field of light together."

With the light of a saint, Don continued. "As such we go out into the world and teach living in Heaven on Earth. We share our heart's and soul's love, we are open here on Earth to our deepest aliveness, where our souls touch each other in the Heavens." He looked over at me again, this time tears were lightly filling his eyes, and love shone forth from the depth of his heart.

Tears welled up in my eyes, too. Don had just presented such a pure and clear understanding of the meta-matrix of the purpose of all our trials and tribulations. Don hadn't condemned me as an adulteress. Instead, he had solved the puzzling question that has plagued men and women for millennia: "How can I love more than one person?"

Although most people do love more than one person, an overriding taboo has covered the hearts of men in women in our societies for eons. This misunderstanding of love and sex has made it very hard to understand the deeper meaning behind true soul love.

Although Don and I have had our share of encountering the fire of passion with others as well, Don had realized that the overriding principle behind the question of loving others is "Becoming Enlightened Beings Together."

Sharing our soul's light weaves us collectively into the matrix of a team of masters walking in Heaven on Earth.

I had struggled at times with myself, judging myself as not being orthodox enough, not straight enough, because I yearned to merge in Oneness with others, men and women alike. Yet over time Don and I have transformed our perils into a tale of mastership.

Don loved me more than I could ever have asked for and he was at peace with my nature. And just maybe union of soul is our birthright and our truest nature.

"You keep us alive and flowing with reality, instead of becoming stiff from ideologies," he often said to me.

"Without your gypsy nature I might have become much too predictable," as he smiled a masterful smile.

I had followed my design and intuitively tried to pull all my relationships into the heart of God. That is where we truly reside. That is where we are truly at Home.

May this book encourage you to deepen your soul connections that you may already have, or to deepen the experience of your own soul and expand your personal connection to God.

Mystical explorations help us discover what lies behind the curtain of this dreaming universe.

To this end I wish you a great journey into Oneness.

Contact:

Ilona Selke

Information about Ilona Selke:
http://www.ilonaselke.com

E-Mail:
info@ilonaselke.com

Order books and CDs online at

www.ilonaselke.com

or call:

1-800-758-7836 / 1-360-387-5713

Books:

Wisdom of the Dolphins

Alin Learns to Use His Imagination

Video:

Living From Vision Course

Living From Vision® is a miraculous Online or Home Study DVD course to help you feel powerful and manifest your greatest dreams so you can live happily and fulfill your purpose in life.

Life is about developing depth of soul; it's about understanding the laws of the universe, the 101 of creation. It's about learning to love and co-create reality.

If you want to develop your power to create, to live in harmony with your intuition, and explore your life form the inside out, then THIS is the course for you! If you have seen or read The Secret, this course will allow you to put the Secret to work in your own life. Imagine that you are one of the people in the Secret telling their success story. This is the power of Living From Vision.

This course Living From Vision® teaches whole brain thinking, imagery, relaxed focusing and immediate action.

No matter how many trainings you have taken, this course will give you wings. "It is a grand recipe that actually works!" (quoted by students worldwide)

This course really delivers! A structured five-week course leads you to actually live what you truly envision. By dealing clearly with the feedback you encounter as your actions begin to manifest, obstacles are easily resolved, and the natural flow of creation comes through you.

This is a powerful course for anyone who wants more from their life, and is willing to commit to a process of creating it.

You will practice:
♦ How to manifest your visions, goals, wishes
♦ How to find and express your personal purpose
♦ Step-by-step methods to ensure your goals come to life
♦ How to make negative emotions work for you
♦ Ways to handle stress effectively
♦ How to create a happy life, & sit in the driver's seat of your life
♦ Develop your creativity.... yes, ... write, sing, travel....
♦ Have the financial dreams of yours come true
♦ Develop your emotional and intuitive IQ
♦ Have time for yourself again   ... b r e a t h e ...
♦ Make the special projects you've dreamed about come true
♦ Face your fears.... turn them around to become your allies
♦ Feel empowered

Living From Vision Self Study Course

Now available as an online course.

Now you can download the Living From Vision course and immediately begin learning how to now create the life you want to live! You will get an online day-planner that incorporates the Living From Vision principles and daily audio exercises, as well as a Daily Diary that is searchable by key words. It can also be used as a Dream Diary to keep track of your important dreams and search for common themes in your nightly adventures.

Music:

Himalayan Soul

Romantic Wonder

Mind Journey Music

Inner Spheres

In One We Are

Yoga with Ilona
DVD and CD set

This series of easy Yoga exercises will transform you body gently and easily with daily practice. Learn the positions and the flow of the asanas (positions) by following with the DVD. After you have mastered the progression of the exercises (usually within a week), you can use the provided CD and listen to Ilona guide you through your morning routine with some beautiful background music from Inner Spheres.

Guided Meditation CDs

1. Mission in Life / Healing your Body

2. Time Travel / Abundance

3. Spiritual Partnership / Dreamtime Awakening

3. Healing the Earth / Dolphin Consciousness

To order please visit www.ilonaselke.com

or call toll free:

1-800-758-7836

or
1-360-387-5713